Psychology Revivals

The Psychology of Everyman

First published in 1935, *The Psychology of Everyman: Nerves and the Masses* was written as a short and simple treatise on 'Functional Nerve Disease' for doctors in general practice. The main object of the book was to enable the busy Practitioner to recognise psychological conditions and to treat them confidently along lines that they could understand. With focus at the time only on the physical symptoms of illness, it was making an important point to doctors that they must realise the psychological state should also get due attention. Very much of its time, today it can be read in its historical context.

The Psychology of Everyman

Nerves and the Masses

George Devine

Routledge
Taylor & Francis Group
LONDON AND NEW YORK

First published in 1935
by Hutchinson & Co. (Publishers) Ltd

This edition first published in 2025 by Routledge
4 Park Square, Milton Park, Abingdon, Oxon, OX14 4RN

and by Routledge
605 Third Avenue, New York, NY 10017

Routledge is an imprint of the Taylor & Francis Group, an informa business

Publisher's Note
The publisher has gone to great lengths to ensure the quality of this reprint but points out that some imperfections in the original copies may be apparent.

Disclaimer
The publisher has made every effort to trace copyright holders and welcomes correspondence from those they have been unable to contact.

A Library of Congress record exists under LCCN: 36003643

ISBN: 978-1-032-94446-3 (hbk)
ISBN: 978-1-003-57081-3 (ebk)
ISBN: 978-1-032-94450-0 (pbk)

Book DOI 10.4324/9781003570813

THE PSYCHOLOGY OF EVERYMAN

Nerves and the Masses

by

DR. GEORGE DEVINE

HUTCHINSON & CO.

(Publishers), Ltd.

LONDON

PRINTED IN
GREAT BRITAIN,
AT THE ANCHOR
PRESS, TIPTREE,
: : ESSEX : :
1935

CONTENTS

THE PSYCHOLOGY OF EVERYMAN

FOREWORD

THIS short and simple treatise on Functional Nerve Disease is written for the doctors in General Practice. These gentlemen are the shock-troops in the front line of Life's Battle against human ills, and the writer will consider himself amply rewarded if the ideas advanced here help even in a small way to aid them in the conflict.

There is no desire entertained of converting an admirable General Practitioner into a bad Nerve Specialist. If the doctor feels the urge to devote himself to the treatment of nervous troubles, he must abandon general work completely and so devote himself, because he will find his new role a full-time job.

The main object of the book is to enable the busy Practitioner to recognise readily the PSYCHO-NEUROTIC state and to treat confidently that condition along lines which he can understand in contradistinction to fiddling with the case on principles which he imperfectly understands or does not understand at all.

Another important point which the physician must realise is that the psychic state of his patient, whether that patient be surgical gynæcological, or purely medical, is of paramount importance always, and effective results can only be obtained when the psychic side gets its due attention.

The writer feels in no way rash in committing himself to the definite statement that within the next decade the psychological side of medical treatment will be so prominent, so universal, as to make the present-day purely physical treatment seem as antiquated as the bow and arrow.

Let us implement this statement by illustrating a surgical case.

To-day we are content to imagine that a successful appendicectomy closures everything for that particular condition. Once healing has taken place the patient

9

is allowed to wander forth with a few chosen words of advice to treat his abdominal wall gently for six or twelve months lest a rupture occur through the operation site. It never seems to occur to the majority of our profession that a general anæsthetic, plus severe intra-abdominal handling, may have damaged the psychic fabric of the individual. The patient with this bruised mental fabric is tossed back into life's vortex again without even a precautionary whisper that he is not fitted for a time to endure ordinary mental stress and, as a result, he often, very often, crashes nervously sooner or later.

This crash causes all-round amazement, but it should not do so—the reason is perfectly obvious to those who take the trouble to search for the reason—it is due to utter disregard for what has happened to the all-important side of the patient—the psychic side.

The purely physical side of the treatment of disease must hold its place obviously. Infections must be combatted, injuries repaired, abscesses drained, etc. It must never be lost sight of, however, that SUB-CONSCIOUS FORCE is the supreme, the sole controller of any and every physical condition in its maintenance, its well-being and its repair. Consequently, the psychic state, which is only another name for SUB-CONSCIOUS FORCE, should receive the maximum of consideration if it is going to give its maximum of efficiency.

The theory advanced in this book as to the causation of Functional Nervous Conditions is purely the theory of the writer.

As an ardent admirer of Freud, who first taught him the principles of psychic investigation, he followed the Master's teaching assiduously for three years in the treatment of cases of PSYCHO-NEUROSIS and failed—failed utterly.

That this failure was due to his technique, or more probably his lack of it, the writer is prepared to admit, but at all events, he abandoned the purely Psychic

Theory of Freud for a Psycho-Physical Theory based on his own personal observation and study.

The theory is evolved exclusively from cases personally treated from start to finish along lines dictated by actual psycho-physical conditions, and happenings clearly demonstrated by patients suffering from PSYCHO-NEUROSIS.

In other words, whilst one is compelled to conjecture as to the positive æteological factors in the PSYCHO-NEUROTIC states, an effort is made to employ all the palpable evidence demonstrated by these cases. This in effect means that in treatment the physician is able to maintain his feet on the solid earth of common sense where he is confident and feels himself at home. From this platform he is much more likely to obtain results which after all is the sole object, rather than from drawing bows at a venture whilst soaring through the psychic strathosphere of another man's fancy.

The theory in a nutshell is :—

(1) All human activities, psychic and physical, are dependent upon SUBCONSCIOUS FORCE.

(2) That our nervous stability and consequent mental and physical well-being is dependent on a sufficiency of SUBCONSCIOUS FORCE.

(3) That the sufficiency of this FORCE is dependent upon the adequate output of our Endrocrine glands.

(4) That the PSYCHO-NEUROTIC state must supervene when SUBCONSCIOUS FORCE is below normal in quantity.

Let us briefly analyse the four points put forward in this theory.

(1) *All actions, psychic, and physical, are dependent on SUBCONSCIOUS FORCE.*

Physical action—We desire to rise from a chair and accomplish this by certain muscular actions. We know that muscle is in itself inert and incapable of movement until stimulated. We know that nerve fibres *per se* are inert and their function merely conductors of stimuli. It must be conceded, consequently, that the stimulus is the basic factor in the action, and as this stimulus is born of volition, which is dependent for its existence on subconsciousness, we must conclude that the stimulus originates from FORCE in subconsciousness.

Psychic action—That thought processes demand the employment of FORCE is manifested by the fatigue which supervenes after prolonged mental effort. All movement demands the employment of FORCE. Cardiac movement is unceasing from the beginning of life until the moment of death. The FORCE employed is extra-volitional and cardiac action is in the main extra-conscious.

That this FORCE is subconscious is easily proved by the fact that emotional stimulus acting on the subconscious causes this FORCE to be poured out in excessive quantity and heart movement greatly exaggerated as a consequence.

The above is sufficient to prove that all human actions, PSYCHIC and PHYSICAL, depend on SUBCONSCIOUS FORCE.

(2) *Nervous stability and physical well-being are dependent on sufficiency of SUBCONSCIOUS FORCE.*

When SUBCONSCIOUS FORCE is present in sufficient quantity psychic actions must, consequently, be orderly and efficient.

When SUBCONSCIOUS FORCE is deficient psychic action is poor and lethargic, giving us the exhaustion symptoms of PSYCHO-NEUROSIS, or spasmodically hysterical, giving us the extravagant hyper-action of the PSYCHO-NEUROTIC condition.

(3) *The Endocrine glands are the elaborators of this FORCE.*

We are all conversant with the psychic and physical activity of the hyper-thyroid subject and the marked opposing condition in the patient suffering from a deficiency of the Thyroid endocrine.

An effort is made in this work to prove that other endocrine glands also play their part and, doubtlessly, research in time will demonstrate this effectively.

The solution of the mysteries of emotional reaction, or such solution as limited human consciousness will ever arrive at, lies entirely in the laboratories. In other words, the future will demonstrate that bio-chemical activity makes saints or sinners of us all.

(4) *That the PSYCHO-NEUROTIC state does supervene when SUBCONSCIOUS FORCE is below normal* is well demonstrated by the fact that exhaustion, both psychic and physical, is a cardinal symptom of the condition. In other words, there is not sufficient SUBCONSCIOUS FORCE to maintain normal psychic and physical effort.

This skeleton of the theory is put forward here in the FOREWORD deliberately, not with the hope that it will make an appeal to any significant number of psychological investigators, it may even be rejected universally, but it does furnish a new angle of approach to the psychic problem.

Many doctors practising as Specialists in Nervous Disease (Functional Type) imagine that any belief held outside Freud or Jung is heretical and should be banned with bell, book, and candle. The author does not believe for one moment that either of these gentle-men holds that idea and would laugh to scorn the conception that their brilliant theories were the last word in the exploration of the SUBCONSCIOUS MIND.

Let any man who has adopted this branch of Medical Science pause for a moment and stand on the edge of that limitless expanse—the Field of the SUB-CONSCIOUS MIND. Soon he will realise that human understanding, after æons of ages of endeavour, can scarcely hope to map out effectively its vastness or explore it in its entirety.

There is unlimited room for every investigator and it is only by a sum total of the results obtained that we can hope to arrive at a common base-line for even tentative effective treatment.

That Freud ploughed a furrow in virgin territory no fair-minded investigator will deny, and that great good has resulted from it will also be readily admitted. Yet, it is but a furrow and it is the duty of all of us to have the courage to undertake a similar independent line of action if our ideas justify us in doing so.

The foregoing is urged upon the reader with the intention of giving him confidence in approaching these cases.

It is absolutely useless to undertake a case if the doctor's underlying thought is that it requires the personal attention of a Freud or a Jung.

The Psycho-neurotic is abnormally sensitive (that is why he is a Psycho-neurotic) and will detect any evidence of lack of decision on the operator's part.

If the case is undertaken it must be undertaken with full assurance that benefit can and will be conferred. There is an invariable rule in the treatment of Psycho-neurotics, and that is that a patient who is not progressing is losing ground, and every effort must be made to counteract this by change of procedure, change of surroundings, or some other medical measure. A patient who loses interest in his treatment cannot progress, because without the patient's interested assistance the operator's effort will avail but little— hence every method and means possible have to be employed to keep the patient tuned up to help in his own recovery.

There is a chapter in the book devoted to suicide, and it is a chapter of supreme importance to the man in General Practice.

Few things can be more distressing to a doctor than to find a man who was a patient, and perhaps almost a friend, as a consequence of this put an end to his own existence. A great percentage of these cases are definitely saveable and a little extra care and attention may bring this about.

Overwhelming depression suddenly panics the vast majority of suicide victims in the author's opinion, and if the doctor early on insists on a brain rest, as outlined in the Chapter on Treatment, the danger would be averted. The majority of these cases are untreated or badly treated Psycho-neurotics who, if given a respite from their temporary mental torture, oftentimes are enabled to adopt a totally different mental attitude and face circumstances with renewed hope.

The Maniac-depressive type contributes heavily to the toll of those who destroy themselves. As has been fully demonstrated in the chapter devoted to Depressive Mania, there are certain well-defined characteristics in this group which makes the diagnosis fairly simple, and every care should be taken to avoid mistaking them for Psycho-neurotics.

The Psycho-neurotic manifesting evidence of profound depression can be treated quite efficiently in his own home, or better still where it is possible in a Nursing Home. After a two or three weeks' rest the suicide idea is, as a rule, very definitely quashed.

The Depressive Maniac very definitely needs Institutional Treatment and under no circumstances should a doctor assume responsibility for this type of case once he has sufficiently satisfied himself of the patient's condition.

Alcohol and drug addiction are fully dealt with in their respective chapters.

That these can be effectively handled in General Practice does not seem possible, and where it is at all feasible, treatment in a Nursing Home should be insisted upon.

These patients belong, as a rule, to a class which can afford Nursing Home and Specialist treatment. At all events, their vices consume a considerable amount of money, a much larger amount, as a rule, than they are willing to expend in medical treatment.

The doctor in busy practice has not the leisure to devote to this type of case and, although good results can be obtained by employing the Lambert Method, the time required after this to restore them to a state of physical and nervous well-being is enormous.

In conclusion, the author wishes to tender his grateful appreciation for the assistance derived, not only in the production of this short treatise on the Psycho-neurotic states, but for the help the works of the undermentioned have been to him in treating cases of Functional Nervous Disease.

In the forefront stands Doctor Sigismund Freud, the great Master who taught the writer the ground-work of psychic investigation. If the pupil had the temerity to hunt a line of country of his own, let that temerity be ascribed to characteristics in part racial and in part to an irrepressible honesty which could not follow even a great leader when he branched off into country which the writer considered both impossible and impassable.

Doctor T. A. Ross, in his admirable work " The Common Neuroses," by his application of Pavlov's Conditioned Reflex to mental reactions gave the writer a lucid understanding of psychic happenings and a clear-cut picture of the development of those reactions.

On the non-medical side, Mr. W. R. Masters, of The Fleetway Press, London, spared no pains in his efforts to help the author to produce this work. He is ever ready to lend assistance in matters medical, as is evidenced by his activities in helping to build the magnificent new hospital at Southend-on-Sea.

Mr. F. Holmes, of The Marlborough Studios, Carnaby Street, London, was most helpful in producing the photographs and by his skill and care succeeded in portraying vividly the salient features of the subjects exhibited in Chapter X.

Lastly, the author's deepest gratitude is extended to Miss Doris Whipps, his secretary, through whose untiring efforts the work was completed in a very short period.

CHAPTER I.

THE ÆTIOLOGY OF THE PSYCHO-NEUROSES

Opening remarks.

Ætiology—

    The Existence of Psychic Force.
    Conscious Psychic Force.
    Subconscious Psychic Force.

Description of the perfect human mind working on full store of Psychic Force.

Description of the Psycho-neurotic mind (Acquired P.N.).

CHARCÔT was the pioneer in the investigation of the Pyscho-neuroses, and gave us our first picture of Hysteria. He maintained that all cases of this type inherited the malady.

Under hypnosis Charcôt was able to produce paralysis, but asserted that this could only be done in the hysteric. The main point of interest for us in this is that paralysis can be induced by ideas implanted in the subconscious, artificially cutting off the PSYCHIC FORCE governing the movement of defined muscular groups.

This proved that PSYCHIC FORCE is the activating agent in ordinary muscular movement. This point is stressed because it becomes of supreme importance later when we come to examine the phenomenon of exhaustion in its relationship to the Psycho-neurotic condition.

Freud, following Charcôt in his examination of Hysteria, advanced the theory that the causative factor was a past trauma of the psychic, and that this trauma was of sexual origin. He regarded these traumata as painful memories buried by an effort of the will in the subconscious of the subject. This will-effort he termed " REPRESSION," and if this "repression" were fully successful, the trauma was wiped off the mental fabric and neither harmful results nor mental discomfort ensued. Where the burial was not completely successful, the trauma remained in the subconscious as a painful area and gave rise to HYSTERIA and other symptoms of the Psycho-neuroses.

Freud thus practically limits the origin of the Psycho-neuroses to sexual traumata of the psychic, either in infantile or adult life.

He lays stress upon the ANXIETY states—ANXIETY-NEUROSIS and ANXIETY-HYSTERIA. The former he regards as a condition where physical symptoms predominate and express themselves in the shape of tics, tremors, speech disorders, etc.

In ANXIETY-HYSTERIA he considers psychic abnormalities are the outstanding features, with depression, dreads, obsessions, and hysteria as the chief exhibits.

ANXIETY-NEUROSIS Freud attributes to the repressions of painful sexual memories arising out of acts in the present, and ANXIETY-HYSTERIA to the repression of sexual ideas evolved by the subconscious in early childhood.

That this sexual theory of Freud plays a part, and a prominent part, is undeniable, but that it plays the entire part, or even the predominant part, is by no means proved.

Let us examine the pan-sexualistic theory from our knowledge of the ordinary individual. Take the ordinary normal physically healthy celibate, for example, amongst whom the author has had wide experience. Is the incidence of the Psycho-neuroses more prominent here than amongst the general run of mortals? The author's experience is that the reverse is true, and that the Psycho-neuroses in this group are not only less common but less severe in type. Yet here we have the ideal type for experimental demonstration of Psycho-neurosis with a sexual basis.

They are recruited, as a rule, from a class of average or above the average in mental capability. This entails high imaginative qualities, which translated means strong subconscious stimuli. They are sensitive, which translated means that their reaction to subconscious stimuli is intense. Again, they are generally in good physical condition, as the conduct demanded of them ensures this. Consequently, there is abundant resource, physical and psychic, to supply the material for sexual activity if a demand is made from the subconscious.

Taking all these factors into consideration, the average celibate must be under the continuous bombardment of sexual stimuli, and he is. He clamps them down firmly by a conscious will-effort—"Repression." In his pursuit of the ideal, sublimation undoubtedly aids him, but the main effort must come from determined "Repression" unremittingly exercised.

On the Freudian basis, this group, or the major portion of it, at least, should exhibit pronounced symptoms of ANXIETY-NEUROSIS. Do they? In the overwhelming majority, by the placidity of their behaviour and their mental contentment, one is forced into the belief that the exact opposite holds.

Freud's theory must be accepted as a cause, and a very important cause, in bringing about a hypersensitive or irritable condition of the subconscious, making it the easy prey to FEAR or any painful stimulus. The result of such stimulation is that the irritable subconscious calls upon an absurd and unusable amount of SUBCONSCIOUS FORCE to combat a supposed threatened danger. There being no danger sufficient to employ this FORCE let loose, the subconscious is compelled to mobilise its Escape Mechanism to empty itself of this surging FORCE, and the resulting manifestations give us the syndrome we term the PSYCHONEUROTIC state.

The mental state of the celibate is known to every serious investigator and constitutes the grounds for objecting to the acceptance of Freud's " REPRESSION " THEORY as blanketing the origin of all the PSYCHONEUROSES.

We have accepted Freud's SEX TRAUMATA THEORY as being one of the principal factors in giving rise to an irritability of the subconscious mind and thus making it hypersensitive to the onslaughts of adverse stimuli.

In order to understand the happenings which arise from the subconscious in this state we must first pass on to an intimate consideration of that PSYCHIC FORCE which puts in motion every thought, every action, conscious or subconscious, which takes place within us.

ÆTIOLOGY

The ætiology of the PSYCHO-NEUROSES as outlined in this work is of more than ordinary significance. It not only embodies the theory of origin, but this theory is the framework around which an attempt is made to construct the vivid working mechanism of functional nervous disease, and the basis on which this condition is treated.

An effort is made also to keep the causative factors in PSYCHO-NEUROSIS as simple as possible, to explain their construction as lucidly as possible, and to demonstrate as clearly as possible the why and the wherefore of the steps taken to alleviate or cure this condition.

*   *   *   *   *

The theory advanced is that the PSYCHO-NEUROTIC state is dependent for its existence on two basic factors :—

(a) The insufficiency of PSYCHIC FORCE at the service of the individual;
(b) The inefficient control of that FORCE.

Incidental factors—heredity, sex, emotional strain, age, disease, and accident—have a direct bearing on PSYCHIC FORCE and if that bearing is sufficiently powerful produce the condition we know as PSYCHO-NEUROSIS, but fundamentally their individual role is only that of an exciting agent. The PSYCHIC FORCE in the subconscious is the axis around which the neurotic states revolve.

What proof have we of the existence of this FORCE ? When the umbilical cord is severed the child begins its separate existence. The heart beats, pulmonary, diaphragmatic and intestinal movements commence and go on unceasingly until the final respiration of the individual.

All movement requires FORCE for its accomplishment, and as the movements mentioned are entirely outside conscious appreciation, and the subconscious is the only other possible locale of the FORCE, we may fairly term it SUBCONSCIOUS PSYCHIC FORCE.

As the child grows it gradually develops the power of voluntary physical movement. The desire to bring about this movement arises as a thought process in subconsciousness, is transferred over to consciousness for voluntary accomplishment, and the action is completed.

As consciousness has played the conspicuous part in this, we name the FORCE employed in the movement CONSCIOUS PSYCHIC FORCE.

Both these FORCES have a common origin in the psychic of the individual. Therefore, we may legitimately group both under the heading PSYCHIC FORCE.

It is this PSYCHIC FORCE, in its quantity and in its method of employment, on which our nervous stability rests.

No one will be found to quarrel with the existence of this PSYCHIC FORCE, but what proof is there to justify its division into the two groups—CONSCIOUS and SUBCONSCIOUS PSYCHIC FORCE ?

CONSCIOUS PSYCHIC FORCE

CONSCIOUS PSYCHIC FORCE, as we have seen, is the FORCE which consciousness or *will* employs in order to produce a definite muscular movement. Its employment can only affect muscular movement. It acts solely through the ordinary Motor Nervous System and has no influence whatsoever on the Sympathetic Nervous System of the individual.

This Force is entirely at our voluntary disposal. We can use it economically and avert fatigue over a period of time consistent with our personal power index. We can use it vigorously and precipitate physical fatigue early. It is dependent for its quantity on four principal factors :—

(*a*) Age,
(*b*) Health,
(*c*) Temperature, and
(*d*) Food,

all of which have a marked influence on physical output·

AGE

It may be taken for granted that the greatest output is between the ages of 16 and 35. This is the high plateau of physical achievement in the graph of life. From 35 there is generally a steady, never-halting decline until death.

HEALTH

In good health our output is up to the limit of our personal index. This falls in gradual proportion in persons suffering from any debilitating condition.

TEMPERATURE

Temperature in both its extremes markedly affects our energy output.

FOOD

Food as an energizer is an element of such importance that it would require a treatise to itself. There are many standard works written on food values in relation to work output, and the reader is referred to any of these. Food is a factor of supreme importance in maintaining physical energy at its highest possible level.

Let us take the argicultural labourer as an exponent of one of the heaviest types of arduous physical effort. He sets forth in the morning in the prime of life, in good health, under normal natural conditions and well fed.

to begin his day's work. His CONSCIOUS PSYCHIC FORCE (i.e. the FORCE at his voluntary disposal) index is 100%. By midday, after his severe physical effort, this index has been reduced, let us say, to 60%. He rests for a period, during which he has his midday meal, and when he resumes his energy index has returned, shall we say, to 80%. By the end of the day he has expended a further 60%, and now has only an energy index of 20%. What is his condition, physically and mentally, at this moment ? His body is in a state of well-defined physical fatigue and he looks forward to rest with pleasure. His mental condition gives no evidence of exhaustion. In other words, he is not depleted to any marked extent of SUBCONSCIOUS PSYCHIC FORCE. He may be sleepy, as the result of the by-products thrown into the blood stream from his exhausted muscles, but this mental condition is really euphoric. Mental distress, anxieties, worries, dreads or fears, do not arise from his exhausted physical condition and are a million miles away from this type of mind. After his evening meal he retires to rest in a condition of placid contentment. His head has scarcely touched the pillow when he drops into a profound sleep, and in the morning he has replenished his CONSCIOUS PSYCHIC FORCE back to its normal 100%.

Here we have a picture of CONSCIOUS PSYCHIC FORCE used almost to the point of depletion which leaves no harmful scars on the individual's mental fabric. On the contrary, this expenditure of physical energy under the drive of CONSCIOUS FORCE is, in reality, beneficial to the mind.

It would be well to relate a short story here as illustrative of the benign part played by physical effort in the restoration of subconscious harmony, i.e. in the treatment of PSYCHO-NEUROSIS.

A story is told of a certain Scottish Nobleman, in the hectic days of the Regency, who returned to his estates in Scotland thoroughly exhausted, physically and mentally, by London life. One morning, shortly after his return, whilst riding round his estates, he chanced to meet the local doctor and stopped to speak to him. During the conversation, on the doctor remarking to him that he was looking far from well, the Duke replied " I am far from well, and that despite the fact that I have been in the hands of one of London's most fashionable physicians for the past three months." I have no belief left in doctors " continued his Grace, " or, at all events, I have just as much belief in you and your common sense as I have in these so-called eminent doctors in London. Do you think you can do anything for my condition ? " " Your Grace," replied the doctor, " I can cure your condition, but I doubt me much if you would tolerate my method and it is the cheapest form of treatment " " I will do anything," replied the Duke, " if you think you can restore me to health." " Well," said the doctor, " Live on a shilling a day, and earn it ! "

This interpreted meant that the Duke had to engage in the same hard physical labour as one of his own estate workers and to maintain his existence on the plainest of food, its plainness and simplicity being assured by the fact that the total amount which he had for expending on it was his remuneration of one shilling per day.

As the Italians say, if this story is not true it deserves to be, and the advice of that old Scottish doctor ought to form a goodly part of the method which any physician, specialist or general, should employ in the treatment of the Psycho-neurotic state.

To sum up, what we have termed CONSCIOUS PSYCHIC FORCE has a single defined role, and that is on the muscular movement of the individual. If used to the point of utter exhaustion, under conditions which do not involve anxiety or mental strain, it only produces physical exhaustion and consequent sleep. It has no adverse influence on the psychic of the individual and is dismissed here finally from any participation in the mechanism of the PSYCHO-NEUROTIC STATE.

SUBCONSCIOUS PSYCHIC FORCE

We have jettisoned definitely CONSCIOUS PSYCHIC FORCE from the picture in Psycho-neurosis, so we are compelled to accept SUBCONSCIOUS PSYCHIC FORCE as the sole factor responsible for this state. It is advisable here to give irrefutable evidence of the existence of SUBCONSCIOUS FORCE. This is easily done, because it does not depend for its existence on theory.

Let us repeat what we have said at the beginning of this chapter. The heart beats, the lungs inflate and deflate, the diaphragm moves, the stomach and intestines engage in peristalsis, and these happenings on the physical side are brought about without any conscious effort on our part.

These efforts are made by SUBCONSCIOUS PSYCHIC FORCE never resting, waking or sleeping, from when we draw our first breath until our final expiration in death.

On the psychic side, this FORCE sits in judgment on the external stimuli which enter subconsciousness through our sensory channels, elaborates our thought processes into understanding and conviction, the result of this being our intelligence index.

As we have stated, this FORCE is entirely beyond our conscious power of command, although it can be influenced by such adventitious aids as alcohol and drugs, a fact which will be demonstrated later on in this work.

We have seen how, by the employment of CONSCIOUS PSYCHIC FORCE we can deplete ourselves voluntarily down to the point of practical physical exhaustion, and in this state we exhibit evidences of physical weakness and physical inability to continue our labours.

Our SUBCONSCIOUS PSYCHIC FORCE we cannot voluntarily deplete, but under the stimulus of emotion we can reduce it to a point where psychic debility manifests itself and we become unable to sustain psychic effort. This accounts for that exhaustion

(under continued emotional stimulation) which is such
a marked feature in the condition of Psycho-neurosis.

We have stated that SUBCONSCIOUS PSYCHIC FORCE
is under the dominion of our emotions.   What proof
have we of this ?   We have just stated that the heart's
action is controlled by SUBCONSCIOUS PSYCHIC FORCE
acting through the medium of the Sympathetic
Nervous System.   Everyone knows that under the
stimulation of a joyful emotion the heart's rate becomes
markedly accelerated.   This means that the emotion
of joy must have let loose an additional supply of
FORCE in the subconscious mind which stimulates the
heart's action through the medium of the vagus nerve.
This stimulation, in the hypersensitive mind met
with in the Psycho-neurotic, may be so excessive as to
produce a condition of faintness or even temporary
insensibility.

Let us try to interpret what this insensibility means
in its full significance.   The emotion has flooded the
subconscious mind with an unjustifiable amount of
its available FORCE and insensibility supervenes as a
protective measure until that FORCE is partially
restored.   Even where the victim does not become
insensible, the sub-acute demonstration of emotional
display is invariably followed by a period of manifest
exhaustion, demonstrating that there is a temporary
sub-normal quantity of SUB-CONSCIOUS PSYCHIC FORCE
available, and all active subconscious effort must
remain for a time at its lowest output, until normality
or near normality is restored.

Even starting from a simple fainting fit evoked by a
simple joy stimulation we see caricatured in miniature
a temporary picture of the Psycho-neurotic state, due
to sudden drainage of SUBCONSCIOUS PSYCHIC FORCE.

There is the extravagant uncontrolled excitement as
a preliminary stimulating agent, followed by temporary
exhaustion, headaches, and general physical and mental
lassitude—in other words, a temporary Psycho-neurotic
syndrome.

In a crisis or emergency, where some great danger arises or life itself is threatened, we have all experienced personally, or have seen evidence of a manifestation of power definitely superior to any possible voluntary accomplishment. An example will illustrate this :—

A swimmer is caught in a current and gets into difficulties. He suddenly realises that he is not making headway, in fact that he is drifting away from safety. He knows that unless he can beat the current he must drift out to sea and lose his life. He puts forth his strongest voluntary effort—it is insufficient, the current is winning. FEAR—FEAR of imminent death, suddenly surges into his subconscious mind and floods his whole being with a radiating thrill. His muscles take on an unknown power and speed : inch by inch the grim battle is waged and he fights successfully through the current to safety. He falls on the beach prostrate, utterly exhausted physically. He lies motionelss where he falls.

If the struggle has been sufficiently intense he exhibits symptoms of dire psychic as well as physical exhaustion. He loses consciousness.

These symptoms, physical and mental, are evidences of the swimmer's excessive expenditure of PSYCHIC FORCE, both CONSCIOUS and SUBCONSCIOUS. If this expenditure has reached the absolute or danger limit, there may not remain sufficient SUBCONSCIOUS PSYCHIC FORCE to sustain cardiac movement and death from syncope results.

Was the PSYCHIC FORCE expended by the swimmer in his successful effort to reach the beach not the CONSCIOUS PSYCHIC FORCE which is normally under his control ? No. Oblivious as he is, in all probability, of even the name PSYCHIC FORCE, his own story of the happening is illuminating. Listen to his recital of the event :—

"When I first found myself drifting in the grip
"of the current, I increased the power of my
"stroke to counteract this and found it unavail-
"ing. I then put forth my utmost effort (in other

" words he was using to the full all the Conscious
" Psychic Force at his voluntary disposal) only
" to find that I was still making no headway.
" Suddenly I realized that my life was in acute
" danger and something swept over me, thrilling
" me to the depths, and with no realization of
" how I accomplished it, I won through to safety."

His mental reaction to the occurrence is interesting:—
" No prize in the world would induce me to run
" such a risk again. I could not reproduce that
" miraculous strength to come through alive
" a second time."

Although he does not know the psychological explanation, it was the stimulus of the strong emotion FEAR which exploded his SUBCONSCIOUS PSYCHIC FORCE from its locale and placed it temporarily at his disposal to enable him to overcome the threat to his life.

When after a time the prostration symptoms have disappeared, the swimmer displays the syndrome commonly called SHOCK. It is a psycho-physical manifestation exhibiting temporarily many or all of the marks of Acquired Psycho-neurosis.

PHYSICALLY there are   Muscular tremors,
Bodily fatigue,
Dilation of the pupils,
Palpitation of the heart, and often Anorexia.

MENTALLY ...   ...   Elated and voluble, or depressed and lachrymose,
Headaches,
Mental weariness,
Insomnia,
Disturbing dreams probably reproducing the occurrence.

When a mention of the distressing event is casually made by a physician or someone else, a pain spasm flits across the features, a shiver passes over the body, and the victim actually turns away his head as if trying to avert his gaze from the place of occurrence. His heart palpitates, his muscles tremble, and cold perspiration breaks out over his body.

This is evidence of definite psychic trauma. FEAR is the agent which has created the damage and manifestly is still alive and active in the subconscious. The direct consequence of the activity of the original FEAR was a stimulation of the SUBCONSCIOUS FORCE and its expenditure for the specific purpose of saving his life. As long as this trauma (FEAR) exists in the subconscious, any exciting circumstance, physical or psychic, which arouses it causes an escape of SUBCONSCIOUS PSYCHIC FORCE to combat a potential danger. This is an example of the Conditioned Reflex of Ross, to which we refer later in this work.

The above is an example of an Acquired Psychoneurotic condition brought about through the agency of FEAR. It is possible, as far as the author sees, to read any sex element into the occurrence as an exciting agent.

We also see FEAR enthroned, at least temporarily, in the individual's subconscious and definitely manifesting its active presence under the circumstances recalling Ross's Conditioned Reflex.

Where no danger exists and, consequently, there is no situation to absorb the SUBCONSCIOUS PSYCHIC FORCE let loose, psycho-physical manifestations result and give us the psychic and physical symptoms of ACQUIRED PSYCHO-NEUROSIS.

We shall endeavour now to substantiate this statement :—

It is easy for us to understand now how a subconscious, inflamed by sex traumata of the Freudian type, is irritable, hypersensitive, and specially prone to react extravagantly under the impulse of adverse stimuli such as FEAR or WORRY.

When sex trauma is the exciting cause and can be curetted from the subconscious by the psycho-analytic method of Freud, it will be readily seen what an effective instrument this is in restoring the subconscious to normality and gaining a perfect result.

The pan-sexualistic theory, as the sole causative factor in Psycho-neurosis is untenable, and it is suggested that there are numerous causes outside sex in this vale of tears which are capable of implanting pathologic emotions in the subconscious and so reducing it to a state of irritability where its extravagant reactions to painful stimuli are just as marked as those which occur under the Freudian theory.

In the normal individual we may regard the SUBCONSCIOUS PSYCHIC FORCE as efficiently guarded. The subconscious mind draws on it for necessary expenditure and uses it judiciously and economically in the maintenance of all the subconscious physical activities—heart, lungs, stomach, intestinal movements, etc., etc.

All these functions are kept at level sustained efficient working capacity, rendering perfect service without conscious effort or strain.

In addition to the above, this same SUBCONSCIOUS PSYCHIC FORCE activates all conscious and subconscious mental processes. Here again this FORCE is expended in an ordered and effective manner. The resultant mental processes are orderly, normal, and entirely free from extravagances or phantasies.

The above is a concise description of the perfect human mind, working on a full store of SUBCONSCIOUS PSYCHIC FORCE and using that FORCE in an orderly and economic manner.

Such a mind has no fears, no dreads, no anxieties, and in addition is maintaining the Sympathetic Nervous System in full working efficiency.

*   *   *   *

Let us look at the PSYCHO-NEUROTIC mind in contrast.

We shall take again our example of the swimmer. FEAR, as we know, has taken up its habitation in his subconscious and is evidenced by his reaction at the mere mention of the occurrence.

This unwelcome resident causes an irritability of the subconscious. It is no longer an efficient guardian of SUBCONSCIOUS PSYCHIC FORCE. No longer does it react smoothly and in an orderly manner to ordinary adverse stimuli of which it formerly took little or no notice.

Spurred on by FEAR, it opens the hitherto jealously guarded floodgates of the reservoir containing the precious SUBCONSCIOUS PSYCHIC FORCE and pours this into itself to repel an imaginary foe.

The first effect is a psychic, physical, or psycho-physical reaction of ludicrous intensity by the sub-conscious.

The second effect is a temporary active and visible manifestation of the Psycho-neurotic Syndrome.

The third effect is the inevitable exhaustion condition. Can we give logical proof of these different occurrences ?

When FEAR panicked the subconscious to pour out her FORCE in a protective effort against the supposed danger, the immediate instinctive employment was to enable the individual to flee from the place of peril.

This is illustrated by the jump or jerk the individual gives when first startled.

With regard to the second effect, i.e. the Psycho-neurotic manifestations, we must visualize the state of the subconscious at this moment. It is filled with a surging boiling flood of unwanted and economically unemployable FORCE. The absurdity of the supposed danger has been exposed and there is obviously no necessity to employ the released FORCE in effecting unnecessary precipitate flight and so making use of it in physical effort. It is released, however, and must be absorbed by some other means.

The subconscious, anxious to rid itself as quickly as possible, opens up CHANNELS OF ESCAPE, and calls on its ever active servitor, the Sympathetic Nervous System, to its assistance.

(a) The vagus becomes hyperactive and the heart palpitates ;

(b) The pneumo-gastric falls into line and breathing is accelerated ;

(c) The sympathetic fibres stimulate motor nerves and muscular tremors result ;

(d) The same system stirs up the sweat glands and perspiration ensues.

Other functions play their part, but those mentioned will serve to illustrate how the subconscious employs these channels to rid itself of a spate of FORCE with which it cannot deal in an orderly and specific manner.

As to the third event, i.e. the exhaustion manifestation, its presence is a natural sequela. The subconscious, after these manifestations, is temporarily drained of SUBCONSCIOUS PSYCHIC FORCE, well below its customary level, and the subconscious either slows down its activities until normality is restored, or definitely refuses to part with any great measure of the FORCE remaining at its disposal until time has replaced the foolish expenditure. Hence we get those exhaustion symptoms—apathy, lassitude, indifference, and a desire to go to bed and rest.

When we look at the effects produced and physically demonstrated by a case as in Ross's ex-soldier, we see immediately that the amount of PSYCHIC SUBCONSCIOUS FORCE so unprofitably expended was huge. To produce the same physical state—

Palpitations,
Breathlessness,
Perspiration, and
Muscular tremors,

would necessitate the expenditure of a great amount of CONSCIOUS PSYCHIC FORCE, so we are compelled to conclude that SUBCONSCIOUS PSYCHIC FORCE has been lavishly expended.

The above is a short summary of how the subconscious employs its ESCAPE MECHANISM to rid itself of a quantity of PSYCHIC FORCE released by panic and incapable of being used in an orderly and methodical manner.

The subconscious also employs the psychic of the individual as a part of the GENERAL ESCAPE MECHANISM, and many and various are the channels thus opened. Ranging in variety from HYSTERIA, through the FUGUES, AMNESIAS, PHOBIAS, COMPULSIONS, down to the " WOOL-GATHERING " mental state of the individual who is unable to concentrate, the subconscious mind employs them all in its efforts to rid itself of any unwanted amount of PSYCHIC FORCE let loose in the mind under the stimulus of FEAR.

The case of the exhausted swimmer is a complete example, according to the author's idea, of ACQUIRED PSYCHO-NEUROSIS. It is simple in its construction, starting as it does with a man getting into difficulties. FEAR enters his mind, stimulates and floods him with practically the last drop of his SUBCONSCIOUS PSYCHIC FORCE. By this means he is bled white of that FORCE and for a time remains in a condition of physical and psychic prostration. When partially recovered he exhibits all the symptoms of a classic case of PSYCHO-NEUROSIS.

After these symptoms, at all events in their acute form, have disappeared or seem to have disappeared, there remains a definite trauma of the psychic at least for a time. In other words, there is an implanted FEAR buried in the subconscious. This can be evoked into consciousness and its recalling gives a temporary exhibition of PSYCHO-NEUROSIS :—

Pain manifestation in the features and muscular tremors ;

Sympathetic hyperactivities, etc., etc.

C

Any circumstance carrying a threat of danger, supposed or real, is capable of exciting the activity of this FEAR. This activity causes an extravagant release of economically unusable SUBCONSCIOUS PSYCHIC FORCE, and its absorption is brought about by extravagant psychic or physical reaction, which we designate the PSYCHO-NEUROTIC SYNDROME. The penalty exacted by this profligate misuse of PSYCHIC FORCE is exhaustion.

The victim of PSYCHO-NEUROSIS is drained of energy by continuous FEAR stimulation, and there is a rapid falling off in the quality and quantity of his work, or even he may become temporarily or permanently incapacitated.

We have given evidence now of the existence of CONSCIOUS PSYCHIC FORCE, its method of expenditure, and touched upon the means by which it is restored to normal.

We have given proof of the existence of SUB-CONSCIOUS PSYCHIC FORCE, its method of normal expenditure, and demonstrated how, in an emergency, under emotional stimulus, it pours itself forth in extravagant amount.

Let us further examine SUBCONSCIOUS PSYCHIC FORCE in a normal individual. Let us suppose we are dealing with an individual whose superterrestrial good fortune has endowed him with good health. ensuring full capacity of SUBCONSCIOUS PSYCHIC FORCE, free from fears which would cause an irrational expenditure of that FORCE, and free from vices which would have a similar effect.

We have supposed the perfectly normal human mind equipped with its full complement of PSYCHIC FORCE. Untrammelled by ill-health, FEAR or VICES, we see it use this FORCE in a judicious, orderly and economic manner. All mental processes are evolved normally, and are free from confusion. The perfect output of a perfect subconscious.

All the functions sympathetically controlled are carried out in absolute harmony and with ideal efficiency.

On the other hand, we have visualized the PSYCHO-NEUROTIC mind, the mind where FEAR has enthroned itself in the subconscious. Here we see useless profligate expenditure of PSYCHIC FORCE under the lash of FEAR. Painful ideas, worrying thoughts, harassing dreams, compulsions, phobias, and other morbid mental artifacts tumble over each other in confusion and disarray.

The Sympathetic Nervous System, caught up in the horror discord, works itself to distraction and gives us the visceral manifestations we associate with the PSYCHO-NEUROTIC state.

All these manifestations are the efforts of the harassed subconscious mind to rid itself of the deluge of unusable PSYCHIC FORCE let loose by the goadings of FEAR.

It may enable us to understand the subconscious better if we take a normal or as nearly normal as possible subject and break down that subconscious artificially step by step.

When we state that we are about to break down the mind artificially only those means will be employed which everyone will readily admit take place in everyday life amongst us. Let us visualize our subject as a man in the prime of life, thirty years of age.

After a good night's rest he starts his day with his SUBCONSCIOUS PSYCHIC FORCE capacity full. He is in excellent health, free from worry, domestic or financial, free from vices, sex, drugs or alcohol, he is Captain of his Soul, and there is nothing on his mind to prevent the judicious employment of his SUBCONSCIOUS PSYCHIC FORCE.

In his office during the morning, whilst life is all coleur de rose, he receives a cablegram telling him the stock market has crashed, and his main Foreign Investments are heavily involved in the debacle. His SUBCONSCIOUS FORCE being at capacity, he controls his feelings and remains calm. In other words, reviewing the situation in detail he realizes that it is grave, but he is not unduly disturbed.

He does his work because his work must be done, whatever the state of his external affairs. His mental efforts are not quite so smooth working. A certain amount of pushing is needed to make them operate, i.e. more SUBCONSCIOUS PSYCHIC FORCE than usual is being expended on the same task. His thoughts, do what he will, keep harping back to his investments.

When the midday break comes the mental efforts do not relax and rest as formerly, giving the FORCE expended on the morning's work a chance of recovery. Thoughts are over-active, i.e. mental processes are over-active, and this activity means the expenditure of additional SUBCONSCIOUS PSYCHIC FORCE.

The afternoon task is approached not with a mind so invigorated by the midday meal and temporary rest as formerly. The task itself, as usual, demands the employment of a stated quantity of SUBCONSCIOUS PSYCHIC FORCE, and he draws from a source upon which there has been already an unaccustomed drain. He feels this drain. He becomes uneasy and he does not really know why. WORRY, " the moth of the mind," has made its first appearance in the subconscious.

When the victim returns home he feels fatigued, quite exhausted as compared with former evenings after doing a similar day's work. He has his evening meal and settles down to rest and read. He finds concentration difficult. The WORRY keeps his thoughts (mental processes) active. They are becoming beyond his control—SUBCONSCIOUS PSYCHIC FORCE is leaking away.

To escape these harassing ideas, or, more correctly put, to get them back under control, he goes for a walk. Temporarily he masters them for a moment, but they keep returning. Finally, he determines to go to bed and sleep, thus effectively shutting them out.

Sleep does not come readily as before. Do what he will, these worrying ideas still persist, become more insistent, more virulent in fact, now that he has nothing to divert them. When he does sleep they may still harass him in the form of disquieting dreams. He wakes in the morning, but not with a mind refreshed.

A more than ordinary amount of SUBCONSCIOUS PSYCHIC FORCE was expended on the previous day, and the insufficient night's rest had made but a poor effort at its replacement. He has no zest for work because he has no abundance of SUBCONSCIOUS PSYCHIC FORCE. In reality he dislikes the idea of going to work, but he has got to go. Not only has he got to go to work, but he will have to work even harder in his altered circumstances. His SUBCONSCIOUS PSYCHIC FORCE is not at full capacity as he starts his daily routine. The worrying thoughts never cease to make their presence felt, making work more difficult as they absorb a portion of the SUBCONSCIOUS FORCE he so badly requires for the carrying out of his business.

He gets over the first half of the day and breathes a sigh of relief when the time for a temporary rest occurs. During this time, however, he cannot relax, his worries do not permit him to and, consequently, there is only a feeble replenishing of the FORCE he expended on the morning's work.

Resuming in the afternoon, he does not feel like continuing, but the task must be done, and he urges himself on—in reality WORRY urges him on.

Returning home he feels more exhausted than even on the previous day, and he truly is more exhausted because the SUBCONSCIOUS PSYCHIC FORCE at his disposal is at a lower level.

This procedure goes on unrelentingly day in and day out. The worrying mental processes are a continuous drain on the SUBCONSCIOUS PSYCHIC FORCE, super-added to the ordinary drain demanded by his work.

Eventually the danger line is reached.

It is advisable to have a look at the victim's mental condition as he stands on this danger line. He tells us he is worried by his altered financial state, which is quite intelligible, natural, and specific. He is confident, however, that he will pull through eventually. This demonstrates that his mental attitude is normal up to

the moment and there is no evidence of PSYCHCO-
NEUROSIS.

His expenditure of SUBCONSCIOUS PSYCHIC FORCE has
been controlled and regular in the performance of his
duties. His thoughts may have been worrying, but have
been arranged in an orderly manner and not yet allowed
to get into fantastic positions.

He is now, as stated, on the danger line, his SUB-
CONSCIOUS PSYCHIC FORCE approaching the lowest
level of safety. He goes to work in the morning with
an effort, and after a short spell he finds it difficult to
continue. He has no energy left ; he squeezes energy
out of himself ; he can hardly concentrate ; he com-
pells himself to concentrate by force of will in order
that he may complete his day's work. By these two
efforts of will, spurred on by WORRY, he makes a further
heavy call on his SUBCONSCIOUS PSYCHIC FORCE.
This FORCE now sadly depleted, the will-power keeping
the worrying mental processes in order fails. No longer
are they marshalled in orderly array, but tumble
indiscriminately over each other in panic and confusion.

FEAR has made its entrance into the psychic and the
morbid processes of the PSYCHO-NEUROSES have made
their beginning.

FEAR bursts upon the mind with the suddenness and
devastation of a thunderbolt. It clothes itself in the
form of depressing thoughts, as for example, the loss
of his ability to make good. This idea gets a melan-
choly support by morbid reflection on the fact that
work has become of late increasingly difficult, until now
the end looks as if it has come and future work looks
impossible. The panic soon overwhelms the conscious
mind, it ceases to function and remains momentarily
in that condition which we term as stunned.

The subconscious mind now, as in future, is prodded
into a condition of hyperactivity by FEAR and gives
visible indications of its reaction.

There is a profound mental depression often accompanied by dreads. There is agitation, as evidenced by
the inability to keep still and wringing of the hands.

Mental lassitude and persistent headache are conspicuous features at this period.

On the physical side we see shivers, involuntary tremors, and usually vaso-motor hyperactivity is demonstrated by irregularity of the heart's action and outbursts of cold perspiration over the body.

After the first sudden shock has passed—shock caused by the entry of FEAR into the subconscious a large amount of voluntary control is gradually re-established. The victim resumes his work, drawing the SUBCONSCIOUS FORCE required to accomplish this under the stimulus of the ever-active FEAR. The work done suffers both in quantity and quality as Nature has not really much more to give. Curiously, a patient at this time will say he is "living on his nerves."

If conditions improve, the worrying thoughts become less intense, and consequently, use up less SUBCONSCIOUS PSYCHIC FORCE, leaving more for application to work and thus generally lightening the burden.

If the exciting cause is intensified, or if it is added to by domestic, health, or any other adverse circumstance, the SUBCONSCIOUS PSYCHIC FORCE becomes less and less and gives but a feeble response to the spurrings of FEAR, and collapse and confusion result. Mental processes (thoughts) get out of control, giving birth to extravagant impulses, and the final act—suicide—is frequently dictated by one of these extravagant impulses.

This disintegrating process is carried out to its tragic conclusion without the intervention of one sex manifestation, and though the picture is artificially constructed, it is undeniably true in its materials.

It is an ACQUIRED PSYCHO-NEUROSIS of purely psychic origin, and the condition is brought about by the abnormal expenditure of SUBCONSCIOUS PSYCHIC FORCE under mental strain.

We have endeavoured to prove by the foregoing that the PSYCHO-NEUROTIC state is brought about by the

extravagant expenditure of SUBCONSCIOUS PSYCHIC
FORCE and the resultant syndrome is merely an
extravagant psychic and physical manifestation of this
expenditure.

At the same time we advanced the theory that the
PSYCHO-NEUROTIC condition may be precipitated if
the SUBCONSCIOUS PSYCHIC FORCE at the disposal of
the individual falls below a certain quantity standard.

We have seen how, after an exhibition of intense
emotional strain, there is a manifestation of psychic
and psycho-physical exhaustion, due to this FORCE
being temporarily depleted.

At the same time, we maintain that if the agencies
upon which this FORCE depends for its existence are
unable to keep it at the required level, we get immediate
evidence of exhaustion PSYCHO-NEUROSIS.

To take the simplest example first—if food is withheld over a long period, definite psychic and psycho-
physical symptoms make their appearance.

On the psychic side the patient's mental processes
(thoughts) tend to fall into disorder, and they give
rise to flights of ideas ; hallucinations of hearing and
vision may develop.

On the physical side, the pulse rate and tension
falls and digestive activity is markedly lessened,
pointing to enfeebled sympathetic activity.

Then again, after exhausting toxæmias, such as the
infectious fevers, the body engaged in rehabilitating
itself has less material to spare for the maintenance of
SUBCONSCIOUS PSYCHIC FORCE and the patient displays, apart from his physical weakness, definite
evidence of psychic debility in the form of peevishness,
headaches, inability to concentrate, etc.

As the formation of PSYCHIC FORCE is considered
fully in the Chapter devoted to the Ductless Glands,
it is not proposed to pursue this subject further here,
and we merely mention that insufficiency of SUB-
CONSCIOUS PSYCHIC FORCE, arising from any cause,
gives rise to the PSYCHO-NEUROTIC state.

In conclusion, may we summarize the theory we have advanced, viz. :—

(a) That basically the PSYCHO-NEUROTIC state is entirely dependent on PSYCHIC FORCE at the disposal of the subconscious.

(b) That the CONSCIOUS PSYCHIC FORCE which is under our voluntary control takes no part in the mechanism of PSYCHO-NEUROSIS.

(c) That the SUBCONSCIOUS PSYCHIC FORCE alone, when it is extravagantly dissipated, either through inherited psychic weakness, emotional strain, age, disease, or accident, gives rise to PSYCHO-NEUROSIS.

This theory in no way combats the brilliant " SEX-REPRESSION " theory of Freud, as FEAR must surely be the activating agent in repression.

Before passing from a consideration of the case of ACQUIRED PSYCHO-NEUROSIS illustrated above, it is advisable to point out here the irritability which also exists in the subconscious of the victim of INHERITED PSYCHO-NEUROSIS.

Under the stimulus of some strong emotion, these people perform herculean tasks until the SUBCONSCIOUS PSYCHIC FORCE stimulated is in a great measure used up. When this occurs they become apathetic : their interest dies as abruptly as it formerly fiercely blazed, and they become absolutely indifferent to that which originally excited their interest.

It is during these spurts of abnormal energy that great ideas have been born, great achievements in Art and Literature accomplished, and great schemes evolved, but the unfortunate victim of INHERITED PSYCHO-NEUROSIS is rarely capable of sustained effort.

We have now the theory advanced that in PSYCHO-NEUROSIS " FEAR " has taken up its permanent residence in the subconscious mind, and any circumstance, conscious or unconscious, which stimulates that FEAR into activity causes an abnormal release of SUBCONSCIOUS PSYCHIC FORCE.

We have advanced the opinion that the employment or absorption of this unwanted quantity of FORCE gives rise to the subjective and objective symptoms of the PSYCHO-NEUROTIC state. Let us analyse these theories in the light of ordinary everyday cases of FUNCTIONAL NERVE DISEASE and see whether they will stand the test.

Take a soldier of the late war. It is unnecessary to select a case of gross neurosis, such as shell-shock. Any ordinary soldier who has served his time and come through the ordeal unwounded and unshocked will suffice as an example.

A motor backfires in the street—watch the behaviour of our subject.

He jumps excitedly, and even after he has definitely recognized the innocent cause of his commotion, let us cursorily examine him.

He remains with visible muscular tremors involving the whole body.

His heart is temporarily markedly accelerated.

His breathing is hastened, and moist perspiration breaks out over his face and torso.

No one can deny that the display of these phenomena demanded the employment of FORCE. Everybody must admit that the FORCE employed came without voluntary effort. We are, consequently, compelled to accept that it is what we term SUBCONSCIOUS PSYCHIC FORCE.

That this FORCE let loose is considerable in quantity must be conceded when we consider that to produce these four physical manifestations, viz. :—

(a) Muscular movements (tremors),

(b) Sweating,

(c) Tachycardia, and

(d) Accelerated breathing,

would require the expenditure of a substantial amount of the PSYCHIC FORCE under our voluntary control (CONSCIOUS PSYCHIC FORCE).

It is interesting to note that this display of FORCE

is succeeded immediately by a manifestation of exhaustion.

This completes in detail the picture of a case of established PSYCHO-NEUROSIS.

What caused this sudden explosion of FORCE entirely subconscious in its location ?

It is impossible for any fair-minded person to deny that the sudden noise of the back-firing motor awakened the slumbering FEAR of a horror state still unforgotten.

As this may seem the reawakening of a FEAR based on crude physical happenings, let us examine briefly a case quoted in extenso later on in this work.

The patient, a young man accused, and rightfully accused, of masturbation, was threatened with dire pains and penalties, ranging from ill-health to certain future impotence.

On his marital bed the surroundings roused his subconscious mind to the performance of the sexual act. These exciting elements in the subconscious suddenly awakened the FEAR with which they were formerly so intimately associated. The result was failure to perform one of Nature's strongest impulses. The Conditioned Reflex of Ross was the mechanism in operation here.

The consequence was an immediately established PSYCHO-NEUROSIS of the most painful type, which brought the subject to the point of suicide.

In this case we have an example of the subconscious mind suddenly flooded, under the stimulus of FEAR, by a pathologic idea sufficiently strong to stifle successfully Nature's most intense emotion. The result was continuous mental exhaustion, culminating in a state of affairs which practically incapacitated the unfortunate victim until the condition was cleared up.

As we have seen, FEAR broaches the Reservoir of SUBCONSCIOUS PSYCHIC FORCE and floods the subconscious mind with a FORCE which cannot be used in other than an extravagant manner. Now, as the amount of FORCE produced by all of us is strictly

limited by age, health and other physical conditions,
it stands to reason this profligate expenditure of
FORCE must be followed by a consequent proportionate
exhaustion.

Exhaustion symptoms, as we know, are characteristic
features of the PSYCHO-NEUROSES. On the psychic side
we have :—

Headaches,
Fatigue,
Loss of power to concentrate,
Lethargy,
Apathy,
Irritability, and
Insomnia.

On the physical side we have :—
Gastric disturbances,
Constipation,
Eructation of wind, and
General and progressive muscular weakness.

On the vaso-motor side we have :—
Palpitation,
Præcordial pain,
Irregularity of the pulse, and
Abnormality of blood pressure.

All these are classic exhaustion symptoms pointing
to the fact that the subconscious, deprived of its
FORCE, upon which all these factors are dependent,
has only a limited supply of that FORCE to donate after
its reservoir has been ravaged by its implacable enemy
FEAR.

In bringing forward these two FORCES :—
CONSCIOUS PSYCHIC FORCE, and
SUBCONSCIOUS PSYCHIC FORCE,
it is to be noted that CONSCIOUS PSYCHIC FORCE can
act only on the general nervous system and has no
influence whatsoever on the Sympathetic Nervous
System. SUBCONSCIOUS PSYCHIC FORCE, on the other

hand, exercises its function practically exclusively through the Sympathetic Nervous System.

Another factor which is worthy of being brought forward here is that the endocrine glands in their function are entirely under Sympathetic nervous system stimulation. As the power for this stimulation is derived exclusively from the subconscious mind, it has to be conceded that a great intimacy exists between subconscious activity, Sympathetic nervous system activity and endocrine glandular activity.

The Conditioned Reflex

Ross's adaptation of Pavlov's Conditioned Reflex is of the utmost importance in understanding the action of implanted FEAR in the subconscious.

Pavlov exposed a dog's stomach to observe the flow of the gastric juices.

When food was brought to the dog the gastric flow started immediately the food came within sight. This was an emotional reflex.

Pavlov rang a bell before bringing in the food and continued this over a period of time. Eventually he found that when the bell was rung the gastric flow immediately started.

This he called the Conditioned Reflex—the flow of gastric juice was induced by conditions which formerly accompanied the administration of food.

A fear implanted by any circumstance in the human mind will light up into reflex activity if any external condition associated with the original circumstance stimulates it.

In the case of the soldier, the explosion of the back-fire, intimately resembling the explosion of shell or rifle fire, reflexly stimulates the FEAR implanted.

In the masturbation case the condition of the marital bed put in motion the same psychic machinery which formerly operated, whilst committing the act of masturbation and reflexly recalled the guilt, shame and remorse feelings in intensity sufficient to stifle his natural impulse.

CHAPTER II.

THE PRODUCTION AND EXPENDITURE OF PSYCHIC FORCE

The Origin of Psychic Force—
    Rest.
    Food.
    The Ductless glands—
        The Thyroid.
        The Pituitary.
        The Suprarenals.
        The Male Gonads.
        The Female Gonads.
    Steinach's experiments.
Abnormalities associated with the endocrines—cretinism Ex-Op. goitre.
Cases of delayed and arrested development.

WE have endeavoured to prove the existence of PSYCHIC FORCE as dictating all our actions, conscious and subconscious, from the earliest moment of separate existence until final dissolution.

We have seen how conscious PSYCHIC FORCE, operating through the ordinary nervous system, activates solely the muscular movement of the striped muscle group.

We have put forward a suggestion that all mental processes are activated by what we term subconscious PSYCHIC FORCE and that all subconscious movements are activated by the same FORCE acting through the sympathetic nervous system.

We have advanced the theory that subconscious harmony is dependent on two factors :—

(a) the presence of an adequate amount of SUBCONSCIOUS FORCE;

(b) the judicious, economical, and orderly expenditure of that FORCE.

In other words, if this FORCE through any circumstances is expended in a profligate, injudicious, or disorderly manner, we get bizarre subconscious reaction resulting in subconscious disharmony which is followed by exhaustion symptoms. This disharmony and its unvarying accompanying exhaustion gives us the syndrome we know as the PSYCHO-NEUROTIC state.

If we can stimulate the production of PSYCHIC FORCE, we must, consequently, strengthen the power of the subconscious and conscious PSYCHIC FORCES and decidedly lessen if not wipe out entirely the fatigue element in PSYCHO-NEUROSIS.

With regard to the origin of PSYCHIC FORCE, let us examine the sources from which we actually know it springs. We do know definitely that PSYCHIC FORCE, both of the CONSCIOUS and SUBCONSCIOUS variety, is replenished by rest and food. This assertion cannot be legitimately criticized. We shall now pass on to the consideration of rest as a factor in the production of both CONSCIOUS and SUBCONSCIOUS PSYCHIC FORCE.

REST.

Rest is the natural producer of PSYCHIC FORCE. Nature is seen at her best in restoring the energy of the body by sleep. Treatment, however brilliant, can make but feeble effort at bringing NERVE (PSYCHIC) FORCE INSUFFIENCY to normal unless Nature co-operates in allowing the body adequate rest at the appointed time.

The normal individual uses up a quantity of his PSYCHIC FORCE, both CONSCIOUS and SUBCONSCIOUS, in doing his daily work. When this quantity is consumed, Nature implants a pleasant feeling of fatigue and disposes the body and mind to sink into a condition of beneficient rest and oblivion whilst she replaces the used FORCE in full.

Where this expenditure and replacement is normal, no neurotic embarrassment can arise and life passes pleasantly unhampered by nervous disturbances.

Thus the working man expends a portion of his energy at his daily task, returns home desirous of his evening meal and afterwards to relax comfortably before retiring to rest.   He retires to bed and awakens in the morning with his PSYCHIC FORCE restored to full capacity.

Let us throw a monkey-wrench into the smooth working machinery of such an existence and watch the results.

On his arrival home in the evening, his PSYCHIC FORCE well depleted, he may be met with the necessity of going out to fulfil an unexpected dinner engagement. His whole fatigued being rises in revolt, and as he dresses he growls unsparingly at the circumstances which drag him out of his house when his predominating desire is to remain at home and rest.   He looks forward with gloom to what he is sure will be a boring evening because he has not the energy to enjoy it.

When he is ready he goes to the sideboard and fills himself a stiff whisky and soda or some other stimulant, and in ten minutes is pleasantly radiated with quite a new feeling.   The fatigue has marvellously disappeared and he feels fit for anything, newly energised and looking forward to enjoying himself thoroughly.

As the hours pass, this energy sags from time to time, but repeated stimulation carries him on and the evening is spent quite pleasantly.

Has the alcohol been the source of energy ?   Let us examine the case in detail.

On his return home in the early hours of the morning, the subject retires to rest and is soon asleep.   Let us carefully examine his physical and psychic state when he awakens in the morning.

Physically his whole body is weary and reluctant to undertake the physical exertion which he knows he must put forth in the discharge of that day's work. His CONSCIOUS PSYCHIC FORCE is not present in a sufficient quantity to enable his physical body to produce his normal power index.

What more immediately interests us is his psychic condition. He is irritable, headachy, apathetic and lacking in energy. This condition is in reality a reproduction in miniature of a temporary PSYCHO-NEUROSIS, and is due to the fact that his SUBCON-SCIOUS FORCE wantonly spent the previous evening is subnormal in quantity and insufficiently strong to produce his usual subconscious harmony.

As we saw in Chapter I, our subject presumably had used up his CONSCIOUS PSYCHIC FORCE to the extent of 80% of its total quantity doing his day's work. He had no rest to replenish this from his return home until his retirement, say, at 4.0 a.m. During the evening's entertainment he had expended an amount of CONSCIOUS PSYCHIC FORCE equal if not in excess of that which he had used doing his day's work. Whence did he derive this additional energy? The alcohol had raided his supply of SUBCONSCIOUS PSYCHIC FORCE and had thrown it over and placed it at the disposal of his will enabling him to undergo extraordinary physical effort. As this FORCE was burnt up from time to time during the evening, further stimulation of the SUB-CONSCIOUS PSYCHIC FORCE by alcohol supplied him with additional jolts of energy and enabled him to carry on.

Now we have his PSYCHIC FORCE in both its forms the following morning at a very low level. Hence his disinclination for physical exertion as he had insufficient CONSCIOUS PSYCHIC FORCE at his disposal and his subconscious was in a state of disharmony owing to the abnormal depletion of his SUBCONSCIOUS PSYCHIC FORCE under the influence of alcohol.

His inclination is to remain in bed and to keep himself warm. He does this instinctively because he is cutting off all possible expenditure of PSYCHIC FORCE (both varieties) and, at the same time, giving the repair forces of his body time to elaborate his daily customary amount of PSYCHIC FORCE and so restore the body to physical normality and the mind to normal harmony.

D

During this process of restoration it is most interesting to watch how Nature goes about the active repair. The SUBCONSCIOUS PSYCHIC FORCE receives primary attention. The temporary PSYCHO-NEUROTIC manifestations fade away first, and when this has been completely accomplished, the physical fatigue symptoms then begin to disappear. It would seem as if Nature, knowing the supreme importance of the subconscious function, gives her chief attention to this and only concerns herself with the coarse physical side when the higher state has been restored to normality.

This manifestly is a clear proof of the important role which REST plays in the elaboration of PSYCHIC FORCE.

FOOD AS A SOURCE OF PSYCHIC FORCE

FOOD is one of the vital sources of PSYCHIC FORCE. We all know how towards the middle of the day our natural FORCE has steadily diminished. After the midday meal there is an immediate rise in the production. This rise gradually falls until at the close of the evening the energy curve is at a low level, due in part to normal exhaustion plus the necessity for food.

Food as an energiser has of late been studied to such an extent that it is in itself an exact science to-day. It is useless to attempt to deal with its importance in a work of this nature and anyone who is interested in food in its role as a producer of PSYCHIC FORCE is referred to any of the numerous standard works on the subject.

In what manner does food act as an energizer ? It undergoes its marvellous chemical elaboration and enters the blood stream in that form in which it can be assimilated by the different tissues for their nourishment, maintenance, and function.

The author's theory is that the *endocrine glands* are the actual transformers of this material into PSYCHIC FORCE. An effort will be made to prove that this theory is correct from what we actually know of the parts played by these glands in the production of both CONSCIOUS and SUBCONSCIOUS PSYCHIC FORCE.

Thus far we have endeavoured to demonstrate that subconscious harmony is dependent upon the presence of an adequate amount of SUBCONSCIOUS PSYCHIC FORCE and on its economic and orderly expenditure. If we can satisfactorily prove the origin of this FORCE within the body, if we can stimulate its production and curtail its lavish expenditure, we have gone a long way to solve the problem of the successful treatment of the PSYCHO-NEUROTIC state.

THE DUCTLESS GLANDS

What part do the Ductless Glands play in the production of PSYCHIC FORCE ? Unfortunately, the information at our disposal regarding the endocrines is only in its earliest infancy. We are acquainted with but elementary knowledge of their potentialities. One need not be a prophet to forecast that the Golden Age of medicime will have arrived when we understand the functions of the endocrines in their entirety and the function of the Sympathetic Nervous System in its relation to these mysterious secretions.

That the secretions of the Ductless Glands are the *fons et origo* of all our energies, mental and physical, is the established belief of the writer. That the administration of extracts of these substances to replace deficiency of the corresponding substances in the human body has not had the measure of success we could all wish for has to be admitted. That this failure is due to faulty administration technique or faulty technique in the preparation of the glandular extracts is the probable explanation.

The Ductless Glands referred to here as being most intimately associated in the production of PSYCHIC FORCE are five of outstanding importance, viz :—

The THYROID,
The PITUITARY,
The SUPRARENALS,
common to both sexes, and
The TESTES in the male, and
The OVARIES in the female.

This gland grouping is taken because, as will be demonstrated in succeeding chapters, there is an intimate relationship in their actions during important psychological and physiological periods in life.

It may be advisable to set forth here in short but clear detail the anatomical and physiological characteristics of these glands. We shall then be in a better position to estimate the psychological manifestations directly linked up with their hyper- or hypo-function.

We shall take them in the order in which we have named them :—

The Thyroid Gland is situated in the front of the trachea and is composed of two lateral lobes and a connecting isthmus. The follicles of the organ are lined by a secreting epithelium which gives us the active principle of the gland.

The internal secretion from the THYROID has a more obvious and dramatic effect on the body than the internal secretion of any other gland. Its outstanding characteristic is, of course, its influence on the mentality of the subject, its insufficiency giving rise to a condition of idiocy or near idiocy. On the other hand, where the secretion is produced in excess of the normal we get the opposite mental state—excitability, nervousness, and, as a rule, a high degree of intelligence.

It is well to note here the characteristic lethargy and lack of energy in the subject deficient in THYROID secretion, just as it is to notice the restless ungovernable energy displayed by the person who has got THYROID in excess.

Where the quantity of THYROID secretion is manifestly insufficient, as indicated by a cumbersome body, we have a corresponding lack of desire for any activity, mental or physical. In extreme cases of hyperthyroidism, as exhibited in Graves Disease, we have associated hyperactivity both of mind and body, and this may occur to an almost pathologic extent.

Here we have evidence, irrefutable evidence, of the THYROID endocrine as a source of PSYCHIC FORCE. When we take a myxodematous subject, with his elephantine body overladen with fat, deficient in muscular power and incapable of normal activity, and when we consider that the mind of the individual is in an exactly similar state, we surely would have to admit that therapeutic administration of any substance which would normalize such a body and such a mind is an energy producer of paramount importance.

It is undeniable that the active principle of the THYROID gland does this.

In face of this evidence it can be asserted indisputably that the THYROID gland is definitely an agent in the production of that PSYCHIC FORCE which influences our psychic and physical activities.

The Pituitary Gland is situated in the Sella Turcica of the skull. It is a small highly vascularized body divided into three portions—the posterior and anterior lobes and the pars intermedia. The anterior lobe and pars intermedia are diverticula from the oral cavity of the embryo, and the posterior lobe is an outgrowth from the brain.

The *posterior* portion of the PITUITARY gland therapeutically is used in midwifery, being injected subcutaneously in labour after the second stage has commenced. It has no defined place in the general scheme of things relating to the Nervous system except this specific action on the uterine muscle through the Sympathetic. It is on record that the removal of the posterior portion of the PITUITARY by surgery is not productive of fatal effects such as occur when the anterior portion is removed.

The *anterior* portion of the PITUITARY gland, in addition to its all-important influence on skeletal development, has also a distinct influence as a gonad stimulating agent.

Mazer and Goldstein, in their admirable treatise "CLINICAL ENDOCRINOLOGY OF THE FEMALE," state:—

> ". . . The high percentage (60%) of meno-
> "pausal women with excessive amounts of
> "anterior pituitary sex hormones in their
> "blood argues for a compensatory hyper-
> "function of the hypophysis in the menopause.
> "However, the compensatory hyper-function
> "of the sex stimulating glands of the ANTERIOR
> "PITUITARY lobe is relatively temporary.
> "Women in whom the menopause is established
> "for years do not show an excess level of the
> "anterior pituitary sex hormone in the blood."

Though the above-mentioned work deals only with the physical phenomena of the menopause, it is interpolated here to demonstrate the close working union between the GONADS, the THYROID, and the PITUITARY glands.

Has the internal secretion of the PITUITARY, either as an entire gland or by its anterior or posterior hormones, any influence on the production of PSYCHIC FORCE in the individual? Unfortunately, it has to be admitted in the light of our present knowledge, that this influence is not convincingly demonstrable. It can be asserted, however, with confidence that abnormality of the gland giving rise to the condition we know as Acromegaly, is generally if not always associated with a marked diminution of both physical and mental energy. When Acromegaly is a late manifestation, due to tumour formation of the gland, there is a gradual decline of mental alertness as the increased bone formation progresses.

In all patients with an abnormal PITUITARY condition, a definite lethargy, both mental and physical, can be noted. They tire easily on either mental or physical exertion and in the late developing acromegalic this gradual decline in psychic power keeps pace with the gradual decline in physical strength.

Is the PITUITARY gland in its normal state, therefore, a source of PSYCHIC FORCE ?

When one watches the obvious decline in mental and physical energy which takes place when the normal functioning of the gland is interfered with, it is impossible to deny logically that it plays some part. Headaches, depression, insomnia, and other exhaustion symptoms are characteristics of PITUITARY irregularity.

The author examined the Italian boxer, Carnera, when he came to England.

At first glance his heavy lower jaw and large hands and feet strongly suggested Acromegaly.

His height was 6 ft. 6½ in., and his weight was around 20 stone.

His torso was gigantic, but not out of proportion to his height, and there was no striking disproportion in the long bones.

His agility was equal to the agility of any athlete of his age and far superior to that of the average man of his age.

His muscular movement was alert and lightning-quick considering his vast size.

In hats he took 7⅝ths, which is nothing out of the ordinary.

Mentally his reactions were average, possibly a little plus, and certainly superior to a great percentage of the men who follow his calling.

Co-ordination between mind and muscle was perfect. He was a good defensive boxer, appreciated to the full the development of an attack, and guarded against it in the orthodox manner.

In every way from a mental standpoint he could not be classified otherwise than as a " good average."

Carnera, in the writer's opinion, is not an acromegalic in the true pathologic sense. He is getting a hyper-supply of anterior hormone from a normal PITUITARY gland in hyperactive function. His physical characteristics have benefited accordingly and developed accordingly along gigantic lines in perfect symmetry. This development has taken nothing away from his proportionate physical strength and activity as happens in the true acromegalic. There is no diminution in his mental force.

Carnera was described by the writer as "the only normal abnormal man whom he had ever examined."

It has to be admitted that, up to the present, we have not much to go on as proof that the PITUITARY gland is a potent factor in the production of PSYCHIC FORCE. Where, however, Acromegaly due to tumour formation is of late development, the gradual but pronounced loss of energy, both mental and physical, and the evidence of steadily advancing apathy and physical weakness suggest strongly that both the mind and the body are feeling sadly the loss of the normal secretion of the healthy gland.

THE SUPRARENALS

These glands, as the name implies, are situated over the kidneys. Structurally, they are composed of two parts, the cortex and the medulla.

Again, unfortunately, it has to be admitted that our knowledge of the physiology of these glands is very limited.

The MEDULLARY portion gives us a very useful substance we know as ADRENALIN.

Goldzicher-Hartmann and Swingle and Piffner report the isolation of a hormone from the ADRENAL CORTEX which prolongs the life of adrenalectomized cats. Control animals without the hormone died within fourteen days after bilateral adrenalectomy. (Mazer and Goldstein.)

Hartmann was able to maintain adrenalectomized cats in good condition indefinitely by the use of this hormone called CORTIN, the potent hormone of the ADRENAL CORTEX. (Mazer and Goldstein.)

Rowntree and others report marked improvement in patients suffering from Addison's Disease by the use of a CORTICAL extract of the SUPRARENAL gland. (Mazer and Goldstein.)

Goldzicher-Hartmann state, however, that at the present time the hormone available for clinical use is so meagre as to be practically unavailable. (Mazer and Goldstein.)

One fact emerges from this, and that is that the CORTEX of the SUPRARENAL gland secretes a hormone which is essential to life. In other words, the CORTEX hormone is a vital factor in the production of that PSYCHIC FORCE essential to maintain existence.

Let us look at Addison's Disease. The outstanding features of this disease, as described by Doctor Thomas Addison, of Guy's Hospital, at the time of the Crimean War (1854), are chronic abdominal pain, progressive weakness, brown pigmentation of the skin, progressively low rapid pulse, mental lethargy and, finally, death.

Post-mortem examination usually reveals cystic, cancerous or tubercular degeneration of the SUPRA-RENALS.

The outstanding feature is gradual increasing debility, both physical and mental. On the physical side the patient rapidly degenerates until eventually he is unable to get out of bed. Even the simplest physical effort to help himself is beyond his power. This can mean but one thing—a gradual loss of conscious PSYCHIC FORCE.

On the psychic side there is a gradual decline in mental activity until interest is lost in all surroundings and complete apathy is the condition before death grants release. This can only be due to a loss of SUB-CONSCIOUS PSYCHIC FORCE due to failure of the same hormone—that of the CORTEX.

Hartmann claims that by the injection of CORTIN, the hormone of the CORTEX, he has maintained in good condition cats from which he has removed both SUPRARENAL glands, whilst control cats which he had adrenalectomized had died.

In view of this evidence, how is it possible to deny that the SUPRARENAL CORTEX, by its internal secretion, plays a vital role in the maintenance of PSYCHIC FORCE both in its CONSCIOUS and SUBCONSCIOUS forms ?

THE GONADS

In the group of Ductless Glands under discussion the GONADS hold a position of importance from their specific function alone. The reproductive side is simple, but the role played by the endocrine secretion of these glands has given rise to more hopes and subsequent disappointments than any of the other Ductless glands in this group.

THE MALE GONADS

Brown-Séquard, who may be stated to have been the pioneer of Organotherapy, claimed that he had practically rejuvenated himself by the injection of TESTICULAR EXTRACT.

For a period he became a world figure as a result of this pronouncement. Other investigators who followed him rejected the claims which he had made and plainly stated that there was no justification for them.

Although Brown-Séquard may have let his enthusiasm outrun his prudence, there is no question but that he started something which one day will prove to be of the utmost value in the treatment of psychic and physical ailments in the human.

Organotherapy, especially that part which involves the use of TESTICULAR EXTRACT, has been very much derided in the world of medicine. It does not require profound investigation to discover the cause of this. The administration of TESTICULAR EXTRACT has utterly failed to rejuvenate from a *reproductive* point of view. Every doctor knows the repeated requests made to him for his assistance in this direction. The majority of us who are not interested in aiding the romantic side of humanity simply as a romantic side, contemptuously reject requests for assistance of this nature. Very few of us, even if it were in our power to do so, would stoop to prostitute science in such a manner. Those who lend, or attempt to lend, assistance in this way have met with nothing but complete disappointment. Under the lash of this disappointment they pour scorn on the administration of TESTICULAR EXTRACT, completely forgetting that the interstitial part of the gland produces an endocrine of supreme importance.

In the investigation of the MALE GONAD the two leading figures in this branch of medical science are Voronoff and Steinach.

Voronoff's experiment is world famous. He implanted a testicle in an old ram suffering from marked senility. The animal could scarcely walk and had incontinence of urine. After two or three months there was a complete transformation. The ram became strong, the general tremors disappeared, also the incontinence of urine. His whole actions were stamped with evidence of virility, and an ewe which he covered gave birth to a strong vigorous lamb. When the graft was removed the ram reverted to its former senile condition. Once again Doctor Voronoff grafted another testicle taken from a younger animal, and the ram was once again rejuvenated.

The MALE GONAD produces two secretions—the external or reproductive secretion, and the internal secretion from the interstitial part of the gland.

In the human being we see active physical energy and general mental activity at its peak between the ages of 15 and 35. During this period the GONADS are in the full flush of their power, just as the SUPRARENALS, THYROID and PITUITARY, must be at their best at this period.

It has never been the author's fortune to have come in contact with a case where castration has been performed for disease or injury, and it is extraordinary how scant the literature is on cases of this nature.

We have all heard of that strange religious sect in Russia where castration was an essential part of the religious ritual.

If castration occurs before puberty, the sexual instinct is definitely lost. The eunuch often grows to be

very tall. The voice retains its high treble, the body
is covered with soft flabby fat. There is said to be no
change in the mental characteristics of the individual.
This is hard to believe in the face of the very definite
changes we recognize in the castrated animal. The
latter loses its prominent sex characteristics. The
capon loses the wattles, comb, spurs and plumage of
the cock. The characteristic crow of the latter is also
absent.

In the animal there is a tendency to skeletal over-
growth, and the appearance of fat to an extraordinary
degree. The mental attitude is listless, apathetic and
non-combative as compared with its full-sexed brother.

STEINACH'S EXPERIMENTS

Steinach, in his experiments, ligated the vas deferens,
thus cutting off the production of the external secretion
(the reproductive element), and the result was a stimulation of the interstitial cells and an increase in the
quantity of the hormone from these.

Steinach claimed that this brought about an immediate rejuvenation, both physical and mental.

In the light of our present knowledge regarding the
MALE GONAD we are unable to make as yet a specific
assertion as to the role it plays by virtue of its internal
secretion. We can only hope that biochemistry in the
near future will be able to demonstrate to us the entire
nature of this role, which, undoubtedly, must be one
of outstanding importance.

In conclusion, if we accept, and it is difficult to see
how we can avoid accepting, Voronoff's experiment,
we are forced to believe that he regenerated an old
debilitated ram. Apart from the reproductive side,
which does not intimately concern us, the change
brought about in the physical and mental condition
of the animal was revolutionary.

The implantation of the TESTICULAR GLAND restored
physical energy. The animal lost its tremors, its
incontinence and general weakness. Eventually it

regained its self-confidence and even its youthful combativeness. All these characteristics are dependent upon PSYCHIC FORCE, both CONSCIOUS and SUBCONSCIOUS. This PSYCHIC FORCE we cannot legitimately attribute to any influence other than the secretion of the implanted gland, and the reversion of the animal on the removal of that gland to its original debilitated state, places beyond reasonable doubt our belief that the MALE GONAD is a very important factor in the production of PSYCHIC FORCE.

Steinach's experiment is of additional interest, inasmuch as by inhibiting the action of the reproductive side of the gland and allowing free play to the interstitial tissue which is responsible for the incretory function of the gland, he brought about a similar state of rejuvenation. It would thus seem that it is the interstitial side of the MALE GONAD which alone operates in the production of PSYCHIC FORCE.

Those who decry the use of TESTICULAR EXTRACT because of its failure to bring about increased reproductive potency, forget that the interstitial element must still be a very beneficial agent in the restoration of psychic normality.

THE FEMALE GONAD

That the internal secretion of the OVARY exercises an extraordinary influence on the Psychic and physical system of the individual admits of no doubt.

Starting at puberty, the blossoming of the OVARY into full activity makes itself evident immediately in pronounced physical and mental changes.

On the physical side the soft superabundant fat of childhood tends to disappear ; the breasts enlarge ; hair makes its appearance in the axillæ and on the mons.

On the psychic side the child loses her noisy turbulent buoyancy and replaces this with the grave complacency and steadiness of young womanhood.

In the declining years of life, when the degeneration of the OVARY first makes its appearance, there is an immediate accompanying psychic upheaval, varying in intensity from a simple psycho-neurotic state even to a condition of definite psychosis.

The OVARY, as an endocrine unit, gives us much more demonstrable proof of the role it plays in the formation of PSYCHIC FORCE than does the MALE GONAD.

OVARIAN administration as a therapeutic measure in the psychic and physical disturbances associated with the climacteric is of supreme assistance in helping the patient at this critical time.

As OVARIAN action is very fully covered in succeeding chapters, it is not proposed to dilate further upon it here, except that it gives evidence second only in its striking effect to the THYROID gland as a producer of PSYCHIC FORCE.

*   *   *   *   *

Let us then give a brief resumé of the DUCTLESS GLANDS named and their role as producers of PSYCHIC FORCE.

The THYROID—undeniably a producer of PSYCHIC FORCE, a fact illustrated beyond dispute in the hyperactivity as exhibited in Ex-ophthalmic Goitre and the lethargy as exhibited in Cretinism.

The PITUITARY—its role as a producer of PSYCHIC FORCE is not so manifest, but the lack of that energy as exhibited by cases of Acromegaly of late development, leaves little room for doubt that it plays its part.

The SUPRARENALS—The destruction of the SUPRARENALS by tubercular or cancerous invasion gives rise to the condition we know as Addison's Disease, whose outstanding characteristic is extreme weakness and lethargy until death closures the scene.

In view of the recent experiments of Hartman and others (see pages 56 & 57) we may be prepared any day for the announcement that CORTIN administered in cases of Addison's Disease may have an action equally as specific on this hitherto fatal disease as LIVER EXTRACT has to-day on Pernicious Anæmia.

THE GONADS

Male—Their obliteration by disease or removal by surgical interference results in a marked loss of energy, both physical and mental. This, naturally, leads us to believe that their internal secretions play an impotrant role in the production of PSYCHIC FORCE.

Female—That the internal secretion ol the OVARIES is of outstanding importance is demonstrated by the condition attendant on the climacteric in the female. At the climacteric we have a loss of physical and nervous energy incapacitating the subject over a period of time.

In view of this clinical evidence, are we not justified in assuming that the internal secretions of these glands are one of the main sources from which we derive our PSYCHIC FORCE. Even on the face of the evidence we have at hand at the moment, we cannot reject the theory that it is so.

In the PSYCHO-NEUROTIC states there is invariably some gland or glands of this chain out of harmony with the others. A gland is out of harmony when it is acting in an abnormal manner by either over-producing or not producing sufficient of its internal secretion.

In ANXIETY-NEUROSIS we have accelerated pulse, indicating an abnormal amount of THYROID secretion in the blood. Accompanying this we have generally a gonad hypofunction as indicated by a loss of desire in the male and amenorrhœa in the female.

Let us examine the manifestations of PSYCHIC FORCE in man during a life span of 70 years in relation to the activities of this particular group of Ductless Glands.

In the infant, PSYCHIC FORCE is scarcely if at all appreciable. The baby sleeps all day and there is but little expenditure of FORCE either physical or psychic except when it cries for food. The THYROID is, apparently, the only Ductless Gland of the group of five under discussion manifestly on active duty. That this is so is evidenced by the rapid pulse rate.

The THYROID would appear at this period to be the principal producer of the scant amount of PSYCHIC FORCE needed. After the child has cried sleep seems to be deeper and more prolonged than usual, as if Nature were wishful to replace the expended energy as quickly as possible—a proof that REST is the primary restorer of PSYCHIC FORCE.

At one year there is a great increase in the amount of PSYCHIC FORCE in use. The baby " notices," makes a great effort to amuse itself ; crows with delight when it is pleased and howls with dismay and anger when it is aroused.

On the physical side there is also a great expenditure of FORCE. Legs are kicked about, arms are thrown up and down (again in delight or fury) and determined efforts at concerted movement are commenced. All these manifestations require the expenditure of PSYCHIC FORCE, and Nature ordains proportionate periods of rest to replace the energy expended. The more vehement the exertions the more profound and more prolonged the sleep.

Up to and beyond the age of puberty long hours of sleep are the rule.

The glands of the group now exhibiting activity are—

> The THYROID,
> The PITUITARY, and
> The SUPRARENALS.

The active principle of the THYROID is manifested still in the rapid pulse ; the SUPRARENALS evidence their presence by the fact of the increased tension, and the PITUITARY is dealing with the skeletal growth.

That these other glands have taken over some of the burden from the THYROID would seem to be indicated by the THYROID's lessened labour in not having to maintain the pulse at such a high rate.

At the age of puberty the strain on the THYROID is further decreased and the pulse rate drops to that of adult life.

The SUPRARENALS are active as evidenced by normal arterial tension.

The PITUITARY is attending to its special function and GONADS have entered actively into the general scheme of things.

Physical energy is now at its fullest. The body seems tireless ; there is an urge to be always on the move. There is a superabundance of PSYCHIC FORCE produced by the healthy young glands working in delightful harmony from puberty to the age of thirty-five. This is the zenith of physical energy now available in overflowing quantities. It is the Golden Age of manhood.

It will be noted that the THYROID was able to supply the small quantity of PSYCHIC FORCE needed for the life of the infant. This was followed by the additional FORCE required by the child—a FORCE generated by the aid of the SUPRARENALS and PITUITARY as they gradually entered into collaboration. These three were the sole factors of this group engaged in energy production until the GONADS matured. The advent of the latter seemed to light up the others to their fullest capacity, and their combined efforts gave us the bounding energy of glorious youth.

The expenditure of PSYCHIC FORCE on the mental side is rarely in equal proportion at this period to that on the physical. As we term it, the serious side of life has not yet been entered upon.

Let us now have a look at this particular group of glands at this period in life.

The THYROID is functioning in full normal activity. The mind is alert, vigorous, untiring. The body is fit, supple, active, strong and devoid of fat.

The SUPRARENALS are producing their best work. The arterial tension is excellent. Energy is untiring.

The PITUITARY is finishing rapidly, or has finished already, its building and its secondary activity is linked up with the GONADS. The GONADS are in the full flush of their power. The internal secretions are contributing their maximum effort to the general state.

E

Between the ages of thirty-five and fifty—the Grey Age of Worry, as the writer would designate it—the psychic side of the individual is evolving its greatest output. The PSYCHIC FORCE, formerly largely absorbed in physical pursuits, now seems practically entirely diverted to mental effort and mental production reaches its maximum.

Regarding the Gland Group at this period, the situation is interesting, and abnormalities in any or all of the glands are liable to be seen.

The THYROID, at times spurred on apparently by anxieties, may take on a hyperactivity and Exophthalmic Goitre result.

The SUPRARENALS in all cases show increased activity, and higher blood pressure is evident. In many cases this activity becomes of pathologic importance, and the resultant heightened blood pressure is of serious import.

The GONADS have lost the surging activity of youth and in the female the first definite evidence of natural disintegration appears with no uncertain symptoms. In the male also close observation will reveal many evidences of involution.

At no period in life is there better evidence manifested of the importance of the Ductless Glands in producing mental and physical energy than at the Climacteric in the female. The failure of the OVARIAN endocrine, and the consequent confusion in this particular chain group of glands results generally in psychic chaos for a time.

These gland groups thrown into a state of disorder, owing to the sudden defection of the OVARIAN endocrine, seem unable to produce a sufficiency of PSYCHIC FORCE to maintain the psychic even in an ordered working condition. At this period the psychic output in the majority of these cases is oftentimes pathologic, and takes the form of FEARS, DREADS and other abnormal mental manifestations.

Thus we see PSYCHIC FORCE from the cradle to the grave is dependent on the efficient working of this

Gland Group. That there are other endocrines which play their role we have no doubt, but we can maintain with practical certainty that our mental and physical energy is directly dependent upon the internal secretions of the THYROID, PITUITARY and SUPRARENALS in both sexes, whilst the OVARIES and TESTES play their necessary roles in the respective sexes.

In the chapter on Acquired Psycho-neurosis, whose origin is based on some infectious disorder, the writer suggests that the Ductless Glands are the primary agents of defence against the toxic invasion and bear the brunt of the battle.

The result of this is a marked exhaustion clearly evidenced in the gland group we have mentioned.

The pulse is slow, denoting subnormal activity of the THYROID. It is of poor tension, indicating subnormal activity of the SUPRARENALS.

Desire is absent and remains absent for some time in the male, denoting diminution of TESTICULAR activity, and the menses disappear for a time in the female, indicating a temporary suspension of OVARIAN action.

The physical picture of this condition is a picture of extreme weakness, marked exhaustion. The patient is incapable of even minor physical movement, and any attempt at such movement only results in failure and an attack of dyspnœa.

On the psychic side no interest is exhibited in either past, present or future happenings. The patient is listless and apathetic.

In a word, the picture is one of utter physical and mental exhaustion. The glands, bled white in their efforts to repel the invasion, are only able to produce a sufficient quantity of PSYCHIC FORCE to maintain bare " life service " through the Sympathetic Nervous System. They are unable to produce any plus quantity of FORCE to enable the body to put forward any physical effort.

For the same reason these glands in a depleted state are unable to generate sufficient FORCE to promote subconscious activity.   Hence the emotional indifference characteristic of this class of patient.

* * * * *

In furtherance of the theory of the THYROID as a producer of PSYCHIC FORCE, let us examine intimately what obtains in cases of hypothyroidism as illustrated by the cretin, and the opposite condition, hyperthyroidism as illustrated by Ex-ophthalmic Goitre.

The THYROID gland is taken out of the group we mentioned, inasmuch as it is easy to portray vividly its action in the production of FORCE both psychic and physical.

This detailed examination of the abnormal THYROID states is made not specifically with the idea of demonstrating the active principle of the gland as a therapeutic agent, but for the purpose of proving that this gland is in a key position with regard to the maintenance of nervous metabolism.

If this proof is accepted it will smooth the way for a more benign consideration of the other glands of this group in the roles they play in the production of *nervous energy*, i.e. PSYCHIC FORCE.

In the chapter on Treatment it will be seen that the therapeutic use of these glands is definitely advocated even in the face of our present-day scant knowledge of their efficacy.

CRETINISM.

In the cretin we know that the THYROID is rudimentary.

The condition is of two types—Endemic and Sporadic.

In the ENDEMIC type of Cretinism, as found amongst the inhabitants of the mountainous districts of South and Central Europe and in the Himalaya Mountains of India, we see Cretinism in all degrees of severity.

The somatic changes are marked.   The body development is arrested even to the state of Dwarfism in severe cases.   Myxode matous changes are prominent. Cushions of fat in the supraclavicular and gluteal regions and around the waist line are conspicuous. The limbs are weak, insufficiently powerful to support the lumbering body. The result is that the gait is shambling and awkward. The hair is scant, lustreless and coarse. The skin is dry, harsh, and scaly.

On the psychic side the symptoms are even more pronounced.

In the severe type there is definite idiocy. No interest is exhibited even in the most elementary necessities. No speech develops.

The less severe forms exhibit a small degree of psychic development. There is a fleeting, unsustained interest in the more urgent wants of life. Efforts are made to express elementary requirements in speech, but the vocabulary is limited to a very few words.

This condition is known as CRETINOUS INFANTILISM.

Post-mortem examination reveals a rudimentary condition of the THYROID gland.

Histologically in the degenerate gland there is found a degeneration of the epithelium lining the cavities and an abnormal amount of connective tissue.

SPORADIC CRETINISM is of much more interest from a psychological point, inasmuch as the degeneration is both marked and rapid. SPORADIC CRETINISM makes its appearance in a family all the other members of which are usually perfectly normal.

The child, apperantly normal at birth, makes normal progress up to a point. Suddenly there is definite evidence of arrested development, psychic and physical. Degenerative progress is so rapid that in a short time the presence of Cretinism is undeniable.

The somatic changes are identical with those in the ENDEMIC group. The psychic degeneration is also similar.

The psychic manifestations are of extreme interest and definitely establish the THYROID secretion as one absolute essential in the production of that PSYCHIC FORCE which is the mainspring of all our actions both CONSCIOUS and SUBCONSCIOUS.

The outstanding psychic feature in Cretinism is apathy. There is no emotional display—there is no emotion. In profound Cretinism there is no clamour for food even by sign when speech is absent. There is no registration of this vital want in the subconscious, or if there is registration there is not sufficient PSYCHIC FORCE in the subconscious to give it conscious demonstration.

In the higher Cretinous state—CRETINOUS INFANTILISM—mental torpor, sublime indifference, is the outstanding characteristic. The SUBCONSCIOUS PSYCHIC FORCE is weak and only feebly portrays an emotion.

The physical functions which are dependent on SUBCONSCIOUS FORCE for the discharge of their respective roles, only respond in the feeblest manner.

Bradycardia is a persistent symptom.

Digestion is markedly weak. The body never perspires.

The entire state is due to HYPOTHYROIDISM—insufficient THYROID secretion.

The administration of THYROID EXTRACT changes the whole scene.

On the somatic side the myxodematous fat disappears from the body. The muscles gathering force outline themselves and become sufficiently strong to hold erect the lolling torso on the legs.

The overlarge tongue retires into the mouth.

Hair becomes abundant and, if hitherto absent, the testes descend into the scrotum.

General growth in height is evidenced from the beginning of treatment.

On the psychic side, the metamorphosis, though not quite so dramatic, is abundantly displayed. Intelligence dawns on the face. The eyes light up with an interest in things formerly unappreciated, and where speech has been limited to a few childish words the vocabulary soon becomes increased.

Even though it cannot be definitely claimed that absolute psychic normality has been brought about, surely the results obtained are admittedly marvellous.

It is interesting to note here that the sex development of the Cretin is interfered with. The testes very
often are late in descending into the scrotum, and the
external genitalia seldom exhibit normal developments. Impotence is very common, and even where
potency does exist, there is seldom or never issue.

EX-OPHTHALMIC GOITRE

In this condition we have portrayed for us symptoms
of a state exactly opposite to that which obtains in
the Cretin.

The THYROID gland, now hyperactive, is producing
a plus quantity of its internal secretion, which excites
both the psychic and physical side of the individual
to a point of intensity definitely pathologic.

Let us briefly run over, first of all, the physical
symptoms of GRAVES DISEASE (Ex-Ophthalmic Goitre).
The most conspicuous feature is the prominent staring
in the eyes. The second is the rapid heart rate, which
may vary from 90 to 200. The third is the fine fibrillary
tremors in the fingers. The fourth is the enlargement
of the THYROID gland, which is generally conspicuous,
although it must be remembered that a well-established
case of EX-OPHTHALMIC GOITRE may present no
evident enlargement of this gland.

On the psychic side the symptoms are of intense
interest to the psychologist. Here we have the mind
driving at top speed—anxieties, fears, apprehensions
and vivid imaginings of all types are never absent
features. The psychic of the individual is in a state
of disturbance that nothing seems to quell. Morbid
dreads tumble over each other. Harassing ideas bubble
and surge in the subconscious, and even temporary
tranquillity is hard to establish. Insomnia is a disturbing feature. Incessant headaches are the constant
rule. Weakness and profound prostration, owing to
profligate expenditure of PSYCHIC FORCE, are conspicuous features, in striking contrast to the athyroidic
type. The mind is scimitar edged. Reflex response to

stimuli is exaggerated out of all proportion. The closing of a door sounds like a thunder clap and evokes a condition of terror accompanied by further exaggerated heart's action, general tremors and sweating.

Is the THYROID gland a source of PSYCHIC FORCE, both CONSCIOUS and SUBCONSCIOUS ?

When we consider the near negativism, psychic and physical, of the a-thyroidic type, and contrast that state with the abounding surging energy exhibited by the hyperthyroidic of the same species, we must believe that it is so.

At all events, who would dare to suggest that the mysterious FORCE which activates our entire psychic and physical efforts could be derived from any source in the human body more important than the THYROID ?

There is an undeniable similarity in the syndrome of profound melancholia and the syndrome of the a-thyroidic idiot.

There is a definite, though not so clearly cut, resemblance in the excitement, restlessness, loquacity and insomnia of the hyperthyroid, to the excitement, restlessness, loquacity and insomnia of the patient in the Manic Depressive State.

Unfortunately, up to date we have no method of estimating the variation of the THYROID content in the blood during the existence of these psychotic states, but, taking the clinical manifestations, it is difficult to deny that there may be a very definite alteration.

*   *   *   *   *

CASES OF DELAYED AND ARRESTED DEVELOPMENT

Though there is no connection strictly speaking between the condition we know as DELAYED DEVELOPMENT and the PSYCHO-NEUROTIC states, it is of interest to look into this condition, inasmuch as it also arises from hormone disfunction.

We have seen how THYROID insufficiency gave rise to the condition we know as CRETINISM, and cases are frequently met with which seem to indicate a combined hypofunction of the THYROID, SUPRARENALS, PITUITARY and the respective GONADS.

The author wishes to present here two cases, one in a male and one in a female, illustrative of delayed development due to hypofunction of these gland groups.

Case No. 1

The patient, R—— C——, a boy of ten years old, came under the writer's care in 1928. The parents were excellent types mentally and physically and in good circumstances.

The boy was the eldest living child and had a brother two years younger, the latter a magnificent specimen in every way.

Physically, the patient was undersized as compared to his younger brother.

The head was of good size and well formed. The eye was intelligent enough, but lacked fixity or concentration power. The palate was high and narrow.

The torso was of fair development, its most marked feature being the abnormal development of the breasts, which were as prominent as those of a well-developed female of sixteen years.

The skin was of exceedingly soft texture.

The pelvis was abnormally broad for a male, and the illiac crests and hips hidden by pads of soft fat.

The legs were spindly and manifestly weak—so weak that he was unable to go down stairs without the assistance of the hand-rail.

Fine movements, such as buttoning up his garments, etc., were impossible.

Mentally, he was a mixture. His memory for what had been taught him or what he had heard was good, but his outstanding characteristic was inattention. When asked a question his mind seemed incapable of pulling itself together and answering. He was usually silent and preferred to sit alone. His mother stated that he had outbursts of temper during which he was ungovernable.

Physical examination revealed :—

Heart rate	...	...	... about 50
Blood pressure ...	...	...	just over 100
Pupils ...	...	...	... normal
Patella reflexes ...	...	...	normal

The left testis had not descended into the scrotum.

This case is prominently placed here, inasmuch as it portrays vividly the position which the gland group of which we have been talking occupies.

The THYROID manifestly is not producing a normal quantity of its endocrine, as evidenced by the pulse rate of 50.

The SUPRARENALS are also hypofunctioning as shown in the low blood pressure.

The PITUITARY is deficient in activity, inasmuch as the patient was a full two inches shorter than his younger brother, in addition to which his bone development was poor.

His GONADS, as we have seen, were under-developed for his age, one not having descended.

The PSYCHIC FORCE picture he presented bore out dramatically the theory that PSYCHIC FORCE was dependent upon the normal glandular secretions of this group, and as these glands were palpably hypofunctioning, an insufficient amount of that FORCE was being produced, resulting in the patient's subnormal mental state.

On the psychic side, although his memory was retentive, he was restless, indifferent, inattentive, and unwilling to express himself except under pressure.

On the physical side he was lazy, preferred sitting around to exercise and, in consequence, his muscles were in a state of comparative disuse-atrophy.

He was not a weakling in the true sense of the term. He ate as much or probably more than any child of his weight and his excretory functions were in perfect order.

It is impossible to attribute this condition, i.e. his lack of PSYCHIC FORCE, to anything other than endocrine deficiency.

His subsequent progress under endocrine treatment bears out to the full this assumption.

The patient was started on :—

Orchitic desiccated ...	...	grs. 2
Pituitary (wh. gland) ...	...	grs. 2
Thyroid desiccated ...	...	gr. $\frac{1}{4}$
Adrenalin	...	gr. 1-150th

three times daily in capsule form.

In addition to this he received an injection of Orchitic Extract equivalent to 80 grains of the fresh gland twice a week.

To strengthen the frame generally, as he was disinclined to take exercise, it was recommended he should ride a tricycle.

General physical strength improved from the beginning, but for the first six months there was little or no advance in the mental condition.

About this time the absent testis began its tardy descent and by three further months was permanently located in its orthodox position. It was small, being only about half the size of the right testicle.

With regard to the rest of the body, the redundant fat gradually started to disappear, the breasts lost their prominence to a large extent, and the legs became quite competent.

After twelve months' treatment there was a decided sharpening of the intellectual faculties. His speech, which at the beginning was slow and scarcely intelligible became much clearer and decidedly faster in time.

An annoying habit which he had of scratching a sore on his breast or leg and continuing picking it with his nails was completely discarded.

During the second twelve months' treatment progress was slow but maintained.

There is no lightning advance made by these cases, and it requires a wealth of patience, both in the parents and in the practitioner, if successful results are to be obtained.

When evidence of commencing puberty appeared, all gland therapy treatment was suspended. Nature displayed unmistakable signs that active normal developments were taking place, and her work is not being interfered with.

When last seen, the intelligence displayed by the boy was remarkable when his original condition is taken into consideration. His tutor says that his work has improved out of all knowledge and that his conduct is exemplary.

Except for the speech defect and possibly a shyness engendered thereby, it would be impossible for anyone to brand this child in any way subnormal.

If he has a normal puberty now, and all the signs predict it, there is no reason why he should not be in every way a normal citizen.

Let us analyse this case and see whether its salvation was due to normal development or to treatment.

That the child was without doubt definitely below normal when first seen is evidenced by the fact that a prominent Specialist told the mother that the case was hopeless, and that her best procedure would be to send him to a home for defective children. This indeed was the author's idea also, and had not examination betrayed the undescended testis, the probability is that the same advice would have been tendered. Whether Nature would have thrown down the testis in six months' time or whether its descent and subsequent development were due to the endocrine administration, the writer makes no attempt to say.

One thing, however, that is definitely claimed is that from the moment of its appearance and gradual development there was marked improvement in the psychic state of the patient until to-day normality can be said to exist.

It substantiates, in some degree, therefore, the claim made in this work that the psychic condition of the individual, whether that state be one of PSYCHO-NEUROSIS or of retarded development, is closely linked with the condition of the sexual organs.

Case No 2.

The second case was a female patient, J—— M——, aged 18 years.

Born in South Africa, the mother stated that the child had been markedly backward from the beginning, and the only further history that the mother was able to give was that the doctor had said she was a case of " closed head " at birth. The author had never heard of the expression before and took it to mean that there was premature ossification of the fontanelles.

The child had received no treatment in South Africa ; in fact, had never been under the care of any doctor there, as her general health was so excellent.

When first seen she was eighteen years old, and of normal height. Her weight—11 stone 10 lb.—was excessive in a girl of her age.

Physical examination revealed several interesting features.

She was decidedly microcephalic. She had pronounced hyperplasia of both breasts, and these could not be described other than enormous.

Her pulse rate was slow and her blood pressure about 100.

Mentally, her intelligence index was that of a child of two or three years old. She could appreciate fully what was said to her, but required to be spurred into a special concentration effort to enable her to do so.

Her menses had appeared at the age of sixteen, but were scanty and of short duration. Their subsequent appearance, according to the mother, was most irregular, nothing being seen oftentimes for months on end.

Frankly, the case was taken on by the author with little enthusiasm. It looked like a case of established infantilism, with a very poor outlook for a beneficent result.

The patient was put on routine organotherapy treatment. OVARIAN and THYROID extracts were given in heroic doses. After a time hyperthyroidism revealed itself in a greatly accelerated pulse, so the quantity of THYROID had perforce to be reduced.

At the end of six months but little progress had been made on either the psychic or physical side, though the weight had come down.

She was sent to school on the deliberate suggestion of the author to see what her reaction would be to her new surroundings. Of necessity she had to enter amongst the youngest pupils, and it was very gratifying at the end of a week to find that she actually resented this. She demanded to be withdrawn immediately or threatened that she would run away if this were not done.

This action on her part denoted that the mind was alive, at all events, to crude pain stimuli, and gave some hope that something could be done.

On her return home the same monotonous grind of organotherapeutic treatment was resumed, and the next month the menses appeared. Two days before this the patient became sullen, irritable and generally intractable. These mental characteristics were quite foreign to anything which she had exhibited before, as she was usually pleasant, placid and almost apathetic in disposition.

With the appearance of the menses she reverted to her customary state immediately.

Treatment was continued along the same lines and the patient was put on a course of Swedish exercises as an additional aid. The menses for three months appeared at the proper time, became more profuse, and lasted longer.

The patient was now steadily losing weight, and there was a definite shrinkage in the breast substance.

At the end of twelve months' treatment there was manifest physical improvement. The weight had dropped to 9 stone 7 lb., and there were periods of distinct mental improvement, alternating with reversions to the old mental conditions.

The services of a governess were now requisitioned, and an attempt was made to teach the patient elementary things. It was a herculean task for the lady teacher, but at the end of a month she claimed definite progress. This progress was not very evident to the writer.

She was taken to theatres, cinemas and other places of amusement. She was taught to dance and to ride. No effort was spared to arouse her interest in outside things during the succeeding six months.

The hormone treatment, naturally, was unremittingly continued, and at the end of that time she had made undoubted mental progress.

Physically, her weight consistently fell, and the hyperplasia of the breasts had practically disappeared. Of course, the evidence of that condition remained.

At this time she had dropped the uniform placidity of disposition which was characteristic of her at the beginning, and showed decided signs of temper when her will was opposed.

She learnt reading and writing, and at the end of her two years' treatment could write a simple letter which, in a rambling way, conveyed what she wished to express.

At the end of over two years' treatment her condition could be summarized as follows :—

She had advanced from conspicuous infantilism to a certain grade of mental acuity which could not fairly be described as normal. That the advance halted at this point the author is reluctantly compelled to admit, judging from letters he has received from her since her return to South Africa.

The treatment was justified, highly justified, when it can be said that it rescued a mentality from noticeable deficiency to a state where, at any rate, it would pass muster and not excite pitying comment.

That the improvement was due to pluriglandular treatment admits of no doubt in the author's mind, and although the case, unfortunately, could not be claimed as a definite victory, there was sufficient psychic and physical advance to stimulate the hope that organotherapy will one day develop to a point where, if administered, it will be specific in these cases.

CHAPTER III

CLASSIFICATION OF THE PSYCHO-NEUROSES

Inherited Psycho-neurosis.
Acquired Psycho-neurosis.
Acquired Psycho-neurosis (Psychic type).

IN classifying the PSYCHO-NEUROSES, the writer makes two divisions only, viz. :—

(a) *Inherited Psycho-neurosis,* where there is definite evidence displayed in the family history that one or both of the parents betrayed irrefutable evidence of the Psycho-neurotic taint.

(b) *Acquired Psycho-neurosis,* where there is irrefutable evidence that the condition resulted from :—

(a) Definite trauma of psychic origin, or
(b) Definite trauma of physical origin.

* * * * *

INHERITED PSYCHO-NEUROSIS

Inherited PSYCHO-NEUROSIS will be disputed by few and no apology is offered here for the unalterable belief that the Psycho-neurotic taint is transmissible. The assertion is not made that this invariably occurs, nor that the inheritance is in the same degree of severity, but that it does occur will be granted by the majority of observers.

After all, we look for the physical characteristics of the parents in the offspring, then why not the psychic ? Although it must be admitted that outstanding geniuses of the past or our own epoch have usually failed to transmit the divine spark to their offspring, still careful research will reveal that the offspring is invariably up to the level of the normal at least, and in the majority of cases well above that level.

The congenital Psycho-neurotic as a type is easily recognizable. On the average the physique is poor, the skin velvety and pallid, the eye large, luminous and timid, the hands long, delicate and tapering. The head is usually large and with very good frontal development These are standard characteristics.

Physical action, as in walking, lacks snap, energy, and determination. Interest in physical exertion, athletics, etc., is seldom manifested by this type of Psycho-neurotic.

Mentality is generally above the average. The mental attitude towards life is timid, hesitant, self-diffident and retiring. Emotional to a degree, these neurotic victims are the exponents of the facile laugh and the facile tear. Alternately they climb the joy clouds of life and plumb its harrowing depths.

From their ranks are drawn the recruits for art, music, literature, drama and the sciences.

This is readily understood when we concede the high degree of emotionalism found in the individuals with inherited Psycho-neurosis. They are hypersensitive to any stimulus of pleasure or pain. Their reaction to such stimuli is excessive, and under the impulse of this reaction they are able to produce on canvas, stone, or musical instrument, an expression of the pleasure or pain which they themselves experience. Unfortunately for these individuals, that same hypersensitiveness reacts in a similar manner to pain. They suffer an agony of depression and give expression to it, where the more earthly amongst us would simply express annoyance and pass on our way with curt comment about the exciting cause.

It is well that we should note here the part the emotions play on SUBCONSCIOUS PSYCHIC FORCE. The artist, under the spur of his art, will produce and go on producing until he has left himself nervously exhausted, as is often evidenced by people of this type at the end of a performance bursting out in a flood of tears. They live in a see-saw state of high nervous production, explosively evoked by emotion and followed by a condition of temporary nervous bankruptcy on account of such hurricane effort.

F

These people are static neurotics. They allow their emotions to bubble forth because they are incapable of repressing them. Thus they provide the strongest evidence against the wholesale acceptance of Sigismund Freud's " Repression " theory.

Treatment—This condition is radically unalterable and basically cannot be influenced by any treatment. It is as much part and parcel of the subject's psychic make up as his intelligence index. When, however, an overwhelming explosion occurs, due to overwork or some extraordinary emotional strain, change of scene, change of work, rest and gentle exercise is the only treatment which is required to restore this type to their particular form of normality, i.e. constitutional Psycho-neurosis.

Detailed treatment to relieve the painful side of this condition will be considered in the chapter devoted to Treatment.

* * * * *

ACQUIRED PSYCHO-NEUROSIS

(1) *Psycho-neurosis of psychic origin.*

(a) *Mental shock*—This has its beginning in some profound mental shock not involving actual physical injury.

An example of this type is illustrated by a case known to the writer where a son in a drunken frenzy stabbed himself through the heart in his mother's presence after she had refused to give him money.

The trauma to the psychic fabric of the horrified woman produced unconsciousness which persisted for some considerable time. The unconsciousness is Nature's merciful absorption of the blow on the psychic fabric.

When she recovered consciousness, after the appalling happening, she was in a hysterical condition for some days and had to be kept at rest under sedatives in a darkened room. At the end of a week she exhibited marked symptoms of Psycho-neurosis accompanied by Ex-ophthalmic Goitre, and this condition persisted until the time of her demise which occurred shortly afterwards.

Permission is begged to interpolate here that Ex-opthalmic Goitre not infrequently occurs in females after some sudden shock, and it is a further proof, if such were wanted, of the intimacy of the relationship which exists between the THYROID gland and the psychic state.

The case given above is final in all its aspects and affords us no information beyond a picture of immediate complete mental collapse followed by swift physical break up.

There are, however, all too many other instances of sudden mental shock which do not produce such a tragic ending but leave the victim in a Psycho-neurotic state. This state may vary from a simple persistent anxiety, through many stages of painful mental processes, such as phobias, compulsions and obsessions, up to the condition we classify as HYSTERIA.

The predominant symptoms in a case of ACQUIRED PSYCHO-NEUROSIS arising from mental shock are, as one might expect, psychic.

Somatic symptoms may be also, a a matter of fact, generally are present, but their role is subordinate to that of the psychic evidences.

The outstanding feature of PSYCHO-NEUROSIS of this origin is ANXIETY, persistent and torturing. There seems to be an intense irritability of the subconscious with ANXIETY goading FEAR into constant action.

As a result of this FEAR stimulation, the reservoir of SUBCONSCIOUS PSYCHIC FORCE is being perpetually tapped for more and more supplies of unneeded and economically unusable energy, which inundates the subconscious. The overladen subconscious, in its efforts to disemburden itself of this unwanted flood, opens any and every avenue of outlet which presents itself.

If the patient happens to be sitting alone in a room and some unfortunate thought bubbles up from the subconscious recalling the original mental trauma, let us follow what happens. Immediately FEAR is stimulated into frenzied activity. It bursts into the reservoir of SUBCONSCIOUS PSYCHIC FORCE calling for aid to meet an unreal and purely imaginary emergency. The loosened FORCE, with nothing specific to perform, boils and surges in the subconscious mind eager to escape.

Suddenly it dawns on the conscious mind of the victim that the space in which he is seated is enclosed and safety lies only in the open air. A panic desire to flee, to escape immediately is formed.

The tortured subconscious, anxious to free itself of its insufferable invasion, opens up this channel of desire and the victim flees in panic from the room, using up the unwanted flooding force in his efforts to do so.

This is the birth of a PHOBIA (CLAUSTROPHOBIA.)

(b) *Worry*—Worry having its basis in real trouble is a fruitful source of PSYCHO-NEUROSIS of psychic origin.

A differentiation is here made of WORRY having its origin in real trouble as distinct from WORRY which has its origin in imaginary exaggerated troubles, as these latter are merely symptoms of any general Psycho-neurotic condition.

Domestic worry frequenty lays the foundation to ACQUIRED PSYCHO-NEUROSIS, and is resistant to treatment.

Financial and health worries, two additional factors, are very prominent contributors to this form of PSYCHO-NEUROSIS.

(c) *Prolonged Mental Strain*—Mental strain produces PSYCHO-NEUROSIS by a continuous demand on SUBCONSCIOUS PSYCHIC FORCE in a quantity much in excess of that in which it is being normally produced. The impetus behind the strain is always FEAR—the FEAR of not being able to accomplish a task. This FEAR produces a condition which one might describe as an anxiety panic urging the continuous over-use of SUBCONSCIOUS PSYCHIC FORCE.

This eventually has but one ending—the depletion of SUBCONSCIOUS PSYCHIC FORCE to the danger point, when FEAR occupies the entire subconscious mind.

A good example of EXHAUSTION TYPE PSYCHO-NEUROSIS, induced by prolonged strain, is afforded by the following case :—

When the author was at the Neurological Branch of the Ministry of Pensions, an ex-Flying Officer of the Royal Air Force was sent from the War Office for special examination as to his disability pension. From memory, he was round about twenty-eight years of age and held a Master of Arts degree from one of the Universities. He had been employed as a Test Pilot for newly-designed machines and also for Altitude Testings. No more nerve-trying occupation existed in that very nerve-trying branch of the Service.

He gave no history of a gradual loss of nerve during the time he was so employed.

One day, whilst flying at a great height, "something snapped inside his head" as he termed it, and he stated that he must have lost consciousness temporarily. He made a safe landing, however, but his nerve had gone for ever as far as flying was concerned. He never took a machine up again.

His general condition grew rapidly worse, and towards the end of hostilities he was discharged the Service. When seen about a year afterwards, his nervous condition was pitiable. He was apprehensive, tremulous, and quite unable to keep still.

His M.A. Degree would have secured him a billet of some description, but he had entirely lost confidence in his ability to do anything. When his disability pension was reduced from 100 per cent. to 50 per cent. he found himself faced with starvation which did nothing to assuage his mental condition, and he was on the verge of utter collapse.

Examination amply demonstrated the necessity for immediate treatment and the immediate restoration of his pension—he got both, and he gradually recovered his NERVE FORCE sufficiently to enable him to secure a position of trust.

CHAPTER IV

SYMPTOMATOLOGY

Psychic—Lack of concentration.
       Phobias.
       Compulsions.
       Dreams.
       Hysteria.
Physical—Viscereal phenomena.
       Vaso-motor phenomena.
       Musculo-motor phenomena.

IT is advisable before proceeding to the consideration of ACQUIRED PSYCHO-NEUROSIS of PHYSICAL ORIGIN, to put forward briefly the outstanding symptoms of the Psycho-neurotic state.

It is not suggested that in this brief summary even the major portion of the symptomatology is covered but it gives the cardinal manifestations invariably found in the Psycho-neurotic Syndrome arising from any cause, either psychic or physical.

As we have seen, the Mental Moth WORRY prepares the territory and FEAR eventually enthrones itself.

The subconscious now settles down in a state of disordered order. Any external happening of an irritating nature, but really trivial in its significance to the normal mind, enters the subconscious of the neurotic. FEAR welcomes it, raises it to a level of absurd importance, and the result is the disorderly and painful manifestations we group under the name of PSYCHO-NEUROSIS.

A vicious circle is thus established. The trivial external impulse arouses the lightly slumbering FEAR. This stimulates an outpouring of an unnecessary amount of PSYCHIC FORCE for which there is no normal and orderly employment. The FORCE is absorbed by extravagant use and a psychic or physical manifestation of the subconscious activity results.

When FEAR is established as the primary pathological inhabitant of the subconscious, it produces a general subconscious irritability and a consequent susceptibility to any emotional stimulus—JOY, SORROW, PAIN, etc. This susceptibility also excites an overflow of SUBCONSCIOUS PSYCHIC FORCE whose absorption likewise results in an extravagant reaction.

All these stimuli which excite an abnormal expenditure of PSYCHIC FORCE are followed as a natural result by appropriate exhaustion symptoms. A fatigue syndrome is a never absent part of the equipment of your established neurotic.

GENERAL SYMPTOMATOLOGY

PSYCHIC—

Lack of Concentration—Concentration, as the name implies, requires ordered thought. Ordered thought means the adequate control of the PSYCHIC FORCE which produces it. When PSYCHIC FORCE is expending itself in scattered array—day dreaming, or in pursuit of a painful idea, grievance complex, or some other subconscious artifact—there is insufficient power left to bear effectively on a concrete idea.

Phobias—A phobia is a painful idea which suddenly arises when the subconscious is in a panic as to what to do with the spate of PSYCHIC FORCE suddenly released by FEAR and choking it up. It forms a means of absorption, a Channel of Escape for the superfluous energy, and is in constant employment by the subconscious for that purpose.

Compulsions—These are another channel which drains off unrequired and unusable PSYCHIC FORCE.

Dreams—The Channel of Entry of the painful idea is not voluntarily made use of by the victim as a means of exit for the redundant PSYCHIC FORCE its entrance has evoked. The conscious mind, warned by the experience of what resulted when this channel admitted the painful idea, endeavours to seal it up permanently and forget it.   Instinctively we turn away voluntarily from using this particular channel for either ingress or egress as we associate its use with pain.

An airman crashes badly and he remains with a shattered nervous system.   He resolves never to fly again.   In other words, he is closing this channel of ingress through which came his horror experience.

This is REPRESSION.

It is the voluntary or involuntary refusal to operate a channel into the subconscious for either ingress or egress if that channel has been used for the transportation of a painful idea.   Dreams are a further method of escape for superfluous PSYCHIC FORCE.

They have a distinctive and often a beneficent characteristic, viz., they employ the Channel of Entry of the painful idea for the escape in the dream content of some of its malignancy.   Patients, although exhausted by the re-enacting of some harrowing experience in a dream, feel an immense measure of relief at a later period.

It is a well-known fact that anyone who witnesses a disaster or accident of a harrowing nature exhibits immediately a pronounced mental and physical reaction which persists for a period, long or short, dependent upon the individual's personal sensitive index, and consequent reaction.   For example, a hypersensitive individual will give a conspicuous reaction, both mental and physical, reproducing in petto a picture of the Psycho-neurotic Syndrome.

There are muscular tremblings, excitability of speech, sweating, palpitation of the heart, and, after a time, symptoms of exhaustion.   If the individual is taken in hand immediately and compelled to recount the entire happening in all its gruesome details, there is an instant lessening of both the psychic and physical manifestations.

If the relation of the story in full is insisted upon again and again, the eye-witness reaches a point where the occurrence will be related with indifference if not with absolute boredom.

At this point the Psycho-neurotic symptoms will have practically disappeared and the patient returns to a state of comparative normality. This process is known as mental catharsis and is one of the most powerful instruments in successful psychological treatment.

What has happened in the subconscious is that the horror occurrence gave birth to a fulminating attack of FEAR. This emotion, as usual, called forth a surging flood of SUBCONSCIOUS PSYCHIC FORCE, and the efforts of the subconscious mind to disemburden itself of this unwanted and unusable FORCE opened up Channels of Escape, giving us the muscular tremblings, excited speech, the sweating, and the palpitation.

In other words, the subconscious mind called upon its old ally (as it invariably does), the Sympathetic Nervous System, to help it out of its difficulty.

When the eye-witness is made to recall and recount the horror occurrence an enormous conduit of escape is placed at the disposal of the subconscious mind and enables it to discharge the burdensome SUBCONSCIOUS FORCE released without difficulty.

This accounts for the disappearance of the Psycho-neurotic manifestations as their employment is no longer needed.

In this way the dream also acts as a powerful conduit.

The eye-witness of any terrifying disaster or spectacle, who does not disemburden the SUBCONSCIOUS mind by discussing it, practically invariably dreams of the occurrence during the night. By this means some of the superfluous SUBCONSCIOUS PSYCHIC FORCE is jettisoned and the next morning the nervous symptoms of the individual will have conspicuously lessened.

Hysteria—As we know, every action of the subconscious mind necessitates the expenditure of a certain amount of PSYCHIC FORCE.

We have seen that, in the neurotic, under the stimulus of an emotion such as FEAR we have a temporary marked over-expenditure of that FORCE in a crisis.

We have seen that this unwanted accumulation of energy demands immediate employment. The agitated subconscious is unable to do this in an orderly manner and loses control of this FORCE which immediately seeks Channels of Escape on its own account.

The Motor Nervous System is a popular channel for " discharge " of the excessive energy, and hyper-muscular activity, as in tremors, spasms, tics, is a very common symptom.

The " Channel of Discharge " along the neuro-muscular route may select a certain muscle group, i.e., the flexors of the right forearm. The constant stimulation of this muscular group allows for the discharge of a great amount of unwanted PSYCHIC FORCE and the inhibition of the opposing extensor nerves acting on the opposing extensor group is an additional Channel of Discharge.

If during a crisis the contraction is sufficiently conspicuous to be noted by the conscious, it passes directly into the subconscious for registration and a hysterical contraction results.

This is the modus operandi in the construction of hysterical contractures. It is the Conversion-Hysteria of Freud.

The Hysterical condition is fully dealt with in the chapter under that heading.

PHYSICAL—

Viscereal Phenomena—The vascular and digestive systems are affected by the general discharge of PSYCHIC FORCE.

Palpitation and heart acceleration are never-failing features.

In the digestive system there is frequently a very marked upset with vomiting, diarrhœa, constipation, and gastro-intestinal distension. Hyperactivity of the vagus and pneumogastric nerves respectively, over-stimulated by the temporary largess of PSYCHIC FORCE, is accountable for these states.

Vaso-Motor Phenomena—The subject may exhibit marked pallor or its opposite, conspicuous blushing, during a crisis due to excessive function of the Sympathetic, causing constriction or dilation of the peripheral arteries.

It is well to note here that the immediate causation factor is increased activity of the SUPRARENAL GLANDS causing a temporary hyperadrenalæmia.

Musculo-Motor Phenomena—Musculo-motor symptoms—tremors, spasms, tics, pseudo-paralysis, loss of speech—are other methods of absorption of the pent-up PSYCHIC FORCE.

From the foregoing we must conclude that the syndrome we know as PSYCHO-NEUROSIS is the " discharge " of PSYCHIC FORCE accumulated in the subconscious in excessive quantities under emotional stimulus, generally FEAR.

Even at the risk of repetition, it must be pointed out here that the only FORCE employed in the production of all these symptoms is what we have termed SUBCONSCIOUS PSYCHIC FORCE, and that the Sympathetic Nervous System is the sole vehicle by which this FORCE is distributed.

CHAPTER V

ACQUIRED PSYCHO-NEUROSIS OF PHYSICAL ORIGIN

Traumatic Psycho-neurosis—the malingerer.
Toxæmic P.N.
Post-operative P.N.
P.N. following the Specific infections.

ACQUIRED PSYCHO-NEUROSIS of physical origin is that form of PSYCHO-NEUROSIS which has a definite origin in :—

(1) Trauma, as exemplified in railway, motor or other accidents.

(2) Toxæmias—pneumonia, influenza, typhoid fever, etc.

(3) Post-operative states.

(4) Specific infections.

(5) Period psycho-neurotic conditions, and

(6) Intoxications—alcohol and drugs.

*   *   *   *   *

(1.) *TRAUMATIC PSYCHO-NEUROSIS*

Everyday life teems with examples of the PSYCHO-NEUROSIS which follows accidents by motor-car, train, bus, flying, etc.

This form of Traumatic Psycho-neurosis is a very well-defined type, and presents a host of objective and subjective symptoms nearly common to all.

These cases are a never-ending source of income to lawyers as compensation cases, and the lack of appreciation displayed at times even by the Bench of the serious import of the psychic damage is amazing. The extent of the physical damage often gives little or no indication of the all-important psychic involvement. In fact, many of these cases of profound Psycho-neurotic import exhibit very little physical injury.

Cases of Traumatic Psycho-neurosis display a more of less standard type of objective and subjective symptoms on the physical side. For some time after the injury the victim remains in a debilitated condition. He has lost weight and his pallor, partly from being kept indoors, is marked. He exhibits :—

Objectively—

(*a*) General tremulousness, which varies in intensity from a coarse tremor, involving the whole body, to the fine fibrillary tremor as generally associated with hyperthyroidism.

(*b*) His gait is marked. It is jerky, almost to the point of being spastic in severe cases. It is generally hesitant and uncertain, and fatigue symptoms soon appear.

(*c*) The face is pale, haggard and drawn, usually bedewed by a cold perspiration on slight exertion or under the stimulus of some emotion.

(*d*) The body is cold and clammy to the touch.

(*e*) The heart rate is accelerated and at times irregular.

(*f*) The blood pressure is practically always affected, being either subnormal or high.

Subjective—

(*a*) Headache is a troublesome persistent feature.

(*b*) General ill-defined fears and dreads.

(*c*) Restless movements.

(*d*) Silent periods alternating with periods of excited speech.

(*e*) Excitement followed by depression.

(*f*) A tendency to laugh or cry on slight provocation.

(*g*) Insomnia or dream-disturbed sleep.

Physical examination reveals :—

(1) General loss of weight.

(2) Facial expression of general anxiety and all movements restless.

(3) Tongue furred.

(4) Cardiac rate markedly increased. Heart sounds accentuated, oftentimes soft blowing murmur at the apex.

(5) Dilated highly tympanic stomach and abdomen generally.

(6) Reflexes—pupils dilated and sluggish.

(7) Knee jerks—plus plus.

(8) Plantar reflexes—plus.

This may be taken as a standard picture of a genuine case of Traumatic Psycho-neurosis. A patient exhibiting all or the major portion of the symptoms in a grave degree is a case for compensation and treatment independent of the degree of physical injury he exhibits.

*   *   *   *   *

THE MALINGERER

A very interesting type to the psychologist is the malingerer.

His strong suit, naturally, is the subjective symptoms of Traumatic Psycho-neurosis. What he lacks on the objective side he makes up for abundantly by the eloquence with which he puts forward the supposed disturbance of his subconscious mind.

The malingerer should not be able to hoodwink the careful examiner, although at times it is difficult to trip up some of these weak brethren.

In contrast to the genuine traumatic neurotic, the malingerer displays certain characteristics of outstanding importance, which it is scarcely possible for him to cover over successfully.

Only the major points of difference are outlined here, as it would require a volume in itself to detail the many methods by which the pseudo-neurotic endeavours to hoodwink the examining physician.

(a) *The Face*—The haggard, anxious look of the genuine nerve sufferer is difficult to portray, and still more difficult to maintain successfully over a prolonged period. In the malingerer the expression is exaggerated, whilst the suspect is under observation, but as the maintenance of this facial attitude requires concentration, this, naturally, induces fatigue, and there is a tendency to relax when the subject believes himself free from notice.

In the malingerer the anxiety expression is mainly portrayed in the facial muscles. In the real sufferer the anxiety rests in the eyes.

(b) *Weight*—In the genuine sufferer there is almost invariably a loss of weight, due largely to the accompanying digestive disturbance.

The malingerer, on the other hand, owing to the ease enjoyed from the time of the accident, and with a mind contented by the joyful prospect of the harvest to come, tends to put on weight.

(c) *The Tongue*—The tongue is seldom befouled and abdominal percussion reveals no evidence of gastric disturbance or, when it does, careful enquiry would be able to attribute it to causes outside the supposed injury.

(d) *The Pulse*—The pulse rate would be unaffected if care is taken to exclude extraneous aids.

(e) *Blood pressure*—There is no change in the blood pressure if similar precautions are taken.

(f) *Reflexes*—These are unaffected.

The above sum up the main characteristics of the malingerer on the physical side.

Psychic side.—The malingerer presents a psychic picture which on careful examination will reveal itself to be the reverse of that exhibited by the true sufferer.

(1) The malingerer is garrulous. He talks in volumes about the occurrence. He becomes eloquent about his dreadful state during and after the happening ; his awful present and his fearful future.

The genuine traumatic neurotic is obstinately silent : really dreads to recall the accident or even remembered circumstances of the event : he is mute as to his present state and he refuses to speculate on the future.

(2) The malingerer complains of pains, never of a definite character and never consistent in their localization.

The traumatic neurotic does not talk at length about his pain, but exhibits it in certain well-defined movements.

(3) The malingerer waxes enthusiastic over his night suffering. According to him sleep scarcely visits him at all and his dreams are on a par with the horror outpourings of a hashish addict.

The genuine sufferer states definitely that he dreads the night, his sleep is disturbed and he wakes with starts and oftentimes has lurid dreams.

The case of the malingerer is interposed here as it may serve as a rough guide to the Doctor in General Practice. In the circumstances of present-day existence when accidents are so commonplace, any Doctor may be called at any time to give his opinion on the psychic and physical state of an accident victim. No one wants to be other than just to all concerned and, consequently, the few hints above may be useful to serve as a guide in segregating the goats from the sheep in compensation cases.

* * * * *

(2.) *TOXÆMIC PSYCHO-NEUROSIS*

The infectious fevers—pneumonia, typhoid, scarlatina, etc.—having run their course leave the patient in an exhausted state.

The physical exhaustion being manifest is carefully watched and tended, but the nervous exhaustion, cloaked away and hidden in the inner recesses of the subconscious mind, excites no interest and is all too frequently overlooked and neglected.

Whilst a fever is at its height the good physical is on his mettle. He is at grips with the destroyer, disputing every inch of territory, feinting, manœuvring and endlessly planning against the foe.

If defeat awaits him he is philosophic in his acceptance of it : conscious of no effort spared, proud of a stout resistance against an inexorable enemy who, possessed of overpowering advantages, pushed them home ruthlessly and snatched the patient from the grasp of the gallant fighter.

If, on the other hand, victory rests upon the standards of the physician, and he sees the patient whom he has dragged back from the portals of death safe once again owing to his care, then is the time he should redouble his efforts. Satisfied though he may be, his work is scarce half done—the victory is far from complete.

How many nerve victims does one see who date the beginning of their trouble from an attack of pneumonia, typhoid, or some other wasting fever contracted one, five, ten or even twenty years before ?

How often has one felt that it might have been a more merciful thing if Death had won the day on that distant bed of sickness. What an amount of mental anguish might have been spared the poor victim if he had obeyed the Dread Reaper's summons instead of being left to drag out his remaining years a worse than half-crippled thing, a nervous wreck.

The physical fills the whole picture even yet in present-day medical treatment and the psychic of the patient is practically entirely neglected—a reversal of this order of things would constitute the ideal in medical practice.

Here is a typical story of a post-febrile Psycho-neurotic.

At 32 years of age the patient had pneumonia. The disease ran its usual course and the patient had returned to his office within three weeks of the fever's abatement. He admitted that he was physically weak, tired easily and felt that he could no longer do his work with the same facility.

He struggled on and his strength gradually returned, but he noticed that his energy never fully re-established itself.

Concentration on his work was difficult, and head-aches at the end of the day were a prominent and frequent feature. His sleep had never been satisfactory during this time and still was far from good.

In general he stated that he felt entirely below par.

G

He found it impossible to maintain what should be normal pressure of work. He tired easily and was incapable of sustained effort. He was irritated by trifles and required persistent will effort to keep track of important details during the day.

He had lost all zest for exercise or games. Everything was just a bore or worse. He was generally depressed about his business, his health and his future; found himself unable to get up interest in anything ; in fact he stated that he saw the end of his usefulness, if not, indeed, the end of life itself.

This is a typical everyday picture of the post-febrile Psycho-neurotic.

It recurs in the Consulting Room with the regularity of the morning light and its symptoms are as stereotyped and distinctive as the rash in measles.

The gravity of the condition, of course, varies enormously. The mildest type is represented later in life by the querulous Club bore at war with himself and with the world in general.

The severe form is the gradually progressive depressed type whose closure is very often tragic.

Treatment of these cases if seen early gives good results ; if the condition is well established, however, they are most intractable.

Let us examine for a moment the source and origin of this type of Psycho-neurosis in the patient.

Immediately after the subsidence of the fever the physical condition is at low ebb. The face is emaciated, pallid, bedewed with cold perspiration. The eyes are listless, apathetic, and the pupils are dilated—sluggish. The heart's action is accelerated, the pulse soft, small and rapid.

The psychic characteristics are marked :—

There is a depressed indifference shown to all external happenings. Tears easily well up in the eyes and internal emotional upset portrays itself readily. Restlessness and inability to sleep for long periods are prominent features at this stage. Headaches or head-pressure symptoms are frequently present.

As convalescence progresses and strength gradually returns the patient is allowed to sit up in bed, and after a few days to get up out of bed in a chair.

This usually taxes the strength very quickly and a desire to return to bed is soon evinced. Day by day vigour slowly returns. The patient gets out into the open air, exercises are gradually increased and, after a few weeks, normal health is apparently restored.

This is the danger period and this is the period where the patient should enter on definite treatment as for a *de facto* Psychic-neurotic.

It is the author's conviction that whatever role (and their role is of supreme importance admittedly) the leucocytes play in the resistance of infection, that role is activated by the endocrines.

Hyperthyroid secretion causes increased heart's action. In toxæmias heart's action is increased. Is the extra rapidity of the heart due to an increase of THYROID activity stimulating the vaso-motor centre and not, as is generally supposed, that the vaso-motor centre is being goaded by the toxins of the infecting organism? The author believes that the accelerated pulse is due to the vaso-motor stimulation by the hyper-activity of the THYROID and that this same endocrine accounts for the increased leucocyte activity.

SUPRARENAL secretion causes a rise in arterial tension ; the pulse at the height of toxic invasion is increased in tension—hyperadrenalæmia.

There is usually (practically always) a cessation of the menstrual function in the female during and for some time after the fever—hypo-ovarian function (reproductive side).

There is a loss of desire in the male during the same period—hypotesticular function (reproductive side).

Where have these secretions gone?

It is to be assumed that they were present in normal quantities in the individual prior to infection. What has happened to them? Nature wastes nothing.

Let us look at the patient in convalescence from an endocrine point of view.

The pulse is weak and of low tension, pointing to SUPRARENAL insufficiency. It is slow, denoting low THYROID content. The OVARIAN function is suspended Desire in the male temporarily disappears.

Are these secretions, therefore, called upon in the battle raged round the body's defence ? Their disappearance or marked diminution after a toxæmia is very significant, and in face of the clinical evidence we have it is impossible to believe otherwise.

In addition, it has to be admitted that a virile, healthy body in the full bloom of vigorous manhood or womanhood, where these secretions can be presumed to be at their peak, resists bacterial invasion, or if invaded generally wages a successful battle against the attack.

It is well to note here the action of this particular gland group during and after the febrile attack.

Before the infectious invasion it is to be presumed that the ductless glands in question in a normal person of 32 were working at full normal pressure.

When the rise in temperature indicated the presence of the infecting organism, these ductless glands immediately gave evidence of abnormal function—

(a) The THYROID increased its production and threw it into the blood stream, as was apparent from the increased pulse rate.

(b) The SUPRARENALS took on hyperactivity and unloaded this additional amount of secretion into the blood stream, as was evidenced by the rise in blood pressure.

(c) The OVARIES (in the female) relaxed or abandoned their specific function, temporarily suspending all their activities in this direction. This is proved by the disappearance of the menses.

(d) The TESTES (in the male)—Although the evidence here is not so manifest that they have suspended their specific function, it may be assumed by the disappearance of desire in the male.

(e) The role of the PITUITARY we are not as yet in a position to survey in a crisis such as this, but no doubt time will demonstrate that it has led its forces to fight against the common enemy.

Nature never does anything without a definite purpose, and it is the author's unshakable conviction that these gland substances are the active agents in promoting phagocytic action against disease.

After the main part of the battle is over, let us examine the position of these endocrine glands. The entire picture is one of depletion—marked exhaustion.

The THYROID appears to be in a temporary state of hypofunction because the pulse rate has quickly dropped to the normal or subnormal rate.

The SUPRARENALIN (Adrenalin) content in the blood is markedly deficient as the low blood pressure indicates.

In the female the OVARIES, apparently exhausted, make no effort to resume their normal function for some time and the same applies to the TESTES in the male.

We have now the body at its lowest point of physical strength. More important to us, however, the patient, from a psychological point of view, is in a state of profound Psycho-neurosis (exhaustion type) due to lack of PSYCHIC FORCE.

We have here every symptom, subjective and objective, of ACQUIRED PSYCHO-NEUROSIS, and contemporaneous with that state we have temporary exhaustion of the THYROID, SUPRARENALS, OVARIES and/or TESTES.

As the physical strength recovers the Ductless Glands do not keep pace with this recovery, and it is some time after full physical health is established that these glands can be said to be functioning to full capacity. Whilst to outward appearance full health may seem to be restored, the patient's general nervous condition is in a parlous state unless these endocrine groups get time to return to full normality.

Early fatigue, disinclination for work, headaches, irritability and insomnia are danger signals. They point decisively to the fact that the patient's nervous balance has not righted itself, and treatment for PSYCHO-NEUROSIS along the most rigid lines is indicated, the object being to restore PSYCHIC FORCE to its normal level

*   *   *   *   *

(3) *POST-OPERATIVE PSYCHO-NEUROSIS*

When a patient has undergone a severe operation necessitating prolonged anæsthesia, there is a central nervous system shock of the profoundest type, as one would naturally expect. Even in cases where the operation has been entirely successful and convalescence proceeds uninterruptedly, it would be well for the doctor in charge of the case if he considers that, after the surgeon's work is finished, the patient requires from him six months' supervision at least.

It has to be conceded these days that, owing to the high cost of living and general financial depression, the patient and the relatives are inclined to finish with medical attention at the earliest possible moment, and consider a patient upon whom a successful operation has been performed as in every way ready to resume work, or, at all events, as in no way in need of further medical attention.

In a great many cases this is far from being a fact, and a traumatic neurosis of operation origin is an ever-present danger.

There is no desire on the author's part to create a panic feeling amongst the general public that grave operations are necessarily succeeded by a grave nervous state. It must be insisted upon, however, that this is always a possibility, and as its avoidance is so simple when taken at the proper moment, it is desirable that the point should be stressed.

The theory that the ductless glands are actively

engaged in the process of repair has already been pointed out in Chapter II. Whilst their forces are being used up in this function, it is merely common sense to assume that they are unable to lend their aid for the discharge of exacting duties. After all, in each and every one of us ductless glands can but produce X quantity of NERVE FORCE. If nine-tenths of this quantity is required for restoring the nervous system to normal status, and whilst this process is going on, if duties call for an expenditure of what remains, this means exhaustion, and nothing goes to reserve. This exhaustion of PSYCHIC FORCE in the post-operative evidences itself in the usual symptoms of PSYCHO-NEUROSIS.—headaches, exhaustion, irritability, sleeplessness and lack of concentration.

The insomnia prevents the proper accumulation of PSYCHIC FORCE during the normal time of rest and the irritabiltiy and other manifestations make a severe drain on the FORCE accumulated. The result is that expenditure is continually exceeding production, and this has but one end—nervous collapse.

It is only when one spends one's whole time in dealing with nervous cases that it can be recognized how frequently the foundation of nervous exhaustion was dated from a particular operation.

What, then, is the duty of the general practitioner in these cases ? The obvious answer is that he must use every endeavour to prevent the occurrence of the nervous collapse, as this is more easily effected than curing the condition once it is established.

After a severe surgical operation the pain clears up and the gradual return to strength is soon apparent. The patient, naturally, impatient at the more or less long confinement to bed, is anxious to be up and doing. It is manifest to the physician that the strength is more apparent than real, and he advises caution. If this opinion is backed up by physical evidence of insufficient PSYCHIC FORCE, he should insist upon his orders being carried out, pointing out to the patient the danger of hasty action.

A soft slow pulse, dilated pupils and depressed reflexes, combined with muscular tremors, are ample evidence to retain the patient still in a recumbent position. Every opportunity should be taken to get the patient out into the open air, and massage, as the first form of passive exercise, should be commenced.

As the patient's strength grows, and this is accompanied by increased appetite and good digestion, he is allowed to sit up for a short time. This period is gradually lengthened, but at no time should he sit up long enough to experience definite feelings of fatigue. Fatigue is the evidence of lavishly dissipated PSYCHIC FORCE.

Exercise should be begun in the mildest possible manner and gently graded to avoid strain. Here, also, when the patient demonstrates that he has recovered again something approaching his former physical vigour, it is advisable to put him on organotherapy treatment, a mixed gland preparation consisting of gonadal extract, Thyroid, Pituitary (whole gland) and Suprarenalin being given three times daily one hour before meals.

Even after the patient is in good physical condition and his nervous system shows evidence of a return to practical normality, it is not advisable to subject him immediately to any mental strain. A short holiday away from all associations of his illness will be found to be of the utmost benefit. After this he can return to his duties practically secure from a nervous collapse.

The author's practice is to keep these patients in view over a period of 12 months, when one can see if the nervous system is standing the duties imposed upon it in a competent manner.

* * * * *

(4) PSYCHO-NEUROSIS AND THE SPECIFIC INFECTIONS

Whilst due recognition is given to the destruction wrought by the Spirochæte on both the physical and psychic sides of the victim, little or no recognition is taken of the other terrible scourge—the Gonococcus.

As Syphilis is amply covered by the Syphilologist in its psychotic manifestations, it is not proposed in a work of this nature to make more than a passing reference to the nervous condition in the early period of the disease.

In the very few cases seen by the author at the time of the appearance of the primary chancre or, more correctly speaking, after the disappearance of the primary chancre under treatment, it was noted that the mentality of the patient became markedly introspective.

All the evidences of the well-marked psycho-neurotic state soon manifest themselves.

The patient becomes morose, apathetic, loses interest in his pursuits, complains of general malaise and is apprehensive.

The gravity of the infection is, doubtless, sufficient to produce great mental distress and psychic damage, but that the actual toxin in the blood is a formidable factor is illustrated by the following case.

The patient, a widow aged 35 years, presented herself for treatment. She was very definitely psycho-neurotic, with marked anxiety symptoms. Of excellent physique and practical level mentality, she lived a well ordered life, and could not recall any occurrence which might be held responsible for evoking the collapse.

The death of her husband, very much her senior, was a normal more or less expected event, and had occurred three years prior to the onset of her nervous collapse. Nothing in this or any known happening since could explain the onset of the nervous trouble. She made little, if any, progress until she mentioned quite casually that she was troubled by the appearance of a mysterious skin rash. It was not irritating, just ugly looking, and made the wearing of evening toilette impossible. Casually mentioned it was almost as casually examined, and no advice was offered as to treatment.

Overnight reflection gave birth to a suspicion—an extremely harsh and almost impossible suspicion to entertain in the circumstances. An appointment was made the next day and a more careful study of the rash revealed its fatal symmetry.

As everything had to be put outside the possibility of error a blood test had to be performed. This was broken to the patient, the explanation being that her skin trouble necessitated the infecting organism in her blood being definitely recognized.

The pathologist was warned that neither by action, hint nor suggestion was he to convey to the patient that her condition was other than the simplest if she exhibited any curiosity.

The Wasserman was + +

The above is a problem in tactical handling for the neophyte psychologist.

The patient was in a highly neurotic state, and a hammer blow—as a positive Wasserman is truly a hammer blow—on an already strained mental fabric was liable to do irreparable injury.

Unfortunately, the technique employed is individual to the practitioner and cannot be set down in stereotyped fashion. All that can be said is that three weeks were consumed in handling the situation. The picture finally developed itself slowly on the patient's mind. All the horror and the violence of the shock had been extracted during that time. The patient's mind had been scientifically " pickled " against the blow, and no ill results befell.

The remainder of the story is commonplace. Specific treatment was entered upon and the patient made a normal recovery.

The case is interesting from the psychologist's point of view in that it definitely illustrates that the spirochætal toxin has a highly deleterious effect on the psychic of the individual infected even from the beginning. We are all familiar with the coarse psychic manifestations in the closing stages of the untreated or inefficiently treated specific.

This patient was highly psycho-neurotic and could assign no cause for her nervous state. She had probably had the syphilitic virus in her blood for a period varying from months to years. It had exercised a baneful effect on her psychic state and must have done so purely in its toxic capacity, as she was absolutely unaware of her infection, and her mentality was uninfluenced by fear, shame or any allied emotion.

The logical conclusion therefore is that the syphilic toxin *per se* induced her psycho-neurosis.

Gonorrhœa

That Gonorrhœa lays the seeds of a future psycho-neurotic state admits of no doubt in the author's mind, and very few close observers will be found to rebut this statement.

No dramatic revelation is possible in gonorrhœa as occurred in the syphilitic case mentioned, because in the former unconcealed evidence of the disease is manifest from the beginning.

The locality of the disease, the pain, the foul profuseness in its early state, are physical traits which must do definite harm to any mentality, no matter how coarse and resistant. Again, invasion of the testicular tissue with the temporary or permanent destruction of the spermatozoa-forming elements, and the epithelium which generates the testicular endocrine, must do incalculable harm.

On the psychic side the morbid fixation on the genitals induced by the locale of the disorder plays no small part in the sum total of the subsequent nervous state.

In the acute stages the copious foul discharge causes an indefinable fear—general corruption. The cordee makes sleep impossible for a time.

Testicular inflammation, painful and incapacitating, gives rise to dreads of permanent procreative damage —indefinable in its scope, but apparently certain and unavoidable.

Lack of self-confidence, dreads, internal courts martial and ruthless self-condemnations are the usual concomitants of this trouble during the acute stages.

A good example of the Psycho-neurosis brought on, or largely helped by Gonorrhœal infection, is set forth in the following case :—

The patient, a young man under 30 years, presented himself late one evening in 1920. His appearance was rather wild, his manner restless and his speech rambling.

At first glance over-indulgence in alcohol suggested itself, but the truculent persistence with which he insisted that he was haunted by a ghost seemed to point to a more serious mental state.

All efforts to persuade him to go home and return the next day were unavailing and only when he was assured of being received in a Nursing Home and guarded by a male attendant did he calm down.

There was no alcohol element in the case and a powerful sedative was effective in securing a long and much needed sleep.

Seen the following day the patient had shed the greater part of his terrors, but was still apprehensive and still insisted that he was driven frantic by the repeated appearance of an air mechanic killed in his squadron during the war.

Careful enquiry, searching questionings, and a thorough physical examination excluded alcohol. On the contrary, he was in the prime of manhood, in hard physical condition, and kept himself fit by hunting two, and sometimes three days a week. There only remained, therefore, the pure psychic element.

His personal history was as follows :—

His age was 29 years. Family history on both sides sound. He was in the City engaged in shipping—a good business and flourishing. No worries. He was unmarried and temperate, although not a total abstainer. Joining the Army at 23 years of age he transferred to the Flying Corps and had done considerable service flying over the enemy's lines.

He had never been wounded, shot down, or even had what legitimately could be termed a close shave.

The material elicited, of which the foregoing is the substance, did not point in the direction of definite mental trouble.

His story, as eventually obtained, was a succession of exciting but, at the same time, commonplace air duels, reconnaisances, raids, etc., and the patient felt no strain until the back end of 1917.

He had contracted Gonorrhœa in the summer of that year, but he put himself under competent treatment, avoided alcohol, and the attack was not at all severe or of long duration.

He had a period of leave and returned to the squadron.

He did some further flying but noticed that he had lost his zest, if not actually his nerve, at least partially.

He became Adjutant about this time and this life was much less of a strain.

A Subaltern from home joined the Squadron about this time, and whether by ill fortune or natural clumsiness succeeded in wrecking the under-carriages of a few machines by making faulty landings.

The outraged Squadron Commander told the Adjutant to return the young officer to England for further instruction in flying. The Adjutant temporarily forgot the order. Next morning, as invariably happens, the wrecker Subaltern was first in the air, and in making one of his usual landings, ran down an Air Mechanic and killed him instantly with the propeller.

At that time of widespread death an incident ot this kind, though regrettable, excited no comment and was forgotten as soon as the necessary formalities were finished.

Not so, however, by the Adjutant.

His nervous system was in a receptive mood—that is, open to receive any pathologic impression. In other words, he was a post-gonorrhœal Psycho-neurotic in an introspective state searching round for some

tangible brick to hurl at himself.   He found the
pathologic brick in the Air Mechanic's unfortunate
end.

His emotions are summarized from his own relation
of them.

He began by considering himself almost equally
culpable of the death of the Air Mechanic.   Despondent,
brooding and silent, in the course of time he had pro-
moted himself to equal culpability with the clumsy
Flying Officer.   Shutting off his thoughts from everyone, never dreaming of talking to the Medical Officer,
his moroseness became more marked.   Later he cut
the Flying Officer entirely out of the picture and
assumed full responsibility for the tragic happening.

He reasoned as follows :—

He was remiss in his duty as Adjutant.   If he had
done his duty he should have seen the Flying Officer
over night and given him specific instructions not to
take up a machine but to return forthwith to England
for further instruction.

If this had been done, the young officer would not
have taken a machine up and the mechanic could not
have been killed.   Naturally—pure logic ; that is, pure
Psycho-neurotic logic.   Of course he was guilty.   The
Flying Officer could not help a natural inability.
Therefore, he (the Flying Officer) was not responsible.
However, he (the Adjutant) was cognizant of this lack
of ability, in fact he had been warned specifically
about it and ordered specifically to prevent him from
flying, and he had failed in his duty.   In final
effect he (the Adjutant) had killed the mechanic.   The
pseudological ruminations of the Psycho-neurotic.

By this time his work had become deplorable ; his
condition was apparent to all and he was ordered home
to England for a prolonged rest.

His state (untreated) went from bad to worse, and
eventually he was invalided out before the cessation of
hostilities.   Possessed of plenty of money he determined
to amuse himself as best he could in an effort to forget
the war and all that pertained to that period.

Insomnia was a relentless foe and he consulted numerous doctors, at times getting relief, at other times deriving no benefit. It never entered his head to open his mind to any of them and tell of the predominating idea that was wrecking his peace of mind and destroying his happiness. No ! that was a personal thing—a thing of shame which must be buried deep out of the sight of all—a something to be ruthlessly smothered. He did not succeed in doing this. In fact the idea gained vigour daily. The accidental killing at the aerodrome had now assumed the horrifying proportions of murder. A murder committed by himself.

Tortured daily by this idea it can only be assumed that the mental fabric gave way under the strain and a true delusional psychosis temporarily manifested itself.

The condition yielded readily to treatment and he made a perfect recovery.

The question of interest in the above case is : What part did the Gonorrhœal infection play in the temporary psychic crash here ?

In the author's opinion it was the predominating factor.

It will be argued that here was an officer with prolonged flying service subject daily to a mental strain of incalculable severity. He breaks down eventually. What could be more natural ?

Everything is not so simple as this flying strain would indicate.

He displayed no evidence of mental wear and tear prior to his infection.

After successful treatment for his infection and rest he returns to duty. He flies again but notices that he no longer has the keenness he formerly possessed. He notes a gradual inexplicable oozing of that self-confidence of which he was once so proud. He is slipping. He hates to admit it, even to himself, but there is definite evidence.,

The offer of an Adjutancy comes his way and he seizes it with scarcely concealed avidity. There will be

little or no flying now and he is glad of it.   Yes, his
nerve has slowly wilted.

This loss of nerve is not typical of collapse through
prolonged nerve strain.   Here the blow falls with
lightning suddenness and the victim, happy and
free the day before, wakes to the fact that he dreads
going up.

It is sudden, it is final.   Nature has given her all in
this particular direction.   There is no more to give, her
fiat has gone forth.   It is definite.

These are the two pictures presented.   As every
observer of the behaviour of the mind is entitled to his
opinion, it is the writer's unshakable belief that
Gonorrhœal infection had first softened the mental
fabric, and the soddened material had slowly but
unfailingly bulged under the strain until it had
temporarily given way.

The above two cases of Specific Infection amply
illustrate that (apart from the physical effects) temporary damage at least is done to the psychic fabric of
the victim.

In the circumstances it would seem that after
specific treatment is concluded satisfactorily, it would
be as well to regard the patient as a *de facto* Psycho-
neurotic and take care of this feature of the case.

CHAPTER VI

PERIOD PSYCHO-NEUROSIS

PSYCHO-NEUROSIS IN INDIVIDUALS AGED FROM 15 TO 22 YEARS

Psycho-neurosis in persons aged 15–22 years, male and female.
Psycho-neurosis in persons aged 20–35 years, male and female.
The Change of Life, male and female.

THE psycho-neurosis of this age, which may be termed school life, is much more common than is generally recognized. This is a great pity, because even though it may undergo spontaneous cure or, rather, apparent spontaneous cure, it leaves a weakening of the psychic fabric, which tends to give way in later life under the strain and stress of existence.

When examining this type of psycho-neurosis one finds that the great majority of cases come from those in boarding-school life. The cause of this is, apart from physiological causes, the mental strain which some individuals suffer during their boarding-school life as compared with others, and the uniform feeding which, though it may be highly satisfactory for the majority, is definitely harmful to a certain number.

When these patients are brought to the physician it is generally because the parents have been warned by the school authorities that the child has given definite evidence of being physically below par, or, mentally, is falling away from study. In 90% of cases there is clear evidence of physical slip.

At this point it is necessary to divide these cases into males and females, because the sex function so different in each has an all-important bearing on the condition. Let us take the boy first as the simplest type.

H

THE SCHOOLBOY

At about the age of 16, when growth is at its height, his physical resources are strained to the utmost. Hard study and concentration undoubtedly play an important role if the subject is of the studious type. Here we have a picture of a youth of 16, his physical body rapidly growing, his ductless glands rapidly maturing and working at full pressure to play their part in the building up of that body. On top of this the mental strain of concentration is added, and these united factors combine to throw out of gear temporarily the smooth working of the individual's psychic system. The subject becomes irritable, loses flesh and strength, repeatedly complains of headache, inability to concentrate on his work, lethargy and general nervous exhaustion. This condition is usually made light of ; oftentimes calls down punishment by the school authorities on the head of the unfortunate victim, and is seldom or never treated.

It says much for the recuperative powers of the ductless glands that they are able to stand up against this period of maltreatment and eventually pilot the body through to adult efficiency. Though they do this, there is no doubt in the author's mind that the stigmata of the battle make themselves manifest at a later period, when pressure of life increases and give rise to that exhaustion psycho-neurosis which the physician is subsequently called upon to treat.

There is, of course, another element in the male life of this period. Reference is made to masturbation. That this is detrimental to the nervous system of the boy is undeniable. Apart from the physical loss involved, there is the far more important psychological element instilled into the subconscious—shame, guilt, fear, and other morbid denizens of the mind.

Let us finish with the boy student before passing on to the consideration of his sister, the schoolgirl. Where a boy of the studious type, fast growing, and physically weak is manifesting marked nervous symptoms, it is advisable to withdraw him instantly from school. This will entail no actual loss of benefit as regards his work, because he is incapable of absorbing beneficially anything he may study whilst in this state.

Take the child home and cut him off from all mental effort as far as books are concerned. Encourage physical exercise and mental amusement of every description. Give him plain, wholesome food to build up his body and train him to observe everything with which he comes into contact to keep his mind bright and occupied.

If the masturbation element is prominent the greatest care must be exercised in approaching the youth. In the writer's opinion, it is entirely inadvisable for the parent (father) to attempt to do this. If the family physician has a special bent for the psychological understanding of boys he must intervene. If he is brusque, abrupt, non-understanding and unsympathetic, it is advisable to send the boy to a psychologist. Even here every tact and sympathy must be displayed to handle effectively this delicate situation.

It is not suggested that it is necessary to withdraw the boy from school for the latter consideration. This would be a grave error, as it would give the matter gravity in the mind of the boy, and this is not at all desirable. On the contrary, it should be treated in a sympathetic but firm manner, so as to arouse no suspicion of definite harm done and imply no fear of subsequent consequences.

In the case of the debilitated boy, the rest at home away from the drag of studies and the refurnishing of strength by home food and plenty of outdoor exercise will build him up at this critical period. He can resume his school the following term with perfect security. It will be found that the mental rest and the observation training has developed him to such a degree mentally that he soon catches up on the period of time lost.

As a general rule, the boy at this age, when withdrawn from school and heavy studies, builds up his physical constitution under the influence of open-air life and sound home feeding.

The debilitated, nervous, and physical conditions undergo spontaneous cure and disappear, but in the obstinate cases where this does not occur special treatment has to be resorted to.

First of all, a strenuous effort must be made to build up the physical constitution of the boy by special exercises in the open air and diet. Study for the time being is absolutely forbidden. The exercises should be of a type which naturally attract the boy. As, for example, it is futile to put a nervous boy who is frightened of horses to ride. The constant dread of injury would undo any benefit he would derive from such exercise. The exercise he chooses must not be indulged in to the point of over-tiring him, and general body massage after such exercise is strongly advocated.

A careful watch must be kept on his digestive system and everything done to promote free elimination daily.

When the boy shows definite evidence of increasing strength by putting on additional weight, it is advisable to question him closely on his habits and inclinations. This should only be done when the physician has gained the complete confidence of the boy and when it is evident that he relies on the doctor for advice and encouragement.

In addition to this the general treatment for Psychoneurosis must be given, especially gland therapy.

If the breakdown has occurred through over-study, ill-health or any tangible physical cause, a good result can be anticipated at the end of a year at most when the boy may return to his studies insured against a further breakdown.

If, on the other hand, his nervous collapse is an indication of an inherited Psycho-neurotic taint, the case will, undoubtedly, improve under rest and treatment, but the possibility of a complete eradication of the neurosis is more than can be hoped for. There is no reason, however, why a boy of this type should not return to school and qualify himself to fill a role, and perhaps a very distinctive one, in life.

THE SCHOOLGIRL

The schoolgirl at this age is more interesting to the psychologist than practically at any other period of her life. This is the time when she is laying the foundation of her whole nervous future and as this future is so intimately linked up with the development of her ovaries it is an epoch of great interest not unmixed with anxiety to the observer.

The writer definitely states that cases of specific mental disease which make their appearance in late adult life may well have their beginning in puberty irregularities allowed to flourish by lack of treatment or by injudicious treatment during these critical years of a girl's life.

The author recognizes the heavy responsibility he assumes in making a statement of this nature, but when one is confronted by a girl possessing a clean mental family history on both sides exhibiting evidences of schizophrænic taint, it is impossible to shut one's eyes to the fact.

Again and again one listens to the history of marked menstrual irregularity in those early years, accompanied by well-defined nervous symptoms which later develop into definite schizophrænic manifestations. That this state may degenerate later on into Dementia Præcox one is forced to believe.

When these cases are taken in the early nervous condition, or even in the early schizophrænic state, they yield to treatment and yield comparatively easily. It seems lamentable, however, that girls at school suffering from these menstrual irregularities, which are palpably injuring their nervous system, should not be treated and such irregularities put right once and for all, rather than subject them to the dangers of mental collapse in later life.

The writer regards this chapter, especially in its reference to girls between the ages of 16 and 20, as one of the most important in this short work. When a girl at school exhibits definite evidence of a non-smooth working development of her maturity, the girl should be withdrawn from school immediately and put under efficient treatment. As a rule the overriding condition will be found to be of blood origin and home is the ideal place for such cases.

At the beginning rest and the expenditure of the least amount of energy possible must be enforced. Nourishing food and attention to the bowels, kidneys, and skin is the next important step. Everything tending to increase the quantity and quality of the blood must be employed.

As the strength recovers graduated excerises in the open air are planned out. When strength is manifestly replenished and the blood condition is nearly normal, the administration of Ovarian hormone by the mouth and hypodermically should begin at once. The girl should not be allowed to resume her studies until menstruation has definitely regularized itself over a period of six months.

If this treatment has been effectively carried out the nervous symptoms disappear and very rarely, if ever, give subsequent trouble.

The above treatment can be regarded as sufficient for simple cases, and the results are ivaraiably good. There are other cases, however, which owing to the duration of the trouble or some grave complication are recalcitrant to treatment.

The first step in such cases is to withdraw the child from school immediately. The next step is to send her to a gynæcologist and have his opinion about the condition of the pelvic organs. If any abnormality exists here the case should be left in his hands until the position has been satisfactorily dealt with.

Very often when the gynæcologist has treated satisfactorily some irregularity here the whole physical status immediately improves, the menses become regular and the nervous system gradually settles down to a normal placid course.

If the gynæcologist expresses himself as satisfied at the beginning with the pelvic organs, as to their development and position, then the blood condition is the next state into which enquiry must be made. The pathologist's report will clear up the situation and steps can then be taken to put matters right. Very often it will be found that a defective alimentary condition with its allied toxæmia is at the root of all the trouble, and attention must be focussed on putting this in the best possible working order.

The conditions detailed above cover for all practical purposes the exciting causes of the PSYCHO-NEUROSIS met with at this interesting age. These cases, in the girl of healthy parentage, should present no grave trouble to the practitioner. They are all amenable to treatment if this treatment is begun sufficiently early and carried out with due care.

When special treatment for the exciting cause has produced a good result, it is always advisable still to regard the case as one of definite PSYCHO-NEUROSIS, and put the patient on the full treatment as outlined in Chapter XV.

A girl of this age efficiently treated for the exciting cause of her PSYCHO-NEUROSIS and specifically treated for her Psycho-neurotic condition itself, can return to school in perfect security well guarded against any possibility of a further breakdown.

PSYCHO-NEUROSIS IN PERSONS AGED FROM 20 TO 35

Male—From the nervous point of view this is the golden period in the existence of the male. His physical well-being is at its highest ; nervous energy floods his whole being to repletion and he fairly bounds with superfluous vitality. His whole body vibrates strength, force, energy. He strains at the leash to accomplish deeds requiring nerve strength and stamina. Games and exercises in the fresh air keep him at the peak of physical perfection, and the cares and worries of mature responsibility have not pushed themselves forward sufficiently well to become troublesome.

PSYCHO-NEUROSIS of any serious character is never met with at this period. The congenital neurotic, of course, like the poor we have always with us, and apart from this type the only evidence of neurosis in the male at this age is the neurosis subsequent on an accident, operation, wasting fever or a specific disease. As these exceptions have categories of their own, they have no place in the chapter devoted to healthy manhood between the ages of 20 and 35, especially as they are treated separately under their different headings.

This age, therefore, in the young male holds no interest for the psychologist except as a comparative standard of how happy and healthy a man can be before time and worry cast their baneful shadows upon his life.

Female—This period in the life of the female resembles the corresponding period in the male life in its lack of interesting psychological material. That is to say, if the female at this age has had a normal puberty and has escaped disease, injury and especially the specific infections, she rarely if ever exhibits a psycho-neurotic tendency.

At the same time it has to be remembered that this is the child-bearing age, and this condition at times brings in its train abnormal psychic states. These states, fortunately, are not at all common, nor are they truly psycho-neurotic in character, as, for example, puerperal mania met with is a definitely psychotic manifestation, and has no relation to the Psycho-neurotic state.

THE CHANGE OF LIFE IN MEN. DOES IT EXIST?

To the author's mind there is no disputing that a definite nervous metamorphosis occurs in the male between the ages of 48 and 54. No one would uphold for a moment that the change is as definite and clear cut as obtains in the case of the climacteric in the female, but change there is, and that admits of no dispute.

The age at which this change occurs is later in the male than in the female. It is very doubtful if the onset occurs in the average male earlier than the age of 48, and it may be a good ten years later.

The anatomical changes are denoted by shrinkage of the gonads, whose firm elastic touch is replaced by a soft yielding feel on pressure. Disappearance of pubic hair and, as a rule, a pronounced tendency to put on fatty tissue in the neighbourhood of the breasts and buttocks is noticeable. In fact, there is a trend towards general adiposis. The prostate displays a marked change. The spongy secreting tissue of adult life shows definite evidence of degeneration. Fibrous tissue makes its appearance and gradually starts to replace the active tissue of the young gland.

In the majority of males at this age few marked traits of a psycho-neurotic type are noticeable, but in all there is a manifest loss not only of sexual activity, but mental alertness and push also.

At this period very often a complete change in the mental disposition of the subject makes its appearance. Men who have been rigidly abstemious suddenly and unaccountably develop an astounding inclination for alcohol. Others, restrained and rigid in their conduct, exhibit a disposition to launch out in a form of behaviour which in their former life they would have regarded as dissipation. The last category comprises those who have definite pathologic sexual tendencies —tendencies so uncontrolled and indiscreet as to bring them at times into the grip of the law.

A male patient of the mildest type at this period seen in the consulting room complains in a general way of gradual falling off of his abilities—not confined to his sexual abilities. He states that he does not feel that he is at all himself. He has neither the energy nor the desire to tackle his work with the same zest which he formerly had, and he is unable to account for his

sudden falling off. His mental concentration is poor.
He has no confidence in the sense that he formerly
had—confidence in his ability to wrestle with a problem,
and he finds himself irritated by trivial little everyday
events which formerly were regarded by him as of no
significance.

He attributes these occurrences to a head heaviness,
not a headache in the proper sense, but a sort of mental
dullness which seems to hold him encompassed around
at this time.

Then, again, his sleep is not at all satisfactory. He
wakes in the middle of the night two or three times,
and, quite a new thing in his life, he has to void urine
during the night.

These are the cardinal signs of the climacteric in the
average male. They are of no outstanding import and
call for very little treatment.   As a matter of fact,
very little in the way of treatment can be accomplished,
nor is it advisable to attempt specific treatment for
the condition, as it only surrounds it with a significance of which it is not worthy, and may make the
patient introspective, thus doing definite damage.

The author, unfortunately, has never had experience
of the type of case where a patient exhibited hyper-
sexual tendencies, and, as a consequence, remained in
danger of placing himself within the grasp of the law.
If such a case, however, came under his notice, and
showed marked prostatic enlargement, he would have
no hesitation in advising prostatic removal as a
preliminary step.

Prostatic conditions which interfere with the normal
voidance of urine are very often accompanied by
genital irritability, and this irritability disappears
when the prostate is removed. The importance of this
condition is that it is often the basic cause of those
fantastic sexual cases which from time to time appear
in our police courts, where the unfortunate man requires
surgical and not penal treatment.

To the author's mind there is nothing more pathetic
than to witness, as we have witnessed in the past

ten years, the spectacle of a man grown grey in the service of his country and covered with well-merited honours dragged in the evening of his life before his country's tribunal and stamped as a criminal for an offence which is only the outcome of a reflex irritation. The comparatively simple operation (prostatectomy) would definitely destroy once and for all this " criminal " trend and allow the old servitor to sink into his grave with his untarnished honours still thick upon him.

The importance of the general nervous upset which in some degree is present at this period in the life of the male, is the fact that any adverse happening at this period is bound to produce a psycho-neurotic state of a much more severe type than would occur at any other period in the life of the individual. Business men facing a crisis, financial or from any other cause, seem to wilt when it occurs at this critical age.

The nervous system, remodelling itself for the terminal conditions of life, is temporarily in a weakened state. It seems to feel the need of something equivalent to the need exhibited by the female nervous system owing to the falling off of the internal secretion of the ovary.

What is the falling off in the male ? It is to be presumed that it is in the testes and its inseparable ally, the prostate.

We have seen definite evidence of anatomical decline in the first gland as well as definite evidence of fibrous degeneration in the second gland. These degenerative processes point towards a pronounced diminution of secreting tissue in these glands from the procreative angle, and, naturally, it is to be inferred that their internal sections which are so necessary for the maintenance of nervous balance are also falling off. *Vide* " Steinach's and Voronoff's Experiments," Chapter II.

When a Psycho-neurotic presents himself for treatment and he falls within the age generally assigned to the change of life in the male, organotherapy is of undeniable importance in the treatment of the patient. The author is well aware that testicular administration has been pooh-poohed almost universally. To the author's mind this objection is based on the ineffectiveness of male gonad use for the promotion of sex activity. The writer has had no experience of it from this point of view, and, consequently, has no opinion to offer. Of the psycho-neurotic side he has had very definite experience over a long period, and indisputable evidence that testicular extract is of supreme importance in treating these cases.

The general treatment of the psycho-neurosis which arises at this time in the life of a man differs in no marked degree from that treatment outlined in a succeeding chapter. In this class, however, there must be a definite and absolute break from former surroundings. The male would seem to be a much more "groovy" animal in the fifties than the female. He is harder to shift from established position and established procedure. Change is resented fiercely, and it is difficult to convince the business or professional man that he is ill and needs to give up his work when he has not got a temperature or a broken leg to give him demonstrable physical proof that the necessity exists.

If there is difficulty in micturition it is advisable that the patient be sent to a genito-urinary surgeon for advice. Nothing is more inclined, on the physical side, to make a man introspective than the incompetent functioning of anything apparently connected with the genitalia. This apart from the inconvenience and discomfort associated with the condition itself.

If the surgeon advises prostate removal it is useless to commence treatment of the psycho-neurotic state. As long as a large and fibrous prostate remains *in situ* it will always form the starting-off point for introspection.

The relief obtained and the general comfort experienced after a successful removal of the prostate places the patient in a benign frame of mind for general nervous treatment with every prospect of success.

When convalescence after the operation is firmly established, the patient is put on routine exercise in the open air, followed by baths and massage as outlined in the chapter dealing with general treatment.

At the end of the month :—

Testicular extract	...	grs. 20 siccum
Prostatic extract	...	grs. 20 siccum

in capsule form is administered three times daily, and hypodermic injections of testicular extract equivalent to 75 grains of the fresh gland are given daily.

When the patient seems to have shed his general nervous symptoms and feels a desire to return to normal life, he may be allowed to do so with every confidence of his being able to stand normal strain comparable with his age. Where financial and other circumstances permit it, a sea cruise is ideal.

A good example of what is regarded by the writer as a typical case of " Change of Life " neurosis in the male is afforded by the case of the Rev. ——.

This gentleman was admitted for treatment suffering from " *Sciatica* and general nervous weakness," in his own words. He was unable to carry on with his ministerial work and was contemplating retirement.

As his age was only 52 years and his physique excellent, it was obvious that the psychic element in this case far outweighed the physical.

The sciatica, it appeared, had started three years previously, and the leg had been burnt, blistered and generally treated, with little or no relief. The affected leg was markedly wasted, especially in the gluteal region, the sound leg conspicuously hypertrophied in the same region. The body was definitely bent over towards the unaffected leg, obviously in an effort to throw the body weight to that side to avoid pain. As this posture was of 18 months or two years standing it looked as if it had become permanently fixed.

The reflexes were generally exaggerated and the Tendo Achilles reflex in the sciatic leg was present, and equally prominent as in the other leg.

Psychically, the patient was very apprehensive and introspective. His mental diet was worry and he had almost reached the point where he was thoroughly enjoying that diet.

His contemplated enforced retirement was a prolific fount of distress and equally useful as a source of self-commiseration.

He was a typical psycho-neurotic.

It was useless to attempt psycho-therapeutic treatment until something was done for the physical condition. The presence of the Achilles reflex gave hope that the organic element was not very profound, and passive movements and massage were commenced on the affected leg.

Little if any progress was made by this method. The mind was recalcitrant. It dictated that pain was there and pain had to be there. An effort had to be made to win over the mind to alliance.

This gentleman had been something of an athlete and prior to his sciatic attack had kept his body in good condition and taken a pride in it. This athletic mental leaning was now made use of. He had never done any boxing, but it was pointed out to him that as it involved a lot of benign leg exercise and foot work it was the ideal method of attacking his sciatica. The beneficial effect of the exercise and its freedom from pain were strongly suggested before commencing.

A boxing instructor was introduced and the patient was rigged out in full boxing equipment—trunks, boxing boots, the entire paraphernalia, to stimulate the mental interest.

The gloves were heavily padded instruments, incapable of inflicting damaging punishment, but, nevertheless, quite capable of temporary hurtful shock if that were desired.

At the outset the patient was enthusiastic and put a great deal of additional movement into the leg, but he soon tired and was losing interest. During the rest interval the instructor was taken outside and told to hit the patient on the chin sufficiently hard to shock him. This blow has a specific jarring effect on the central nervous system and shocks the entire system from the brain to the heels.

This order was duly carried out and when the momentary physical shock had disappeared the whole psychic of the subject flamed with white wrath. He tore after the instructor, blood battle in his eye. Gone was the Sciatica, gone was the limp, the whole mind had a contempt for all physical handicaps, revenge was all that mattered.

When his fury had abated the patient almost collapsed in amazement when he contemplated what he had accomplished. In his exuberant delight he requested a continuance of the bodily exercise (though he was visibly distressed) and he was permitted to continue.

When he finished he was massaged, a sand pillow being placed under his convex side and an effort made to bring back normal body posture.

The physical improvement went on uninterruptedly, but the anxiety symptoms still persisted. The amelioration of the physical condition was a beneficent aid to the psychic condition for a time, but this was soon neutralized by the dread that the improvement might not be maintained—that there might be a relapse.

The time was ripe now for the customary treatment of Psycho-neurosis.

The hypodermic administration thrice weekly of Orchitic Extract equivalent to 75 grains fresh orchitic gland was commenced. In addition to this, Extracts of Orchitic, Anterior Pituitary, Thyroid, and the Suprarenal glands were given three times daily.

Treatment was continued for eight weeks—the result was good.

The physical condition and activity to-day are normal and there has been no recurrence of the Psycho-neurotic element after a lapse of six years.

It is difficult to rebut the assumption in a cold recital such as the above that the success of the

treatment, both mental and physical, was due to the
primary success of the original physical treatment and
that the organotherapy was of little if any importance.
Close contact and observation of the case over the
period effectively destroys any such assumption.   As
stated, the primary physical improvement actually
caused a temporary psychic retrogression—FEAR OF
RECURRENCE.   After a week's organotherapy there
was a distinct improvement in the whole mental
attitude and this never faltered until the patient's
final discharge.

The above case is a good illustration of how the
Operator must be ready to meet any emergency which
arises in a case.   The patient quoted above had a
marked deformity, his body conspicuously curved to
one side with atrophy of the convex side and hyper-
trophy of the concave.

His mental condition was definitely one of established
Psycho-neurosis.   As long as this physical condition
remained it was impossible to effect a radical result on
the psychic side, the physical deformity always remaining as a source of irritation keeping alive the morbid
psychic state.

When at the beginning of treatment an attempt was
made to correct this deformity, the patient would not
tolerate even simple bodily extension movements.   He
complained that the pain was too great and decided
that if such movements were absolutely essential he
would throw up treatment.   The position looked for
the moment as if a deadlock had been reached until the
boxing idea suggested itself to the author.

The mere idea, though useful, was but a beginning,
as it took a lot of effort to have it accepted in the first
place and later on to have it adopted with enthusiasm.
Then again, strong effort had to be made to attune the
patient's mind to the new scheme.   His mind was
stimulated by the provision of a real boxing instructor,
real boxing gloves, orthodox boxing equipment, even
to the regulation footwear.   All these things had a
marked effect on the psychic of the patient.   He

became deeply interested in boxing, and as a channel through which he was able to extrovert it was admirable.

On the physical side, of course, his enthusiasm made him overcome his fear of pain and as his body grew warm with the exercise the pain tendency naturally lessened. After the exercise, whilst the body was still warm and pliable, massage was soon effective in restoring normal carriage.

This gentleman to-day is able to row, plays a good game of golf, and in his ministerial capacity has an important living to look after, which duty he discharges admirably without any difficulty, physical or mental.

THE CLIMACTERIC IN THE FEMALE

Death itself is not more certain than that the arrival of the Climacteric in the female will give rise to a psychic manifestation varying in its intensity from a simple Psycho-neurotic state to acute Psychosis.

If anything were wanted to drive home to us the important role which the OVARIES, or rather their mysterious internal secretions, play in the maintenance of the nervous balance of the female, surely the climacteric is irrefutable evidence.

Nothing is more outstanding in human existence than the invariability with which every woman exhibits at this period in life the phenomena of profound nervous change.

That two small glands whose acknowledged function is procreation could exercise such an influence on the entire nervous system of the individual seems impossible. Nevertheless, when Nature determines the end of their primary usefulness and decrees involution, the whole nervous system of the subject is thrown into a state of unbalance, presumably due to the loss of the mysterious secretion which was a vital factor in the maintenance of nervous stability.

The histological changes in the OVARIES are well known. There is a gradual increase in the fibrous elements and a gradual obliteration of the epithelial cells.

I

In women who have not borne children this change is more marked and the onset of the Climacteric in these women is earlier than amongst the multiparous.

The time of onset varies roughly between the ages of forty and fifty, and forty-six may be taken as the average.

The changes are both physical and mental and although the former is of no interest in this treatise, it is well to recapitulate them briefly, inasmuch as they markedly indicate the involvement of gland groups other than the OVARIAN in this transaction.

Physical changes :—

(a) The outstanding change is the cessation of the Menstrual flow. This may occur abruptly after the first signs of onset, but more generally it is a question of months—sometimes years.

(b) Atrophy of the breasts.

(c) Tendency to obesity.

(d) Vaso-motor disturbance, pulse hypertension, flushes of heat, shivering attacks.

Psychic symptoms :—

(a) Depression varying in intensity.

(b) Irritability—restlessness and inability to concentrate.

(c) Headaches, insomnia, dreads, morbid imaginings.

The above is a concise grouping of the Climacteric symptomatology, and although some fortunate individuals escape to a large extent their full severity, very few if any of them escape entirely.

These symptoms at first sight may seem to be dependent solely on the gradual decline of the OVARIAN activity, but there is an accompanying disturbance of other gland groups.

" The Climacteric must be considered a pluriglandular manifestation " (Mazer and Goldstein).

In the OVARIES, as we have seen, there is a gradual sclerosis with consequent destruction of the germinal epithelium.

The THYROID, according to the above authorities (Mazer and Goldstein), hypofunctions, although occasionally hyper-thyroidism is evidenced. This deficiency of THYROID secretion and the excitability symptoms of the Climacteric do not blend well together. The psychic symptoms, however, are due to the OVARIAN deficiency.

Mazer and Goldstein, in their admirable treatise " Clinical Endocrinology of the Female," continue :—

> " *The Adrenals*—Basing our view on the " clinical findings, visible manifestations such " as transitory hypertension, vaso-motor disturb- " ance, moderate hyperglyæmia and glycosuria, " it seems likely that a hyperadrenalæmia " exists in this condition."

> " *The Pituitary Gland*—The high percentage " (60 per cent.) of menopausal women with " excessive amounts of anterior pituitary sex " hormones in their blood argues for a com- " pensatory hyperfunction of the hypophysis " in the menopause. However, the compen- " satory over-activity of the sex-stimulating " glands of the anterior pituitary lobe is " relatively temporary. Women in whom the " menopause is established for years do not " show an excess level of the anterior pituitary " sex hormone in the blood."

Though the above-mentioned work deals only with the physical phenomena of the menopause, it is interpolated here to demonstrate the close working union between the GONADS, the THYROID, the PITUITARY and the SUPRARENAL glands.

To have a thorough understanding of the nervous manifestations at this all-important epoch in the life of the individual, it is essential to have an understanding of the physical workings behind the scenes.

The clinical picture, from the Psycho-neurotic view point of the menopausal woman is clear cut in the majority of cases.

The first onset is heralded by the flushes of heat accompanied by a feeling of dread and uneasiness.

When the flow appears it is usually irregular in volume and duration.

There is a temporary cessation of the heat flushing, but a feeling of malaise and lethargy supervenes.

These feelings gradually increase in intensity until a pronounced irritability and querulousness is added to the picture. At this time, in bad cases, life for the patient is almost insupportable and nearly equally so for those in immediate contact with her.

Headaches and vertigo, accompanied by extreme lassitude, are now prominent features. The restlessness increases and the patient cannot even find solace in reading as concentration is an impossibility. Depression, as may be imagined, is an expected sequela.

The patient becomes morose and lachrymose. Everyone everywhere is leagued against her. Everything is designed for her particular torture.

These symptoms may be so pronounced as at times to suggest paranoia.

The symptoms outlined above cover the majority of cases of simple menopausal change and the specialized treatment for the condition before the general treatment for the Psycho-neurotic state is entered upon is detailed below.

The first step in treatment is to make sure that, apart from natural conditions existing at the moment, the pelvic organs are otherwise in a healthy state. If there is any doubt about this the patient should be sent to a Gynæcologist and his opinion obtained.

The patient is put to bed and kept there, specially at the times when the pain and floodings are at their height. Hot stupes locally applied give relief when these conditions are interfering with normal rest and sleep, and, consequently, exacting heavy toll from the already debilitated nervous system.

Particular attention should be paid to the bowels and kidneys, daily free elimination must be insisted on.

The diet should be light and nourishing and the patient should be kept in the fresh air as far as possible.

Organotherapy administration should be commenced as soon as the patient's general physical condition has been got into a satisfactory state. The following is suggested :—

Ovarian siccum	...	...	grs. 10
Pituitary whole gland		...	grs. 5
Thyroid ...	...	...	... gr. ¼

three times daily, one hour before meals.

Hypodermic injections of OVARIAN extract equivalent to 75 grains fresh gland thrice weekly.

As soon as the uterine condition permits exercise should be commenced in the form of walks or non-strenuous games. Great care must be taken not to overtax the strength of the patient at any time, and the exercises should only be very gradually increased.

If the nervous symptoms still persist after three weeks' administration of the hormones detailed above, the patient should be put on full routine treatment as outlined for cases of general psycho-neurosis.

The fulminant nerve cases of this type, naturally, demand much more strenuous treatment. The nervous symptoms here may be indistinguishable from the symptoms of definite psychosis.

The writer recalls a case of a nulliparous married woman, aged 48, whom he saw at the time when he began to treat climacteric cases on this basis. Her history showed that this lady had had an extraordinarily difficult climacteric. To begin with, she was physically of the poor type, and as she had enjoyed life in all its aspects her constitution was far from as robust as it might have been.

At 45 the first onset of the " change " became evident, and she had the most difficult time over a period lasting two years, spending a great part of that time in bed. When the " change " was eventually established, her nervous system, far from righting itself, became gradually worse and worse, until, finally, a doctor was called in. She was certified insane and removed to a private home.

The patient's condition must have undoubtedly improved very much during the six months of her detention, because when first seen by the writer she was clear mentally, well controlled, perfectly orientated, and in every way a fit and proper person to be discharged to the care of her relations. Her discharge was secured and she returned home with a nurse to look after her, as she was in a very debilitated state, apart from her upset nervous system.

Everything was apparently all right for two or three days, when the patient again developed symptoms of marked restlessness and agitation. When visited by the author, after her first restless night, he had many misgivings at having withdrawn her from the home without further investigation.

The patient was markedly agitated, was struggling to get out of bed, attempting to tear her hair out and conducting herself generally in a very obstreperous fashion. A heavy draught was given and soon the agitation disappeared and she went to sleep. This draught was administered three times daily as indicated under the treatment of " putting the mind in splints " (*vide* Chapter X). The draughts were sufficiently strong to keep her quiet and somnolent during the day, ensuring her good rest at night. As usual, in the morning a saline was administered to sweat the drugs out of the walls of the intestines and prevent an accumulation of drugs in the system.

At the end of ten days enforced rest and quietened agitation the patient had regained a lot of her strength, and as a good night's rest was ensured again by the draught, the patient became definitely tranquil and contented. There was still marked evidence of depression and moroseness. She took no interest in her surroundings and evidenced no desire to read or otherwise distract herself mentally in any way whatsoever.

When her strength seemed to warrant it the patient was taken for daily drives and after her return was gently massaged when she had gone back to bed. The night draught was gradually reduced. Her periods in the open air were increased. She was encouraged to walk a little and this exercise was gradually added to as her strength tolerated it.

At the end of a month her physical condition generally was much improved. She was taking a considerable amount of exercise, digested a light diet easily, and slept six or seven hours as a rule without the draught.

Polyglandular administration was now commenced. Exercise, baths, and massage were kept up and the lady steadily advanced to practically normal physical and nervous well-being.

Seen three years afterwards she seemed contented and happy, and although her general physical condition was poor, life on the whole was comfortable and, apparently, contented.

The above case will illustrate the heaviest type of nerve case that one meets with in the Climacteric, and the steps taken in the order outlined should give definitely good results. It is no use jumping in to treat the shattered nervous system as indicated by its probable basic cause—endocrine upset. Treat first of all the immediate nervous symptoms which are making a drain on the nervous energy manufactured within the body by the endocrine glands, remove the excitement, struggling and mental worry, and conserve the Force normally elaborated.

After this treatment and rest period the patient has a definite nervous reserve which is increased very much if fresh air and exercise can be indulged in.

Finally, endocrine therapy gives that definite balance of Force to the nervous system which enables it to function efficiently and calmly without jar.

CHAPTER VII

PSYCHO-NEUROSIS and MASTURBATION

Physical and psychic harm caused by masturbation.
Psychic harm more potent than physical—case quoted in support of this.
Treatment of masturbation.

A WHOLE volume could be written on this subject alone. Keen controversy exists as to whether this sexual abuse gives rise to definite psychosis. In the author's opinion it does not, but it certainly puts a severe strain on the psychic machinery of the individual.

Is the resultant PSYCHO-NEUROSIS due to the actual physical loss, or is it purely psychic in its origin? It is impossible to see where a deliberate assertion can be made with confidence on the point. Let us examine the physical and psychic elements in the act.

On the physical side there is a definite loss of substance. It is impossible to deny that in that lost substance there may be voided the mysterious endocrine content required for the maintenance of general nervous balance.

Nature, however, is a jealous guardian of the glands throughout the body—all the glands. Not only the endocrine group, but glands like the salivary, etc., have a function of supreme importance to fulfil, and Nature does not permit us to abuse them unduly.

Anyone who has attempted to masticate dry Army biscuits without any lubricating fluid makes a severe call on the submaxillary glands. A certain amount of saliva is produced, then there is a cessation and no amount of mental drive can produce more. If an attempt is made to do so, an actual pain in both the glands in question results. In other words, Nature does not allow the organs she employs to be over-driven by us at will.

Is Nature likely to be less guarded in her protection of the gonads ? That the repeated emptying of the Vesiculæ Seminales by unnatural means is other than highly injurious, no one can deny, but it is incredible that Nature would not put the closure on such action before PSYCHOSIS could manifest itself.

On the psychic side ONANISM exhibits outstandingly morbid characteristics—mental exhaustion, shame, depression, guilt. These are heavy blows on the fabric of the mind and cause a gradual destruction of self-confidence and self-control. The patient becomes introspective, hesitant, lethargic and self-diffident.

That these psychic disturbances are of far more pathologic significance than the actual physical loss would entail admits of no doubt in the writer's mind.

A case which amply backs up this theory is illustrated here.

There is no form of SEXUAL PSYCHO-NEUROSIS more painful, more destructive of mental happiness, and more prone to excite suicidal intent than Impotentia Sexualis of Psychic origin. The overwhelming majority of these cases originate in youthful malpractice and for this reason the following case is given in extenso. An effort will be made to reproduce the gradual development of the mechanism of the disorder and the process by which the pathologic mental structure was eventually uprooted.

The patient was a young man of 34 years. He was in excellent health, superbly built, fond of athletics, and kept himself in first-class fettle. Well educated and blessed with wealth, outwardly he had everything this world could give. He served with distinction throughout the War as an Artillery Officer and came through scatheless.

At the age of 32 he married—a girl with whom he was madly in love, and their mutual desire was for a family.

Then came tragedy. There was utter inability on his part to consummate the marriage. In panic he fled from doctor to doctor, in all probability not remaining long enough with any one physician to derive any benefit. After 18 months of what he described as horror, he finally visited a leading genito-urinary specialist who succeeded in assuring him that physically he was 100 per cent. normal, and that his impotence was entirely psychic in orgin. When first seen by the author his outward appearance was pitiable. He was haggard, drawn, and depressed.

He stated that he had lost over 14 lbs. in weight during the preceding 18 months. He lost interest in his business, his physical state, in life itself. As a matter of fact, he had strong suicidal tendencies.

Enquiry elicited the fact that there was no estrangement from and no lessening in his regard for his wife. On the contrary, he considered it almost an honourable obligation to remove himself, as he felt he was ruining her life.

Physical examination revealed increased knee reflexes and sluggishness in pupil reaction, but little else. The testes and penis were of normal size.

Mentally there was extreme depression, introspection, and profound anxiety.

The assurance of the surgeon had lighted a faint flicker of hope and he consented to undergo treatment.

At the beginning progress was difficult. His replies were in monosyllables and his over-riding depression hung like a pall over any interest he had in his present or past life.

His military life was devoid of incident as far as erotic sentiment went except for one occurrence which had little or no bearing on the case. He could not or would not recall anything of pertinent interest in his life prior to going to school at the age of thirteen years. Even his school experiences were dragged to the surface with the greatest difficulty.

Eventually he broke down and poured forth in a perfect spate of words a school memory which had

wounded him deeply at the time and which he had
never been able to blot out effectually from his mind.

At the age of 16 years his Form Master, who happened
to be a friend of the family, asked him to come to his
study. The youth duly presented himself and was
invited to be seated.

The following is the gist of the conversation which
ensued, according to the patient :—

> " *Master*—I have been watching you closely
> for the past six months. You have fallen off in
> your work ; you have lost interest in games ;
> you have become idle, slothful, careless of your
> appearance. I know the cause. You are com-
> mitting the crime of self-abuse. You are ruining
> yourself physically and mentally. Answer me,
> sir, is it not so ? "

The admission was made and the good master, but
bad psychologist, driven by his anxiety for his friend's
boy, let himself go in a perfect tirade of threatening
invective.

He painted word pictures of general ill-health,
possibly early death. The probability of future
insanity was depicted, but the certainty of the loss of
manhood and the impossibility of future marriage
was insisted upon.

He wound up his oration by saying that early demise
would be a good thing if this conduct were persised in.

If this boy had been of the " cabbage " type, little
harm, if any, would have resulted from the terrible
picture. Unfortunately for the lad, however, he had
an ultra fine, sharp, impressionable, easily-injured
mental fabric, and one can readily picture him stumbling
from the study stunned to the very depths of his
soul.

Time passed, and the impulse, when it stirred within,
was rigidly repressed. The instrument of repression
was by means of a morbid emotion—FEAR—born of
that lecture in the study. When, as occasionally
the impulse overcame this Fear and masturbation

occurred, the unfortunate victim was left in the following mental state :—

After the act he was left suffering from mental exhaustion, shame, guilt, and the overwhelming dread of its dire consequences as forecast by the master.

Owing to this mental agony following the act, the period between his indiscretions gradually lengthened, the Fear growing in intensity step by step until the impulse, after some years, was finally stifled. The dread of the mental anguish experienced after the commission of the act was unbearable.

His after-school life, until he joined the Army and during his War service, held no noteworthy incident of an erotic type.

He quickly linked up the gradual obliteration of his impulses with this implanted Fear, and confessed that on the bridal bed he was overwhelmed by an unaccountable dread which left him powerless—the Conditioned Reflex.

Ordinary treatment for his Psycho-neurotic state and building up soon established absolute normality.

Let us examine again the factors in this breakdown.

We have a highly sensitive mental fabric. We have this fabric injured by secret malpractice, shame and guilt being impressed upon its surface. We have the well-meaning but uncouth handling by the master leaving it in a highly inflamed condition—a condition of FEAR—FEAR directly linked up with the sexual act. It shrinks from further injury and bruising which can excite or aggravate this painful state.

The crushed impulses gradually fade in their intensity until the stimuli are so weak that they are unable to set the nervous mechanism in motion which causes erection of the penis.

The salient feature, in cases of this type, is ANXIETY. There is an underlying dread in every case that definite though undefinable harm has been done and is being done.

The physician's attitude must be invariably one of sympathy, of understanding, of patient encouragement. The appeal must be made direct to the manhood of the individual and to the encouragement of games and athletic exercises.

Literature of the emotional type should be excluded and reading of the adventure novel cultivated. The task for the doctor is not an easy one, as indeed it never is in any form of functional nervous trouble. If, however, interest can be aroused and maintained in the establishment of good health and physical fitness, much will have been accomplished.

CHAPTER VIII

HYSTERIA

HYSTERIA is the reaction manifested in the absorption of an excessive amount of SUB-CONSCIOUS PSYCHIC FORCE produced under the stimulus of some strong emotion, generally FEAR.

The theory has been advanced in a previous chapter that SUBCONSCIOUS PSYCHIC FORCE liberated in the subconscious by FEAR surges around until it burrows Channels of Escape. The ENERGY thus released along these Escape Channels gives rise to those multiform physical and psychic symptoms we group under the name of PSYCHO-NEUROSIS.

HYSTERIA is invariably found in the Psycho-neurotic (inherited type). Under the stimulus of FEAR the subconscious mind of the hysteric is flooded with an unusable quantity of SUBCONSCIOUS PSYCHIC FORCE from the reservoir of that FORCE, as happens in Psycho-neurosis. The method of discharge, however, is different. Instead of employing a multiplicity of Discharge Channels, in HYSTERIA we have the employ-ment of one single conduit of sufficient capacity to drain off the unwanted ENERGY. This Escape Mechanism, which is in reality protective, gives rise to the psychic and physical manifestations we know as HYSTERIA.

What are the arguments in favour of this theory ?

(1) Despite the inheritance of the Psycho-neurotic taint, its syndrome rarely if ever coexists with HYSTERIA. In other words, the employment by HYSTERIA of an ample Escape Channel makes unnecessary the use of the number of channels employed in PSYCHO-NEUROSIS, giving rise to symptoms such as tremors, headaches, insomnia, palpitations, etc.

(2) The " belle indifference " of Jânet further demonstrates that the mind, relieved by the ample Escape Mechanism employed by HYSTERIA, is left in a condition of placid ease thereby.

Freud's brilliant Infantile Regression Theory in no way runs counter to the theory expressed above. As interpreted by the author, Freud's theory is that the subconscious mind is in a state of extreme irritability. This irritability would leave it (the subconscious) more vulnerable to an attack by a strong emotional stimulus and, consequently, more prone to give us an exaggerated reaction such as HYSTERIA.

Let us examine the theory of the Escape Mechanism in the light of different phases of the physical and psychic manifestations of the hysteric reaction.

PHYSICAL MANIFESTATIONS OF HYSTERIA
MOTOR

Any group of muscles may be picked out for involvement in this paralysis. The distinction between the paralysis of the hysteric type and true paralysis is very easily made, as in the hysteric type there is no disturbance of the deep reflexes. There is usually a wasting, due to disuse atrophy, and generally some vaso-motor changes as evidenced by coldness and blueness of the affected part.

A case which came under notice in 1919, immediately after the war, will illustrate this theory of Escape Mechanism vividly.

The patient was admitted for treatment some 18 months after his discharge from the army. He was suffering from Spastic Paralysis, obviously hysterical.

The patella reflexes were exaggerated markedly.

The plantar reflexes were normal and there was no true ankle clonus.

The limbs were wasted through disuse atrophy and the feet cold and blue.

The history of the patient was that a shell struck the parapet and he was buried. He was not wounded by the shell, but was sure that it was the sandbags which fell on his back that had done the damage.

When he recovered consciousness he was unable to move his legs owing to the pain and stiffness located in the centre of his back down to his buttocks. He came to the conclusion that his spine was affected and that he would remain paralysed as a result. He was of the refined intellectual and imaginative type, obviously a man who would know that a serious spinal injury would certainly result in paralysis.

Physically, apart from discomfort suffered through his leg condition, he felt very well. Mentally he was bright and cheerful and strongly desirous of being cured of his disability. He had not a neurotic symptom. No tremors, no excitability, no stammering, no headaches. He slept well and his digestion was good.

When he was questioned closely as to what had occurred exactly on the day he received his injury, he gave a history something as follows :—

" On the 7th November, 1917, I was in the front-line trenches."

Questioned as to the time he said that it must have been round about 10 o'clock in the morning because a tea ration or soup ration or some other ration was coming round.

The Germans were shelling the front-line trenches heavily with " whiz-bangs." He recalled such details as Private So-and-so being hit with a splinter, and Private So-and-so being killed beside him.

Further details he was either unwilling or unable to call forth.

The history of that morning's occurrence was elicited day after day and the patient obstinately stuck at the same point and could not recall anything which happened from that point until the time he found himself in the Advance Dressing Station.

It may be interpolated here that there was a considerable amount of emotional display at the recital of these events but no effort was made to move the affected limbs.

It was explained to the patient that if only he could recall events up to and including the actual happening which brought about his condition, that he would undoubtedly recover the use of his limbs. He was reassured that there was no injury produced capable of causing a permanent paralysis of his legs, a fact which he eventually grasped thoroughly.

Despite every effort he continued unable to give any further information and his condition made no improvement.

Eventually he was put under hypnosis. He was given the thread of the story in all its details and told to carry on. He carried on past the former obstruction point, and eventually, with an ear-splitting shout, flung both arms and legs in air so violently that he had to be saved from falling off the couch.

He was wakened up, found himself in a sitting position, could scarcely believe his eyes when he saw he could move his legs.

Let us examine this case in the light of this theory of Escape Mechanism. Everything about the man, his refinement, etc., pointed to the probability of his being a neurotic before military service ever claimed him. When he recovered consciousness after being blown up, his first sensation was excruciating pain in the back. His mind, a sensitive mind, battered and buffeted by this experience, magnified many times the already serious condition of his back. Unable to move his legs because attempted movement evoked an exacerbation of pain, FEAR, now active in the subconscious, gave birth to the idea that, in all probability, his back was broken or at least crushed. This being so he would remain paralysed, whispered his subconscious, unable to move his legs. The probability became an established certainty—yes, of course, he was paralysed. The idea was implanted and all the PSYCHIC FORCE liberated by the FEAR flooded out along this Channel of Escape and the condition of paralysis became established.

A compensatory Relief Mechanism now asserted itself—as he was paralysed at least he could no longer return there. He was afraid, he admitted to himself, but he had done his duty and physically now was no longer fit for active service. This idea brought mental relief and all the SUBCONSCIOUS PSYCHIC FORCE evoked by FEAR poured out along the channel that fed the idea of his fantastic paralysis.

It is significant that no symptom of Psycho-neurosis obtruded itself into the picture whilst the victim was still suffering from paralysis. However, when the paraplegia had disappeared the patient, for a time, displayed many symptoms of Psycho-neurosis. He became apprehensive, worried about his health, his future, and whether he would be able to re-establish himself in life.

This proves that when the large Escape Channel which fed his paralysis had been closed, the plus quantity of SUBCONSCIOUS PSYCHIC FORCE, still evoked by continuous anxiety or FEAR stimulation, had to burrow for itself multiple Channels of Escape, as exhibited by these manifestations.

SENSORY SYMPTOMS

We have Hysterical manifestations affecting sight and hearing, and the glove and stocking anæsthesias are other forms met with from time to time on the physical side.

PSYCHIC MANIFESTATIONS OF HYSTERIA

There are few states which HYSTERIA cannot simulate. The most common cases met with on the psychic side in this condition are :—

> Hysterical fits,
> Amnesia,
> Fugues,
> Dual personality.
> Phobias.

Hysterical Fits—This is a condition very often met with in General Practice, and, as a rule, it is quite easy to differentiate between the Hysteric and the true Epileptic.

In true Epilepsy there is usually an accompanying degenerative mental change. The patient is generally dull, apathetic, and disinclined to interest himself in his general surroundings. The Hysteric, on the other hand, is over-bright, active, irritable, pushing, talkative and excitable.

Physically, the Epileptic of long standing exhibits evidence of gradual psychic and physical degeneration. He is careless and inclined to be slovenly in his clothes and habits. Scars are very often noticeable, especially on the back of the skull. Burns may be seen on the nose and the face. The tongue is scarred and gives evidence of having been frequently bitten through.

The Hysteric is usually well set up, careful of his appearance and scrupulous in his habits. Seldom or never are scars seen and certainly never on the back of the head unless associated with an injury other than a suspected seizure fall. The tongue seldom shows evidence of injury.

Regarding the fits. In the Epileptic nocturnal seizures are frequent, as evidenced by bed wetting. In the Hysteric this never occurs. The Epileptic may fall at any time, in any place, and under any circumstances. The Hysteric, as a rule, selects a gallery. The true Epileptic invariably does himself some injury, invariably bites his tongue, and practically invariably voids urine. The Hysteric invariably does none of these things.

The true Epileptic is disorientated from one to three hours and suffers from an incapacitating headache for a further 6 to 24 hours. The Hysteric is his normal self within an hour.

Amnesias and Fugues—An amnesia is a complete blank period in the life of the individual where memory is unable to recall one single incident. In boxing it not infrequently happens that a man continues to fight round after round without giving any outward manifestation of change in his condition though the next day he would be unable to recall what happened for two, three, or four rounds before the end of the fight.

This amnesia, of course, is organic in origin and due to concussion, but it helps us to understand how a patient suffering from amnesia of psychic origin can carry on normally during these blind spots in his existence and have no recollection whatever of what happened during the period.

Cases of amnesia arise in people of the Hysteric type when they are subjected to prolonged mental strain. The culminating factor is generally a critical happening. The harassed subconscious, unable to withstand the additional blow, to save itself turns deliberately away from the distressing circumstance and blots it out of consciousness.

Many of these cases are found amongst persons with heavy financial responsibility as, for example, Treasurers of Working Men's Savings Clubs. The amount involved may not be great from the monetary point of view, but the responsibility to this class of Treasurer is, nevertheless, a grave one. If a man in this position finds himself short in his accounts and the day of distribution is gradually closing in, the never-ending worry drives his mind to distraction and very often he commits suicide, or the mind, no longer able to contemplate the harassing situation, draws down a curtain and the patient loses entire contact with the cause of his perturbation.

In the second circumstance he generally takes refuge in flight, termed a fugue. The patient wanders away from home. His conduct is not dictated by any concrete idea of escape, as is evidenced by the fact that these cases make no effort at disguise and never attempt to flee the country. In their new mental condition they exhibit no extraordinary behaviourisms. They purchase a ticket in the usual way and travel to some point with which they may not have had any previous connection. They live their lives in an aimless but rational fashion, and when they recover normality they are unable to give any account of what has happened during the period of their absence. Many of these cases wander aimlessly on, neglectful of themselves as regards food and shelter, until finally physical exhaustion places them in the hands of the authorities.

The cynic regards such cases with more than suspicion and, doubtless, there are cases of this type where the impostor hopes to escape or at least mitigate a deserved punishment.

There are many genuine cases of amnesias and fugues, however, who suffer a complete black out of consciousness under the hammer blows of perverse fate. They seem to arrive at a point where the mind, under persistent torture, is threatened with disintegration and death. To avert this there remains nothing but precipitate flight from the persecuting circumstances.

Does this square with the theory put forward to explain the action under the drive of Hysteria? The mind is flooded with excess of SUBCONSCIOUS PSYCHIC FORCE activated by FEAR. If this flood overwhelms the subconscious before it can be dealt with panic results, confusion is enthroned, and suicide is the exit. On the other hand, in the subconscious, under the scourge of FEAR, a desire is ever present to flee from the torturing surroundings, and if and when the surging flood is about to overwhelm it, then usually opens the Channel of Escape. The resulting liberated FORCE urges the victim away from the location of his torments.

Let us look at the patient now. Mentally he is calm, undisturbed, apathetic to everything. His hidden FEAR no longer operates. There is nothing in his new surroundings to call forth its activity. As a consequence there is no flooding of his subconscious with uneconomic PSYCHIC FORCE. On the contrary, after the storm has come a calm and the exhausted SUBCONSCIOUS PSYCHIC

FORCE is scarcely present in sufficient quantity to evoke even ordinary thought processes—This probably accounts for Jânet's " belle indifference."

The victim has forgotten his name, his antecedents, his relations, all things appertaining to his painful past. This is due to there being insufficient PSYCHIC FORCE to activate the thoughts which should recall such circumstances. As time passes the SUBCONSCIOUS PSYCHIC FORCE re-establishes its normality, recovery takes place, and the patient is himself again.

That this crisis is protective is demonstrated by the fact that the patient invariably has improved in his mental perspective and is ready to face the previous harassing situation with a completely changed and better equipped mental attitude.

Dual Personality—Development of this condition is along parallel lines to that which has been demonstrated in the fugue. Here we have the subconscious of an individual driven to desperation by FEAR and flooded with an unusable amount of SUBCONSCIOUS PSYCHIC FORCE poured forth in supposed defence of a threatened personality.

The subconscious deliberately elides the persecuted personality from conscious existence and creates a new personality, using the excessively liberated FORCE to activate it. This new personality appears to take on a new consciousness, a new memory, cutting out completely the old personality and all its painful associations.

It is easy to imagine the normal absorption and economical use of the liberated PSYCHIC FORCE under these conditions, but, apart from the Jekyll and Hyde story, the author has never met with a case of this type. *Vide* Chapter X, "Personality."

Phobias—A Phobia is a fear entirely illogical in its origin which gives an utterly absurd and violent reaction.

We have made an effort to trace the beginning of this painful mental condition in Chapter III (Acquired

Psycho-neurosis of Psychic Origin), and it is undeniably part and parcel of the ordinary Escape Mechanism used to unload the subconscious of a sudden spate or unwanted PSYCHIC FORCE.

The following case has an origin with a more obvious basis in reality than one usually finds in this condition and is of interest from the point of view that this origin is clearly demonstrable.

Private X. presented himself for treatment at the Ministry of Pensions Neurological Clinic, Lancaster Gate, early in 1919. He was in the late twenties, a good type and of fine physique.

At the time he was employed as a temporary postman in the Soho area. He was, however, forced to give up this employment inasmuch as a persistent anxiety was quickly wearing him down. His anxiety took a peculiar form. When he had completed his rounds a sudden idea arose in his mind that he had forgotten to lock the postal boxes, with the result that his anxiety compelled him to make a second round. Needless to say, this double tour of duty soon made itself felt on his physical health and as a consequence he was definitely unable to continue his occupation. Being a regular soldier he had seen long war service having been out with the original Expeditionary Force. Despite this, however, he had no evidence of gross neurosis of the physical type.

Intimate examination of his war experiences after a time revealed an underlying and very interesting memory. He made no effort to bring this memory to the surface on the closest questioning. He happened to remark, upon being questioned about his digestive system, that he had given up eating flesh meat in all forms. Pressed as to the reason for this, he said that he now disliked the idea of flesh meat intensely. So much so that even when passing a butcher's shop he had an uncontrollable desire to vomit.

Eventually the story behind this was elicited. It appears that towards the end of the war he assisted at the capture of a front-line trench and engaged in a hand-to-hand struggle with a German officer in a deep dug-out. He had bayoneted this officer who, apparently, closed with him, and the last memory he had of the occurrence was that in the struggle he had fastened his teeth into his enemy's throat. He was certain of this, he said, because they were both lying on the floor of the dug-out in a death struggle, and he could taste the warm salty blood as he bit into his enemy's throat.

He states that he must have lost consciousness at this time, as he does not remember anything for some hours afterwards. The next time he saw flesh meat it filled him with horror. He did not know why and did not specifically associate it with his life and death struggle in the enemy dug-out.

It was pointed out to him the practical physical impossibility of his having bitten into his enemy's throat, and the warm saltish taste of blood was almost certainly the blood welling out of the bayonet wound he had inflicted on his enemy, which had by some means or other got into contact with his lips.

It must be admitted that there was certainly sufficient material in a happening of this nature to produce a profound psychic trauma. The struggle was a life and death one, and taking place at the bottom of a dug-out, had all the elements of profound horror.

Strange to say the patient did not associate his repugnance for flesh meat with the actual biting of his enemy's throat, but stated that when it came into his mind it caused him a painful memory that such a thing could have occurred. When it was demonstrated to him how impossible it was that he actually could have brought about the death of his enemy in the horrible manner which he imagined, he was immensely relieved, and made uninterrupted progress towards recovery.

There was nothing in the upset itself strikingly connected with his anxiety state which was due, undoubtedly, to prolonged war strain. His hysterical attitude towards flesh meat was directly associated with the occurrence, and undoubtedly was the chief mental trauma in calling forth his general war strain to the surface.

This case vividly illustrates that in an acquired psycho-neurosis of psychic origin the predominating symptoms are psychic. The physical symptoms, such as muscular tremors, exaggerated reflexes, heart palpitations, etc., were not evidenced or were evidenced to such a minor degree as to be of no importance. On the other hand, his anxiety was sufficiently incapacitating to render him unable to carry out his simple duties as an auxiliary postman. Then, again, his hysterical aversion to flesh meat was sufficiently strong to cause anorexia at the mere sight of a butcher's shop.

ANOREXIA NERVOSA

Anorexia Nervosa is not at all infrequently met with in general practice. Young unmarried girls are the exponents of this disorder. It may progress until life itself is threatened.

At the beginning the victims exhibit extraordinary energy, considering this starvation, but soon general weakness manifests itself. Subcutaneous fat rapidly disappears all over the body. The skin becomes loose and wrinkled, the tongue dry and harsh, the breath heavy. The menses disappear.

In treating this disorder the patient must, of course, be kept in bed in order to husband her scanty resources. If it is possible, rectal alimentation should be given, and if this is at all well tolerated the case is sure to prove easy to treat. This method of feeding is very often unbearable even for patients who have no taint of HYSTERIA, so we must approach our victim from the point of view that feeding per rectum has been impossible. Make no effort to urge the patient towards eating. Place some peptonised milk alongside her bed and explain to her that even the smallest amount taken will be sufficient to maintain her strength as being in bed her physical expenditure is practically nil. Impress upon the patient that by feeding herself in this manner, when she feels like it, and making sure to take only small quantities at a time, there will be no possibility of setting up any irritation in her stomach, and, consequently, no possibility of her vomiting. If the patient is able to pass three or four hours without vomiting, a reassurance that her stomach irritability is settling down will do a lot of good.

Make no attempt to increase the quantity of milk taken. Let the patient's natural desire dictate this. On the contrary, rather discourage the taking of even moderately large quantities, informing the patient that there is no hurry and no necessity to rush things, as normality will soon re-establish itself.

Change from milk, in the first part of the day, to light bouillon in the evening, and give the patient to understand that she may have a dry biscuit if she likes to ask for it, and then only giver her half a dry biscuit. Let the requests for food, both in variation and quantity, come from the patient. At no time must the pace be forced, as only harm can result from pressure.

This type of case should invariably be nursed in the open air. It is necessary to confine an Anorexia Nervosa case to bed, but this is simply because the physical debility is so marked owing to continuous starvation.

Where practicable, place the bed in the open air and surround the patient with as little atmosphere of invalidism as possible. The open air is more prone to give edge to the appetite than lying up in a stuffy bedroom, whilst treatment which is deliberately devoid of pampering and softness is the proper method to employ for HYSTERIA of any type.

As the stomach gradually demonstrates that it is dealing effectively with whatever food is given, it is incumbent upon the physician to hasten slowly still.

Promote the patient from peptonised milk to ordinary

milk, from one tablespoonful every two hours to two tablespoonfuls every two hours, and then increase it to four tablespoonfuls every two hours. When this is well tolerated, switch on to bouillon, with one dry biscuit three times daily with milk and fruit juice alternating every three hours.

Gradually this diet is increased. Remember, never be in a hurry to restore this type of case to full diet, only do this when the patient is sufficiently strong to take a considerable amount of exercise. When full diet is restored it should be kept to a restricted scale as regards quantity for at least two weeks.

TREATMENT

There is no object in differentiating between treatment given to the sufferer from HYSTERIA and the victim of PSYCHO-NEUROSIS. A word of warning must be sounded here to those who regard HYSTERIA in the light of malingering. There is no relationship whatever between the conditions. HYSTERIA is a true PSYCHO-NEUROTIC state, and must be handled with the greatest care, and, at the same time, with the greatest sympathy.

Physical examination, to elide every possibility of organic lesion, must be carried out meticulously. The history, both personal and family, must be taken down in scrupulous detail. These people owe their condition to the fact that they belong to the high mental index class, and as such are hypersensitive and necessitate the greatest care in handling.

To give a hysteric an idea by abrupt or brusque mannerism that the operator regards the case as one of feigned illness is fatal. Such an operator could never have any success with a patient of this type so offended. A famous hotel manager once said, "A guest is never wrong." If the operator is not content to accept the maxim that the psycho-neurotic of whatever type is never wrong in his ideas about his condition, success will not attend him whatever effort he puts forth.

CHAPTER IX

SCHIZOPHRÆNIA

Schizophrænia—its probable causes—puberty irregularities;
Symptoms of puberty irregularities.

Quotations from Henderson and Gillespie describing Schizophrænia.

Two examples given to illustrate how Schizophrænia manifesting itself between the ages of 19 and 30 is closely associated with faulty puberty development.

SCHIZOPHRÆNIA has no place in a work which is devoted entirely to the Psycho-neurotic state.

Yet, inasmuch as the author's experiences compel him to advance the theory that Schizophrænia can be a development from a grave and neglected early Psycho-neurosis of endocrine origin, no further excuse is required for the inclusion of this chapter.

Due recognition is given to the gravity of the above statement, and the author is well aware how scornfully the idea will be rejected in many quarters, yet in spite of this opposition, personal experience repeated in case after case leaves him unmoved in the face of any criticism.

It is admitted that the sum total met with during the past ten years has not been anything out of the ordinary, but this number, restricted though it may be, gave proofs too strong to admit of any doubt.

Here it must be stated that the cases met with were, with one exception, females, and the male who was a Schizophrænic (Katatonic type) is only of interest from a treatment point of view which will be related at the end of the chapter.

Before passing on to a few concrete examples of Schizophrænia, the author begs the reader's permission to develop one of these cases as he or she progresses from the onset of the first simple condition of Neurosis up to the definitely established state of Schizophrænia.

It must be understood that the author is simply dealing with the clinical aspect of these cases from onset to climax; regarding the battles raged around the changes in the generative organs in Schizophrænia by the pathologists of the Mott school and their adversaries he has an open mind and awaits with interest the time when something of real assistance is discovered and agreed upon by both parties.

In the meantime, we of the clinical school must do our best with what information the pathologists and bio-chemists have furnished us ; with what knowledge we have elicited by care and observation we must strive to check the progress of this malady at its earliest possible point and prevent its development by all means possible.

As already stated, in the artificially developed case which is now put forward, it must be remembered that the supposed patient is a female.

Whilst holding the theory that Schizophrænic development in males would proceed along lines fundamentally similar, as the author has not had sufficient experience of the malady in the male he does not wish to include him in the picture.

Puberty in the pre-supposedly healthy normal female is the first and greatest crisis in her existence. Her whole nervous future, her position as a child-bearer and the decline of her life is intimately linked up with the circumstances attendant upon her first blossoming into womanhood.

Puberty primarily is the axis-cylinder around which will revolve the whole psychic future of the individual.

It is not to be denied that extraneous factors— accident, disease, etc.—will have an influence, possibly a great influence, on the psychic of the young maiden, but the basis of her entire future mental equipment is laid at puberty.

When the young girl in the full bloom of health approaches this time there are no attendant anxiety symptoms. The menses appear practically painlessly and excite no subconscious emotion other than one of wonderment at the new and extraordinary happening.

The breasts enlarge, hair appears in the axillæ and on the pubes, and the boisterous turbulent child glides into the placid grace of young womanhood.

Hence onward the body gradually grows and fills out to adapt itself for Nature's most sublime experiment—the bearing of children.

Now let us examine the picture where the physical health of the child upsets this magnificent and all-important change. Physically the child looks ill, acts as if she were ill, and in reality is ill.

The face is pale and drawn, and the body, deficient in subcutaneous fat, presents none of the pleasing roundness associated with this period of young female life.

The breasts lie flat on the rib-ridged thorax. The abdomen is concave and skinny. The muscles of the arms are small and flaccid, whilst the thin weak legs tire even on the slight support they are compelled to give the attenuated frame.

The psychic state is interesting, and special attention is drawn to it at this particular point.

(a) The most prominent feature is established apathy. The child loses interest in her work. She simply cannot be bothered to study. Not only does application bore her—she cannot apply herself—Insufficient SUBCONSCIOUS PSYCHIC FORCE.

(b) Companionship with former girl friends no longer attracts her. She prefers to be alone. She has no desire to mix with her old friends. They no longer interest her. She is unable to arouse an interest for them. Again lack of SUBCONSCIOUS PSYCHIC FORCE.

(c) She refuses to play games. She is not amused by them. They are too much bother, besides she does not feel able to play just at present. Lack of CONSCIOUS PSYCHIC FORCE.

(d) As to her health, she never troubles to think of it. She makes no complaints. She states her head worries

her at times but not much, and, at all events, she pays
no attention to headaches. Lack of SUBCONSCIOUS
PSYCHIC FORCE.

Indifference to everything and everybody dominates
the picture.

Let us examine into the history.

The family history may be good or, at all events,
reveal nothing of pathologic significance.

The personal history may be devoid of interest
up to a year or a year and a half before the anticipated
puberty manifestation. Then one is entertained by
stories of slight manifestations of ill-health, generally
with a cold or something insignificant as its starting
point.

The child now exhibits symptoms of lethargy and
petulance. Constipation appears and is an obstinate
feature. The appetite drops away and general bodily
strength is not maintained. The child becomes droopy,
indifferent, easily fatigued and irritable, even without
provocation. Headaches are complained of and
advanced as a reason for the falling off in studies.
Sleep at night is restless and disturbed by starts
and frightening dreams.

It is not difficult to imagine that the approach to
puberty under such condition is calamitous.

The body, which should be at the peak of perfection,
is in alarming disorder.

Insufficient nourishment is absorbed to maintain
the blood at its required volume, and its quality,
poisoned by the reabsorbed gases of long-retained
semi-digested food debris, is away below the standard
in quality which Nature demands at this all-important
epoch.

The result is faulty puberty.

The onset is late and the show is poor in both
quantity and quality. After the first menstrual flow
nothing more may be seen for two, three, four months,
or even longer.

The ovarian and uterine glands, insufficiently
nourished, are unable to perform their normal secretory

functions. They are, consequently, unable to pour their endocrine secretions into the blood stream to complete that harmonious blending we know is essential for the maintenance of normal nervous metabolism.

How could we expect to get a condition other than that of psychic upheaval under these circumstances ? We see it plainly manifested at the other end of the gestation cycle—the climacteric—and accept it as a natural sequela.

Depression, lethargy, general weakness, apathy, must ensue when puberty in the female is commenced under such conditions. If the condition is neglected, or if treatment is not successfully carried out, these symptoms, in the nature of things, must progress, and there must be, and there is, an uninterrupted disintegration of the personality of the victim until the state we know as Schizophrænia is established.

The author makes no apology for the amount of space he has devoted to this particular subject.

This is a period in young adult life, more especially in young female adult life, which transcends all others in importance as regards its bearing on the subsequent psychic of the individual.

Let us go a step further and boldly assert that if adequate supervision were made and efficient treatment administered where needed to the young female twelve months before the anticipated period of puberty, the incidence of Schizophrænia amongst them would fall to vanishing point provided the family history was good.

Let us briefly run over the condition we know as the Schizophrænic state and compare what we to-day might term the Psycho-neurosis associated with the puberty epoch.

Schizophrænia means, literally, "splitting of the mind," i.e., "splitting of the personality of the individual."

Bluer, in 1911, gave this designation to all functional mental disturbance, exclusive of the Depressive Manic states.

Henderson and Gillespie, in their admirable textbook of Psychiatry, state :—

" Schizophrænia, in its typical form, consists in
" a slow, steady deterioration of the entire
" personality, usually showing itself in the
" period of adolescence. It involves principally
" the affective life, and expresses itself in dis-
" order of feeling, of conduct and of thought,
" and in an increasing withdrawal of interest
" from the environment."

The Pshcyo-neurosis which the author associates with puberty, *vide* chapter on Period Neurosis, portrays a fundamental degenerative change, even if only temporary, in the personality of the patient.

Let us compare the symptomatology of the Psychoneurosis which has its basis in a faulty puberty with the symptoms of Schizophrænia.

In the Psycho-neurotic of this type there is a complete and degenerative change—temporary at least. The healthy, playful, athletic girl becomes lazy, listless and disinclined to exert herself physically or mentally.

In the Schirzophrænic (Henderson and Gillespie) :—

" The most prominent symptom is the failure
" of affect or emotional blunting, showing itself
" in apathy and indifference. Another in-
" pressive feature is the disharmony between
" the mood and the thought. Schizophrænic
" patients may express without any show of
" emotion ideas which in the ordinary person
" would produce remorse or pity or profound
" depression. Situations in which they find
" themselves which would normally have a pro-
" found emotional value, as, for example, being
" placed in a mental hospital, are by them met
" with indifference."

The author has taken the liberty to quote extensively from Henderson and Gillespie's textbook, as it gives such a clear-cut view of the Schizophrænic.

The Psycho-neurotics of the puberty type, in their

L

indifference and apathy to things which formerly were of absorbing interest to them, give a reproduction in miniature, if one might say so, of the Schizophrænic type.

The author has not found heredity play a fixed and evident part in any of the cases which have come under his notice.

Kræpelin believed that Schizophrænia had its origin in dysfunction of the sex glands. The author's contention is that a faulty puberty, due to an unhealthy general physical state, impedes normal development of the sex glands.

The consequence is dysfunction of these glands and endocrine upset resulting in puberty neurosis. If this neurosis is allowed to go unchecked, the personality of the individual slowly but gradually deteriorates, until we arrive at the definite Schizophrænic state.

The two cases illustrated here, in the author's opinion, demonstrate that Schizophrænia manifesting itself between the ages of 19 and 30 is closely associated with puberty development. This is further borne out by the immediate improvement, in fact, the immediate cessation of morbid mental processes, when the normal ovarian function was re-established.

This re-establishment of normality is no doubt in a great measure due to putting the attendant physical conditions, such as constipation and general blood conditions, in good order, but nothing can divert the author from his firm opinion that the administration of glandular substances and the injection of the Corpus Luteum played a very important role in successful treatment.

(1) *Miss M———, who came under notice in the spring of* 1926.

She was a school teacher, aged 28, but had been unable to follow her profession during the preceding 12 months owing to a supposed nervous breakdown.

When first seen her condition was as follows :—

Her height was 5 ft. 7½ in., and her weight was about 6 st. 12 lb. She was thin to the point of emaciation, and so weak that she was unable to walk. Her face was drawn and haggard and covered with a thick downy fluff, extending well down the throat region. The thorax and abdomen seemed practically utterly devoid of subcutaneous fat, and the musculature of the arms and legs was pitiable.

Physical examination revealed a dry, heavily coated tongue and sordes about the mouth. The heart sounds were weak and distant ; pulse rate was accelerated— 92, and the blood pressure low—about 116. The pupils were dilated, reacted sluggishly to light. The patella and plantar reflexes were depressed.

The history covering her condition in the two years 1924-26 was a history of struggle against general ill-health. Subsequent questioning elicited the fact that really good health had not been enjoyed by the patient from her fourteenth year, and in 1924 it became almost a physical impossibility to continue on with her work.

According to her sister, trouble started at puberty time. She had been in very indifferent health from about the age of 13½, suffering from continuous head-aches and chronic constipation. The menses made no appearance until after the fifteenth birthday, and were very scanty, accompanied by a considerable amount of pain. After the first appearance nothing was seen for some time, and at no time did the menstrual flow come in normal quantity or with regularity.

There was no treatment even suggested at this time. Her delicate health was attributed to the fact of her rapid growth, and no active measures were taken.

In the twelve months preceding her entry into the nursing home her condition had gradually grown worse, and retirement from her duties gradually became imperative. She refused to take any interest in her work. She became apathetic with regard to her personal appearance. By her mien she was manifestly depressed, although she gave no reason for this and made no complaint. Incidentally, her menses had only appeared about four times during the twelve months, and were well below normal in amount.

Things finally came to a climax when she impulsively attempted to destroy herself by drinking disinfectant, although at no time prior to this had she given any indication of an inclination to take her life.

The family history on both sides was, apparently, satisfactory. Both parents were alive, and there was no evidence to demonstrate any psychotic or neurotic element.

When the patient had entered the nursing home an attempt was made to get a personal history from her. This was a difficult proceeding. When asked about her health her reply was, " I am all right." When asked about her strength she said she had no complaints. The same reply was vouchsafed when questioned about her appetite, her sleep, her work, and her friends —in fact, everything with which she had relationship. Her condition was one of firmly rooted indifference to her entire environment, and it was absolutely useless to attempt to detach her from that attitude.

It was a puzzle how to commence treatment, but as her physical condition was so extremely poor it became evident that unless something was done to improve that condition the patient would, in all probability, die. An attempt was made to feed her per mouth on the lightest and most easily digested diet possible. The attempt was not a success ; she was able to retain but a small quantity. Rectal alimentation was then tried, and had to be abandoned, inasmuch as the patient became hostile to this on the second or third day of treatment.

As an extreme measure cod-liver oil was resorted to, but as this could not be administered orally it was decided to rub it into the abdomen, flanks, breasts, and axillæ of the patient. By the mouth peptonised milk in small quantities was given every three hours, and was retained. The patient had a blanket bath every day, followed immediately by a cod-liver oil inunction. The night-clothes and bed-sheets soon becoming saturated with cod-liver oil, were in constant contact with her body all the twenty-four hours.

At the end of ten days the patient seemed physically stronger and there was a gain of over 1 lb. in weight. The mental attitude was entirely unchanged. No effort was made other than to increase the physical strength. The quantity of peptonised milk was gradually increased, egg albumen was added to this and was well retained. Rectal alimentation was again resorted to and was very satisfactorily tolerated. Naturally, the cod-liver oil inunctions were continued, and at the end of four weeks' treatment the patient had gained 5½ lbs. in bodily weight, and the increase in physical strength was most pleasing. The digestive system grew daily stronger and the diet by mouth was advanced to beef essence, chicken jellies, etc. At the end of two months the patient was over 9 lbs. heavier than on admission. Her strength had increased uninterruptedly. Her digestion maintained its improvement. There was not, however, any visible evidence of mental advance.

The patient, apparently, took as little interest in her surroundings as she did when first admitted ; although she ate, and ate with apparent relish the food she was given by mouth, she never expressed a desire for food when it was purposely withheld to see if she would demand it.

Rectal feeding was abandoned at the end of the second month, but the cod-liver oil inunction was still maintained and the oral alimentation was steadily increased.

At the end of the third month bodily weight had increased by an additional 3 lbs., making a total increase of 12 lbs. since her admission. She was allowed up and encouraged to walk about the room and allowed downstairs after two or three days. As her strength increased she was taken out for short walks and gradually, at the end of the fourth month, from a physical standpoint, she was nearly normal. She had, however, made but little advance from a

mental point of view. She was still listless and apathetic
When requested to get up and dress, though still
indifferent she was not hostile as she had been earlier
on.

At this period it was considered advisable to commence gland therapy, and a capsule containing :—

Extract of Ovary	... ...	grs. 3 siccum
Thyroid, B.P. ...	... ...	grs. 1-5th siccum
Ext. Pituitary whole gland	...	grs. 3 siccum
Adrenalin	... ...	grs. 1-120th

was given by mouth three times daily one hour before
meals, and three times per week an Extract of Corpus
Luteum was injected subcutaneously.

About the middle of the month the patient complained of abdominal pain—practically the first manifestation of external interest she had exhibited. She
was put to bed and hot stupes were applied. The
menses appeared and, although scanty, persisted over
a period of five days. There was marked mental
improvement from the first appearance of the menstrual
flow. The patient actually became talkative, much
to the amazement of everyone in contact with her,
and when the menses had ceased, expressed a desire to
get up and go out for a walk of her own accord.

The cod-liver oil innunction had, of course, been
stopped for some time, and the patient was now on
ordinary full diet. Her digestion was very good, her
physical strength was normal, and her weight had
increased to 8 st. 2 lbs. Every day her mental condition exhibited a gradual advancement. She became
interested in her improvement and desirous of helping
in every way possible. She chatted freely with her
relations when they came to visit her, then with the
nurses, and gradually became quite open and friendly
with the author.

As she had been a long time in the Nursing Home,
she was discharged to the care of her own people as it
was hoped that a change to her old surroundings would
hasten her recovery. She continued to visit the author

twice weekly for injections of Corpus Luteum and still kept on taking the polyglandular capsules by mouth.

A very agreeable feature of the case was that the heavy downy fluff covering the face and neck completely disappeared and her skin became as smooth and normal as that of a normal woman of her age.

At the end of seven months her weight was bordering on 9 stone. She appeared to be in the pink of physical health and there was not a vestige of any mental abnormality. She returned to her profession as a teacher and has never been troubled since.

Just before her final discharge from treatment she was asked by the author if she could give him an idea of the approximate date of origin of her trouble. She kept harping on the fact that her trouble really started in 1924 when she became depressed, etc., etc. When it was pointed out to her that this was possibly only the culmination of her condition, she freely admitted that she had never enjoyed good health whilst at school. She was over fifteen before her periods commenced and she felt terribly unwell at these times, both before the onset of the period and after it had cleared up. The periods were never regular and invariably painful. She said that from her sixteenth year she suffered from physical weakness to such an extreme degree that she really had not the strength to take part in games and robust exercises. As she was a tall lanky girl her teachers and she herself ascribed this to the fact that she had outgrown her strength. She had never thought about the menstrual side of the case, nor did her teachers. She was never examined and never treated. At no time was she able to put on weight and she had been a victim to constipation all her life.

What conclusion can we draw from this case? That she was a Schizophrænic admits of no doubt. She had all the mental signs of that condition, and that it was well established is shown by the fact of its resistance to treatment. Her own picture of her early girlhood demonstrates her entrance into the puberty state under really bad conditions. The penalty paid

was Dysmenorrhœa and menstrual irregularities
brought on by her unhealthy physical state. As no
effort was made to check the physical condition, so
that the sex glands might have an opportunity of
normalizing themselves and fulfilling their normal
function, the nervous condition gradually degenerated
from being an ordinary PSYCHO-NEUROSIS (puberty
type) until it became a definite Schizophrænia.

The method of treatment of this case is very interesting from the point of view that it goes a long
way to establish the theory of this condition being
due to a dysfunction of the sex glands. It goes a
long way to prove that this dysfunction of the sex
glands, in all probability, is based on an actual
physical toxic state, as, in this case, chronic constipation. This chronic constipation, with its accompanying toxic effect, has such a deleterious influence
on the blood that both its quality and quantity
suffers, and the sex glands, naturally, suffer in
consequence.

In the treatment of the above case the physical state
of the patient had, naturally, to be tackled first, as
life itself was dependent on an improvement in that
condition. No special effort was made to treat the
blood as a separate entity, but we see how the blood
normalized itself as the body was brought back to a
good physical status.

That gland therapy played a marked role in the re-
establishment of normal ovarian function admits of no
doubt in the writer's mind. That gradual all-round
physical improvement could bring about a similar
happy result is, in all probability, true, but it is highly
questionable if ovarian normality would result as
quickly without endocrine assistance.

It is noteworthy how even the steady physical improvement was not accompanied by a simultaneous
mental advancement. When, however, the ovarian
function had re-established itself, there was an immediate mental change. and improvement from that
hour went on unchecked.

The second case, that of Miss C——, is in marked contrast to that of Miss M——, inasmuch as the development was quite sudden. In this case a well-established Schizophrænia manifested itself without any marked evidence of earlier preliminary PSYCHO-NEUROSIS. There were both hallucinations and delusions, whereas with Miss M——, if these were present she, at all events, never gave expression to them.

Miss C—— was employed as a Civil Servant and had just passed her twenty-first birthday when first seen.

Physically, she was of medium height and well covered. Her features were pleasant and intelligent.

Cardiac examination revealed a soft blowing murmur over the pulmonary area and the heart sounds generally were soft and distant.

The body was well nourished and the skin in good condition.

Her reflexes generally were normal, except that the patella reflex should be listed as plus.

On the psychic side the patient's general characteristic was distraction. She was absolutely indifferent when questioned about her past, present or future. She was not sullen in her refusal to answer questions. She just seemed bored and utterly indifferent to the whole proceeding. After a period she relaxed a little, or, more accurately, she seemed to take a passing interest in her examination, and in response to the question, " What is your chief trouble ? " she replied, " Nothing." " Was her health good ? " she was asked, and the reply was the single monosyllable " Yes." On being questioned as to whether people were kind to her, she did not make any response, and on this line being pressed home she asserted that she was pregnant.

This supposed occurrence happened at the seaside the previous summer with a boy whose name she could not recall. It was subsequently elicited from the mother that she had not been to this particular seaside resort at the time she mentioned ; in fact, not at all for the previous two or three years.

The patient continued to assert that she was pregnant, and her calm indifference to this situation was
closely symptomatic of the Schizophrænic mental
attitude.

She admitted that she constantly heard voices
alleging that she had had intimate relations with many
men. She stated that her mother constantly upbraided
her with this fact, but that it was a matter of no
importance with her.

There was no foundation whatsoever for these statements, and after being questioned she lapsed into her
customary apathy, apparently indifferent to everything.

Very occasionally a smile would flit across her face,
but on being questioned as to the reason for this she
either refused to reply at all or said that it was nothing
of importance.

As mentioned at the beginning of the history of this
case, the mother stated that she was not a robust
child. Her bowels had given trouble always. The
mother's statements of her condition at the time of
puberty were manifestly unreliable, but from what she
stated of the patient's subsequent menstrual periods
one was forced to the conclusion that at no time was
the menstrual function satisfactory.

About eighteen months prior to her first visit she
began to complain of general weakness, continuous
headaches, inability to concentrate, nervousness and
insomnia. At the end of three months her condition
became so bad that she felt unable to go to work and
applied for sick leave. This was granted for six months,
but the condition of the girl showed no evidence of
improvement. Her physical state became worse, her
physical weakness increased. She was gradually
losing interest in her surroundings and became moody
and depressed. She took no interest in the house and
developed a distaste towards helping in any way in
domestic functions. A further extension of sick leave
was obtained as the patient was quite unfit to return
to work. Her apathy had increased to such an extent

by now that she was disinclined to get out of bed and became irritable and petulant when told to do so.

Her physical condition, as has been stated, despite the fact that she was constantly under the supervision of her family doctor, became progressively worse. Her periods were irregular, scanty and difficult, and four months before being seen by the writer had completely ceased.

She now seemed very depressed and refused to reply when spoken to, and at this time began to develop delusions and hallucinations.

The patient's blood was taken for examination. This revealed a marked reduction in the hæmoglobin, which was down to 60%, and the red blood corpuscles were moderately decreased (3,500,000). There was no marked change in the leucocyte count.

High colonic lavage was started to clean out the intestinal canal, and the diet at the beginning was confined to easily digested food, jellies, beef extracts, fruit juices, etc., and glycerine extract of red bone marrow was given three times daily.

The patient was confined to bed, light massage being administered.

Her physical condition gradually improved, her appetite increased and her diet was soon put on a more generous scale.

At the end of six weeks her strength was obviously getting near to normal, and she commenced walking exercises twice daily.

At this time she was put on a polyglandular compound consisting of :—

Extract of Ovary	...	grs. 5 siccum
Thyroid B.P.	...	grs. 1/5th
Adrenalin ...	...	grs. 1/120th

three times daily, and Corpus Luteum Extract was injected subcutaneously three times a week.

Up to this time there was no very pronounced progress in the mental condition. The patient was still apathetic and listless, but when walking exercises were begun, about the end of the sixth week, she gradually became interested and, in order to hasten her recovery, she was taken to cinematograph shows and theatres.

At the end of three months there was a gain in weight of about 12 lbs., and her mentality had become completely clear. There was not a vestige left of the abnormal mental processes, and the patient, after a time, requested permission to resume her work.

Menstrual irregularity was still present to some degree but, apart from this, the patient has had no further trouble after a period of 18 months.

CHAPTER X

PERSONALITY

Axis Personality.

The Splitting of the Personality in Schizophrænia.

Consideration of the component units of the Axis Personality—
the Predominant Personality Unit and the Dormant Personality Unit.

Analysis of the Personality in a normal subject, with photographs.

Accentuation of the Predominant Personality Unit in Psycho-neurosis (Psychic type).

Accentuation of the Dormant Personality Unit in Psycho-neurosis (Physical type).

How Psychic Force vitalizes the Axis Personality.

Psychic Force and its relation to the Predominant Personality Unit and the Dormant Personality Unit.

Analysis of two abnormal personalities—with photographs.

PERSONALITY might be defined most accurately, though paradoxically, as the invisible and intangible part of us which is visible and tangible to the invisible and intangible part of our neighbours. Personality is our subconscious reaction.

It follows from this that the first noticeable change in the patient suffering from PSYCHO-NEUROTIC or PSYCHOTIC ailments must occur in the PERSONALITY, as the subconscious is the battle ground on which the entire conflict is fought out.

In the PSYCHO-NEUROTIC state we see patients reveal a disposition entirely at variance with that which we had attributed to them before the psychic upset. That this character metamorphosis is no superficial happening is fully evidenced by the basically altered attitude of these patients to their former friends and to their old surroundings.

A patient who, prior to a nervous upheaval has been energetic, lively, sweet-tempered and kindly in disposition, may and usually does become lazy, listless, surly and generally ill-disposed. Here we have a marked overturning of the PERSONALITY of the normal condition.

In the Hysteric the outstanding feature of the ailment, apart from the hysterical overaction, is "la belle indifference." This indifference is a Personality manifestation diametrically opposed to the Personality exhibiting the overaction—so different that one is forced to believe that the subject is the possessor of two Personalities in the Hysteric condition.

This brings us to the point where it is incumbent on us to get a clear-cut working idea of the mechanism of Personality. Without such an idea it is impossible to understand fully the genesis of the Psycho-neurotic state.

We have just seen how the patient in Hysteria presents what seems to be two entirely different personalities. Is Personality, therefore, a dual mechanism? To the author's mind the answer is undisputably in the affirmative. Further than this, the author puts forward the theory that not only is the Personality composed of two distinct units but that these two component units psychologically speaking are sex-differentiated.

To put this plainly, the author holds that in the male, whilst one of the component units in the Personality is essentially a male psychological unit, the second component unit is strongly tinged with female psychological colour.

The same rule, of course, applies to the female.

It must be clearly understood here that this colouring of the Personality of the individual with the Personality of the opposite sex refers only to sex in the psychological sense, and does not carry any significance normally of sex in the procreative sense. At the same time, it does enable us to understand readily how easily sex perversion could arise in such a predisposed territory.

What evidence can we advance in the first place that Personality is a dual mechanism ? It has to be

FACE COMPOSED OF TWO
LEFT HALVES

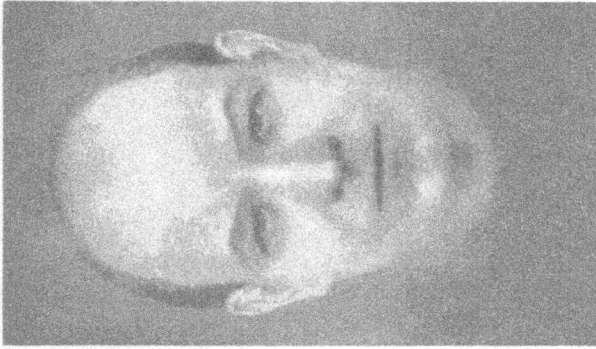

ORIGINAL FRONT FACE

FACE COMEOSED OF TWO
RIGHT HALVES

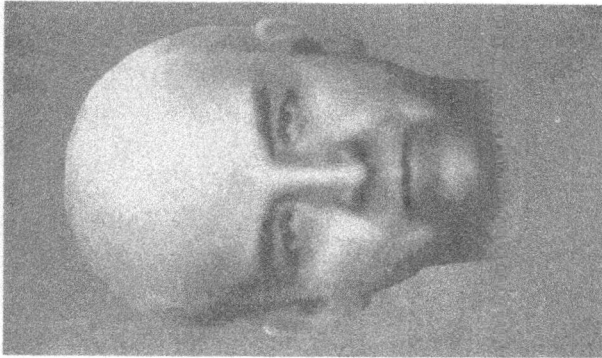

DORMANT PERSONALITY UNIT

The Personality displayed by this face differs markedly from the personalities evidenced by the original and by the face composed of the right halves. This Personality is aggressively male in type and is termed the Dominant Personality Unit in the combination.

AXIA PERSONALITY

A normal subject of excellent type. Note the well-cut, sensitive and refined features. The forehead development is imposing, the eyes intelligent and penetrating.

PREDOMINANT PERSONALITY UNIT

The Personality displayed in this face closely resembles the personality of the original and for this reason is termed the Predominant Personality Unit in the combination. The refinement of the features is accentuated. This refinement in contrast with the Personality displayed in the face composed of the two left halves approaches the feminine in type.

admitted that the brain is the site of intelligence as far as our knowledge brings us, and the face, generally speaking, is the mirror in which we see that intelligence. The vacant purposeless bovine look of the cretinous imbecile is mute but irrefutable evidence of the barely glowing embers of the subconscious fire of understanding within. The tense facial muscles and gleaming eyes of the frenzied maniac almost enable us to see the mounting flames of the mental volcano underneath.

If the physical can be of any assistance in enabling us to understand the underlying mind, we must surely seek for it in the face of the individual.

The most convincing proof is always a visible one— that is something which we can actually see and which admits of no contradiction. For that reason we start with a front face photograph of a normal man. The subject of this photograph is an excellent type physically and intellectually. He is above the average in intelligence, as is manifested by the fine frontal development and the sharp penetrating eyes. The features are pronounced, sensitive and well chiselled

The face generally is a face of intelligence and refinement and he follows an occupation in keeping with these characteristics.

Let us divide the face in the middle line, and let us build up a face composed of two right sides of the original. After this we construct a face made up of the two remaining left sides. (See illustration.)

Placing the two artificial photographs one on each side of the original, let us examine them and compare them with each other from a psychological angle.

A.1 bears a very close facial resemblance to the original "A" There is the same generous frontal development, the same finely chiselled features, but a close scrutiny reveals that there is a distinct difference in the expression. The refinement, the gentleness, the sensitiveness, the artistry of the original "A" has been deepened in the artificial "A.1." The expression is even more refined, more gentle, more sensitive, and more artistic than the original "A." It definitely, very definitely, approaches the feminine.

In other words, the Personality portrayed by the photograph "A.1," psychologically speaking, exudes a distinct feminine aura.

Now let us turn to photograph "A.2." This face is made up of the two left s des of the original "A."

It bears little or no resemblance to the original "A" and not a vestige of resemblance to "A.1." The Personality of photograph "A.2 " is male, aggressively, uncompromisingly male. The personality here is that of a realist, a worker, a strong vigorous materialist who takes care that the dreamer, the artist "A.1," derives substantial benefit from his art.

These are the two component psychological units whose fusion gives us the Axis Personality expressed by the original "A".

As the Personality exhibited by the photograph "A.1 " bears such a close resemblance to the Axis Personality of the original "A", as proved by the close feature resemblance, it is to be presumed that this is the dominating unit in the fusion. To distinguish it from the other unit let us call it the PREDOMINANT PERSONALITY UNIT. Owing to the subordinate part played by the second unit we shall give it the name of the DORMANT PERSONALITY UNIT. The fusion of these two units gives us the Axis Personality of the individual.

It is to be noted here that the PREDOMINANT PERSONALITY UNIT is the unit which is tinged with female psychological colour.

The DORMANT UNIT expresses unadulterated male psychological bent.

It may be asked whether such a tinging of one of the component Personality Units with a foreign sex psychological element is of advantage to the individual. To the author's mind it is of immense advantage, even stronger than this it is an essential.

It permits of that flexibility, that resiliency of mind, which gives us what we term the colour in Personality.

It gives to Personality what tempering gave to the steel of the Damascus blades. It means to Personality what the pink blush means to the orient of the pearl.

It is in this tinging where genius lies, and genius cannot exist without it.

Its presence means refinement, sensitiveness, brilliancy of mind, and its possessors in a high degree lead the world in art, music, literature and the sciences.

It is not to be imagined for a moment that this tinging of the PREDOMINANT PERSONALITY UNIT in the male, for instance, interferes with what we consider the male attributes—courage, resolution and tenacity.

The Hall of Heroes is tenanted in the main, if not exclusively, by the psychologically hypersensitive. The most sublime acts of courage in the late Great War were performed not by the crude Boetians of the Armies, but by the highly sensitized and overstrung Lacedemonians.

Let us experiment on the Personality of the individual and, fortunately, we can experiment on it in a manner easily understood by all.

By the administration of a certain quantity of alcohol to a man we induce a definite temporary psychological change. In other words, we induce a temporary alteration in his personality. Before taking the alcohol our subject was quiet, reserved, inoffensive and unobtrusive. Under the influence of alcohol he becomes noisy, flamboyant, aggressive and offensive.

This is a very definite and very marked temporary Personality Alteration which is undeniable. There certainly has not been a heightening of his PRE-DOMINANT PERSONALITY UNIT—that is gentleness, restraint, etc. These characteristics are temporarily in indisputable abeyance. On the other hand, there is a very marked accentuation of the primitive male instincts —roughness, quarrelsomeness and aggressiveness.

In other words, the alcohol has exercised its entire stimulating influence on the purely male or DORMANT PERSONALITY UNIT.

M

The DORMANT PERSONALITY UNIT is now in complete control, and it is male, one might almost say with truth offensively male, in type. The restraining influence of the PREDOMINANT PERSONALITY UNIT is temporarily over-ridden and we get an exhibition of the male beast naked and unashamed.

Notice must be taken here of the fact that eroticism is markedly increased in this condition as one would, naturally, expect in the circumstances.

Now let us turn to the female subject under the influence of alcohol. Just as in the male the PREDOMINANT (sex male tinged) PERSONALITY UNIT is temporarily bereft of its balancing or restraining power; the DORMANT (or purely feminine sex) PERSONALITY UNIT assumes control, poise is lost, and we are treated to a picture of the primitive female psychological inclination. There is an over display of emotion, the individual becomes sickeningly affectionate, then tearful and finally hysterical. Eroticism also is a pronounced feature in these circumstances.

As far as the writer sees the evidence brought forward by this simple experiment is incontrovertible, and it teaches us many things about the Mechanism of Personality—in other words, the working of the subconscious mind.

It demonstrates that the PREDOMINANT PERSONALITY UNIT or the Unit which is in control under normal circumstances, is tinged, psychologically speaking, with the opposite sex element.

It demonstrates how this tinging makes for balance in the Axis Personality and gives to it poise, flexibility and resilience. It proves to us how impossible the human race would be if the component units of the Axis Personality were of the same sex elements, giving us a race sharply divided into animal males and equally animal females.

This experiment more than strongly suggests that the PREDOMINANT PERSONALITY UNIT of the blend carries the character, the intelligence, and the true psychological germ of the human individual.

On the other hand, this simple experiment suggests equally strongly that the DORMANT PERSONALITY carries in the male the instinct to strive to work, to fight, and in the female the affectionate, protective and motherly instinct.

In both sexes this latter Unit carries the procreative sex instinct in the normal.

It may be interpolated here in support of this theory that the Personality of the individual is sex-tinged, that even the physical confirmation carries evidence of the close relationship of the sexes.

In position, external appearance and structure the breasts of the male resemble closely the female breasts. In fact, they only differ in that having no lactiferous elements they do not secrete milk.

The clitoris of the female mimes the penis of the male, is composed of the same erectile tissue and reacts in a similar way under the influence of stimulation.

In the light of this evidence it does not seem an impossible idea to entertain that there is a passing of the line of demarcation between the Personalities of the sexes.

In Schizophrænia we have a splitting of the Personality. Let us examine this condition along the lines we have used.

The Axis Personality splits into its constituent Units—the PREDOMINANT and the DORMANT. We have seen how under the influence of alcohol the DORMANT UNIT usurped temporary control and the PREDOMINANT or balancing Unit suffered temporary eclipse.

In the two cases of Schizophrænia outlined in the previous chapter we have seen how the Axis Personality of the individual was changed and an individual with an entirely new Personality arose.

What has happened here is exactly parallel to what has happened under the alcoholic stimulation. The PREDOMINANT PERSONALITY UNIT is swamped and the DORMANT PERSONALITY UNIT rises into control.

This is due, in the author's mind, as he has stated in the previous chapter, to a toxic influence brought about in all probability as a consequence of imbalance in the secretions of the endocrine glands.

The start in both cases was signalised by menstrual abnormality. This denoted malfunction of normal ovarian activity on the procreative side, and it is only logical to assume that normal function in their endocrine capacity was also upset. This would bring about disharmony in the secretions of that chain group whose combined secretions we have endeavoured to prove are the essential elements in the maintenance of normal nervous stability. The result is sub-conscious upheaval and symptoms of the Psycho-neurotic state first make their appearance.

At the beginning it would appear that the PRE-DOMINANT PERSONALITY UNIT is the Unit most affected. The individual becomes more sensitive, more highly strung and subconscious reaction is markedly stimulated. The DORMANT PERSON-ALITY UNIT seems to fade to some extent and a general lethargy and listlessness becomes markedly evident.

There is an accompanying loss of sexual desire at this time, giving further evidence of the lessened activity of the DORMANT PERSONALITY UNIT. If this Psycho-neurotic condition persists and grows worse over a prolonged period the DORMANT UNIT in the partnership seems to come under the toxic in-fluence of the altered endocrine secretions and, as in alcohol, suddenly asserting itself assumes control of the Personality.

The Axis Personality has now split. The normally PREDOMINANT PERSONALITY UNIT falls from its position of control and that control is usurped by the hitherto subordinate DORMANT UNIT.

Support to this theory is lent by the sudden mani-festation of sex inclination. The DORMANT PERSON-ALITY which is the locale of this inclination treats the now weakened PREDOMINANT PERSONALITY UNIT with contempt and derides its restraining and balancing influence.

This is evidenced by the conduct of the Schizophrænic individual. This new personality pays no heed to the habits, inclinations, and associations of the old Personality. It shamlessly flouts and scorns the limitations and rules which governed the individual in the normal. This specially applies to the sex procreative side which is rampant and unrestrained in the new state of affairs.

There is exhibited in the Schizophrænic state, therefore, a steady progressive personality deterioration from the normal through the Psycho-neurotic to the definitely Psychotic condition.

From this we can readily visualize a further progressive degeneration unless the condition is effectively checked.

The marked feature in this state, as we see, is the gradual submergence of the PREDOMINANT PERSONALITY UNIT, and the gradual rise of the DORMANT PERSONALITY UNIT.

In Psycho-neurosis, are we entitled to assume that the condition is due to an accentuation of the PREDOMINANT PERSONALITY UNIT? In Psycho-neurosis we undeniably have evidence of over-care which, on free translation, means anxiety, and anxiety as we know is the cardinal feature of the Psycho-neurotic state.

It would seem that this exaggerated PREDOMINANT PERSONALITY UNIT aggregates to itself an unwarranted portion of the Psychic Nerve Force elaborated in subconsciousness in order to help it out in its exaggerated actions and imaginings.

The result of this is an insufficiency of that Force remains over to vitalise and keep normally active the DORMANT PERSONALITY UNIT whose object in life seems to be the production of energy and the maintenance of the procreative sex side.

This idea is supported by the fact that lethargy, exhaustion, and lack of sex desire are static features of the Psycho-neurotic state, and these features appear to depend for their existence on the normal influence of the DORMANT PERSONALITY UNIT.

A case treated by the author as far back as 1919 may be of interest to the reader as the condition Schizophræenia (Katatonic Type) is not too frequently met with.

An attempt, believed to be unique, was made by the author to drive the split off personality of the patient back into the Axis or Normal personality.

The attempt to do this was successful as far as a temporary restoration of the Axis Personality was concerned, but unsuccessful in holding the patient permanently in the normal state.

After successfully restoring the patient to normality on four or five occasions, only to see him slip back again into his psychopathic condition, the treatment was abandoned and the subsequent history of the case is unknown. The experimental treatment is of paramount interest inasmuch as it proves beyond any reasonable doubt the existence of the duality of personality, and how these different personalities evidence themselves under psychologically adverse circumstances.

The patient was aged 23, a dispatch rider invalided from France. He had been blown up in a shell explosion and sent to England suffering from shock. Transferred to the Mental Hospital at Cardiff he was there for some time when the writer was asked to see him. Through the courtesy of Doctor Goodall the author was enabled to visit him there in April, 1919.

HISTORY—The patient was listed on admission, as far as the writer's memory serves, as an ordinary case of shell shock.

On March 1st, some time after his admission, the nurse on going to his bed in the morning found him awake, but he resolutely refused to answer her or to pay any attention to what she said. He refused breakfast, keeping his teeth tightly clenched, and remained fixed in the same position in the bed, his eyes never varying from a specific spot on the ceiling.

This frozen attitude was maintained throughout that day and, in fact, never varied according to his history up to the time he was seen by the writer.

He passed urine and fæces in the bed, making no request for assistance. He never uttered a word, refused all food and liquid and had to be tube fed.

On examination the patient, naturally, was emaciated owing to the difficulty of feeding, but considering this difficulty he was in good condition, his strength fair, and he was free from bed sores—a tribute to the care and attention paid to him.

All efforts to question him were futile. He lay in bed with fixed gaze, entirely oblivious of every effort made to elicit his interest or arouse him from his stuperous state. His patella, plantar and testicular reflexes were present but depressed. His response to slight pain stimulus was absolutely negative.

There was no evidence of Flexibilitas Cerea as far as the writer's memory serves him. (Unfortunately the notes on this case were lost, and the writer is only able to give the salient features with precision.)

After an examination and study of the history a diagnosis of Katatonic Stupor was made.

Nothing was further heard of the case until the following October when the patient was discharged from the army and, at his mother's request, transferred to Camberwell House Asylum, Peckham Road, London, under the care of Doctor Norman.

Here, with the courteous permission of Doctor Norman, the writer was enabled to see him and carry out the treatment detailed below.

Considering that the patient's attitude had never varied over the previous period of nine months, during which time he had to be tube fed, it was astounding to find his physical condition so well maintained. In fact, if this condition had not been so satisfactory it would have been impossible to carry out the treatment determined upon, as there was palpable risk in administering an anæsthetic over a long period to a patient who had been tube fed during the preceding nine months.

The treatment carried out was as follows :—

An anæsthetic of ether was administered until the brain entered into the condition of alcoholic excitement —the pre-anæsthesia state.   It was hoped by the writer that the patient freed from the morbid control of his psycho-pathic state, that is the DORMANT PERSONALITY UNIT, would talk, rave, or shout as do the generality of normal patients under an anæsthetic. The hope was vain.   The patient remained as immobile as in his waking moments.

An electric battery was here introduced and the wire brush was applied over the thorax, neck, and face.

This is a really sharp pain stimulus and insupportable by the fully conscious.   Any patient partially anæsthetised would normally be sensitive to such stimulation, but our subject remained utterly unresponsive.

A request was made for complete anæsthesia—the idea being to catch the patient emerging from the anæsthetic when logically all pathologic subconscious organised resistance must be in abeyance.   The wire brush was again applied at full force and again the result was absolutely negative.

As a final effort the wire brush was applied to the top of the glans penis, and the effect was dramatic in the extreme.   The patient struggled, made a grab at the wire brush and shouted at the top of his voice " Take it away !   Take it away ! "   These were the first words he had uttered from the preceding 1st March, a period of nine months.

He was now thoroughly aroused and began talking volubly and excitedly but perfectly coherently and normally.

The mother was admitted to his bedside and it was interesting to watch the reactions of each of them.   The mother had sat by his bedside day after day for nine months never receiving even a glance of recognition. The son, as he subsequently told the writer, was consumed with a desire to speak to her but was not permitted to do so by the threatening monitor within him—the DORMANT PERSONALITY UNIT.

A noteworthy feature was that the patient, despite the fact that he had had full anæsthesia, was quite rational practically from the time he shouted for the brush to be removed until his mother, Doctor Norman and the writer left him in order that he might have a rest.

As the case was so interesting the writer returned to Camberwell House to spend the night.

No attempt was made that evening to question the patient about his feelings during the time he was stuporous. A general conversation was carried on, the patient asking questions of general interest and replying in an intelligent manner to questions submitted to him.

He fell asleep naturally and in the morning over a cup of tea the writer set himself deliberately to glean as much information as possible from the patient as to his ideas and general psychic reactions during the nine months his normal mental functions were suspended.

He was quite rational and clear cut in his statements. He recalled outstanding events during that period, however, with manifest mental pain, almost horror.

He related that some dominating personality (the DORMANT PERSONALITY UNIT), absolutely irresistible, commanded him to refuse food. At no time did this voice suggest that the food was poisoned—he was simply commanded not to eat and not to pay attention to external happenings of any description under penalty of something calamitous happening to him.

He was powerless to resist these commands, terrified even to attempt resistance.

He stated that his hunger pangs at times were

insupportable, and when he saw trays with food carried past him to other patients he wanted to cry out in his agony but dared not.

He felt acutely the degradation of his personal uncleanliness owing to his inability to attend to his natural requirements, but the overpowering "something" sternly commanded him to take no notice.

In the summer time when flies walked across his face and even encroached on his eyes he was sternly ordered to pay no attention.

His memory for all the happenings during this period was tragically vivid and he even recalled how a cobweb which had settled in a corner near his bed escaped the attention of the maid or nurse when the daily dusting was being done.

The patient was entirely rational, perfectly orientated, and betrayed general interest in external happenings.

As he was exhausted both physically and psychically after such a terrible ordeal, it was not to be expected that he could have the vivid interest of a healthy individual in current events.

The writer laments deeply the loss of the notes on this case as it is only possible to give the broadest features which are indelibly impressed on his memory.

The patient's mental attitude one could see very plainly was one of acute pain, almost amounting to horror, as he reflected on his past condition.

After two or three hours he was allowed to rest and was visited again that evening. He was weak and tired, partially due to his low physical state, and one naturally supposes also partially due to his terrible mental strain.

On the second night he slept naturally and was rational in the morning but less active mentally. He showed evidence still of great mental fatigue and his alertness gradually faded until in the evening he had lapsed back into stupor.

It was a dreadful disappointment to the writer as his progress for about 48 hours gave every hope that he could be restored to normal physical and mental health.

He was roused from the stupor again on two or three occasions and the effort needed to arouse him, as far as memory serves, was less vigorous on each occasion, but his clear periods were not so well defined and not so prolonged.

During these attempts at treatment every assistance was rendered by Doctor Norman, the Superintendent of Camberwell House Mental Hospital, who placed all the resources of the Hospital at the writer's disposal. To him and to Major Leahy of the R.A.M.C. and to Doctor Robert Slaney the grateful thanks of the author is tendered for the help they gave him in what at the time was quite a trying experiment.

The treatment, unfortunately, must be written down as a failure, but there is something to be learnt from it even in defeat.

An attempt, a successful attempt was made to press a split-off Personality temporarily in morbid control back into the original Axis Personality and again to form a harmonious blend.

It is regrettable that this forcible restoration to normality did not hold, but perhaps the effort may stimulate those who have wider opportunity than the writer to carry on the work.

The writer begs permission to submit photographs of two individuals who legitimately from the sociological standpoint may be classified as abnormal.

Here again the front face photographs of the subjects are treated in the manner described beforehand. The result of these experiments would go to emphasise further the marked difference of Personality portrayed and emphasise the author's theory of the sex differentiation existing in the Personality of all of us. (See illustration).

The subject of the photographs was a young man of twenty-four, a notorious bank robber who

committed a number of cold-blooded murders.   He
was a friend and companion of another American
deperado named Floyd, and recently met the same
fate as Floyd, being shot to death by police officers
in the United States.

The original photograph marked " B " shows us a
rather pleasant-faced youth with a vivid eye and
apparent good head development.   There is nothing
evident in this face to denote brutal criminal tendency.
On the contrary there is rather an air of humour,
intelligence, and a generally attractive Personality.

The " B.1 " photograph is a face composed of the
two right halves of the original.   There is a marked
resemblance in this synthetic individual to the original.
There is the same broad sweep of the forehead and
the same vivid humorous eye.   The expression of the
face displays no vicious tendency.   On the contrary, it
is radiant with good humour and a good nature which
is almost feminine.

The composite face " B.1 " closely resembles the
original face, and it is to be presumed that the character
depicted by this face is closely allied to the character
of the real individual and was the PREDOMINANT
PERSONALITY UNIT over the greater part of the
subject's existence.

Photograph No. " B.2 " is the composite face built
up from the two left halves of the original.   This face
bears little if any resemblance to the original " B "
or to the photograph " B.1 ".   The sweep of the
forehead is less pronounced, the eye is larger, more
intense, almost ferocious.   The face as a whole is
firmer, stronger, and with the wide mouth is markedly
masculine.

The Personality displayed by No. " B.2 " photograph
is as different from the personality displayed by the
original photograph " B " or the composite photograph
" B.1 " as its physical difference.

That this personality "B.2 " played as important a
part as that played by " B.1 " Personality over the
major portion of the man's life is difficult to believe.

FACE COMPOSED OF TWO
LEFT HALVES

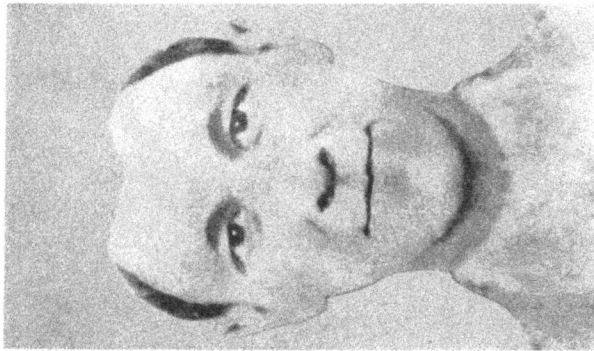

ORIGINAL FRONT FACE

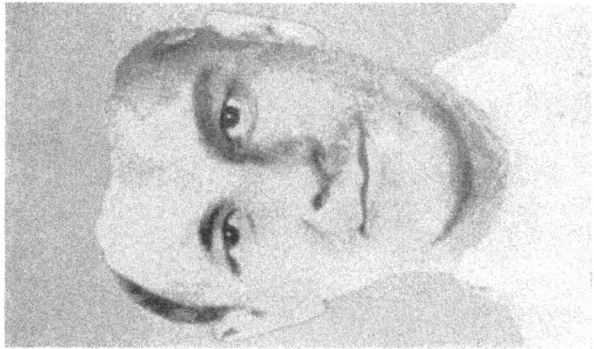

FACE COMPOSED OF TWO
RIGHT HALVES

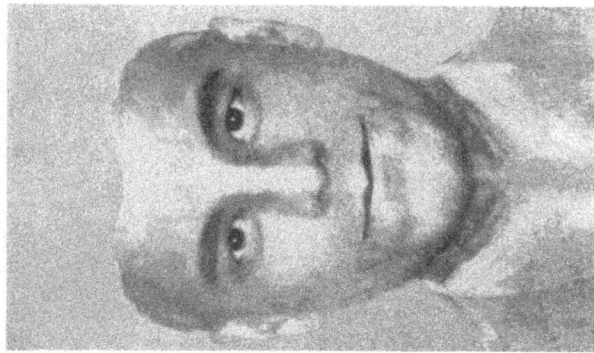

DORMANT PERSONALITY UNIT

It is perfectly apparent that this face denotes a Personality markedly different from the original and also from the Personality displayed in the face composed of the two right halves. It is a strongly masculine face and evidences an undeniable recklessness and ferocity. It is the Dormant Personality Unit, and the Unit which carried the killer instinct.

AXIA PERSONALITY

The above is the normal front face photograph of Miller.

PREDOMINAT PERSONALITY UNIT

The Personality displayed by this face is softer than the original and bears little or no resemblance to the strong ferocious personality as exhibited by the face composed of the two left halves. Owing to its resemblance to the original it must be described as the Predominating Personality Unit in the combination. There is a feminine tinge displayed in this face.

This youth at 24 years was at the Schizophrænic age. Was there a gradual oncoming psychic deterioration from puberty pushed suddenly forward by the strain of his criminal life until his Personality split asunder under the pressure ?

Did this No. " B.2 " Personality, this DORMANT PERSONALITY UNIT hitherto subordinated in the blend suddenly blaze forth ? Did this Personality in its new found freedom scorn its former controlling partner and casting caution to the winds launch itself on a mission of reckless slaughter, heedless of the inescapable penalty.

One fact cannot be denied, viz. that the Personality displayed by No. " B.1 " is clearly the PREDOMINANT PERSONALITY UNIT in the Axis Personality, and must have been in command for the greater period of the youth's life as it has so vividly stamped its characteristics on the face of the subject. Over this long period there has been no murder. Suddenly there is a character revolution. A new Personality arises and a ruthless killer develops.

In the author's opinion this type is definitely Schizophrænic. (See illustration.)

The subject here is a female aged about 50 years. She committed a deliberate and a particularly revolting murder by driving a motor-car backwards and forwards over her victim until life was extinct.

Her normal photograph "C" shows her as a rather gross woman with a strong face giving evidence of considerable intellectual power.

In the composite " C.1 " made up of the two right halves of the face ; there is an immediate and manifest resemblance to the original as portrayed in " C." So close is this resemblance that one would be justified in assuming that they represented the same individual. It may be conceded, therefore, that their Personalities are very closely allied also.

A careful scrutiny of the face depicted in No. " C.1 " displays a decided masculine firmness. This face carried the PREDOMINANT PERSONALITY UNIT which influenced the subject over the greater part of her existence, kept her balanced and made her an ordinary commonplace personage until the tragic occurrence with which she was associated. It is said of her that she was generous and kind to those less fortunate than herself. In fact, her victim had been for years a pensioner on her generosity.

This photograph (No. C.1) represents that side of her Personality and was the PREDOMINANT PERSONALITY UNIT in the combination.

Photograph No. " C.2 " portrays a Personality vastly different from both the original " C " and the synthetic Personality " C.1 " It portrays a coarse, lustful and blantantly feminine individual. This represented the DORMANT PERSONALITY UNIT over the greater part of the woman's life. Balanced and kept in control by the PREDOMINANT PERSONALITY UNIT, it enabled the subject to lead an inconspicuous existence.

What then broke up this harmonious union and allowed the DORMANT PERSONALITY UNIT to assume tragic control, casting off the balancing influence of the PREDOMINANT PERSONALITY UNIT ? Riotous living, alcoholic and other excesses plus the stress of poverty gradually sapped the power of the controlling PRE-DOMINANT PERSONALITY UNIT and allowed the rise of the DORMANT PERSONALITY UNIT.

The result was the emergence of an abnormal uncontrolled mentality, disastrous alike to her victim and to herself.

After a consideration of the photographs of a normal man and two persons abnormal, at all events from the sociological point of view, it is of interest to examine the results obtained by this method in the case of a congenital idiot.

Our subject, as displayed in Photograph M, is manifestly a Mongolian idiot boy.

The expression is the usual expression of the type —plain, flat, totally devoid of interest. M1 is the face composed of the two right halves, and here again we

FACE COMPOSED OF TWO
RIGHT HALVES

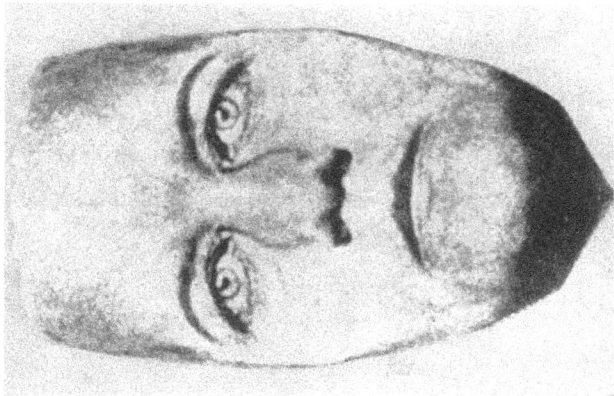

ORIGINAL FRONT FACE

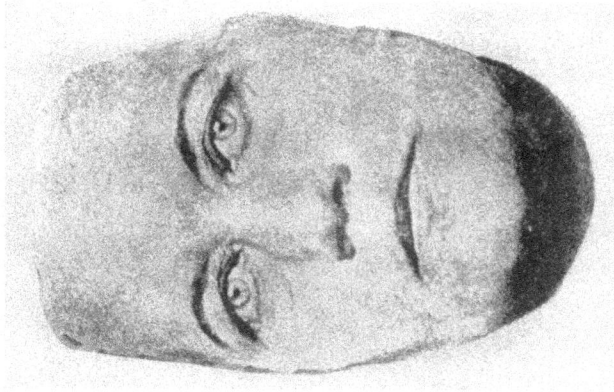

FACE COMPOSED OF TWO
LEFT HALVES

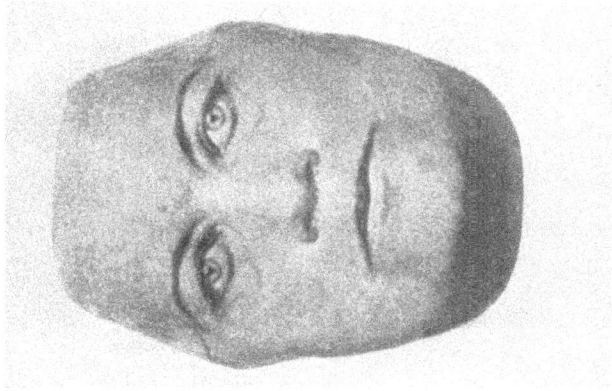

PREDOMINANT PERSONALITY UNIT

The Personality displayed by this face and its general outline approaches the masculine in type. The strong Personality of the original is accentuated.

AXIA PERSONALITY

The normal front face photograph indicates an abnormally strong Personality for a female.

DORMANT PERSONALITY UNIT

The Personality of this face is feminine and gives a strong suggestion of self-indulgent female animalism. It is the Dormant Personality Unit in the combination, and the Personality Unit which carried the killer instinct.

have the same colourless vacant Mongolian expression. M2 is the face composed of the two left halves, and once again the Mongolian apathy is depicted.

It is interesting this lack of differentiation in the defective mental type when contrasted with the marked differences exhibited by the fully developed mental subject.

The Psychic Force in this idiot boy was insufficiently strong to stamp any kind of a personality on his countenance, and the result is a grey, flat, unbroken surface.

Dividing the face in the middle line in an attempt to reach the component Personality Units gave us the same colourless amorphous expression in each—the expression of Mongolian idiocy—complete absence of Personality.

From a criminological view point, this method of photography, in the author's opinion, should be of the utmost importance in the positive identification of suspected persons.

It does not matter what physical alterations are made on the physical characteristics by the individual, it would be absolutely impossible for him to alter the aura of his different Personality Units.

Though the author has not had sufficient experience of this work to attempt even to advance a theory, he puts forward the suggestion that the wider the gap of difference between the component Personality Units the greater the tendency towards Psychic Instability.

Is this examination of the mechanism of Personality of practical benefit to us in our consideration of the Psycho-neurotic and Psychotic conditions? In the author's opinion it enables us to visualise in a practical and easily understood manner how these states originate in the individual.

We have seen that the personality in each and every one of us is a harmonious blend. We have seen that the two units which make up this blend are radically different. We have advanced the theory that the basic difference between these two units is one of sex psychologically speaking. We say, theoretically, that the Personality Unit which carries the foreign sex tinge is the PREDOMINANT partner in the blend, is the index of the intelligence of the individual and gives colour to the character of the individual. The DORMANT PERSONALITY UNIT is the subordinate partner in the blend. Psychologically speaking it carries purely the sex of the individual and harbours exclusively the procreative sex instinct.

In the harmonious blend, both Units playing their roles according to plan, we have normality and consequent psychic stability, i.e., the PREDOMINANT PERSONALITY UNIT governs and stabilises : the DORMANT PERSONALITY UNIT is subordinate, does the rougher work of life and attends to the sex procreative side.

If the PREDOMINANT PERSONALITY UNIT from any cause, physical or psychic, aggregates to itself an inordinate amount of Psychic Force, it becomes exaggerated. The DORMANT PERSONALITY UNIT, robbed of its adequate supply of Force, as a consequence fades proportionately in its vigour and the Psychoneurotic condition results.

If, as in alcohol, a toxic condition is generated by imbalance of the normal endocrine secretions which are the basis of Psychic Force, then an abnormal augmentation of the DORMANT PERSONALITY UNIT may occur accompanied by an equivalent decrease in importance of the normally PREDOMINANT PERSONALITY UNIT.

Thus we have the Axis Personality riven asunder and two Personalities vitalised and active appear on the scene. Being fundamentally different conflict must ensue and the result is Psychosis.

Viewed from this angle, does it not give us hope that nervous and mental troubles occurring in the offspring of normal parents have their origin in some specific toxic state on the physical side, or some specific leakage on the Psychic side of a combination of both these conditions ? This being so, we can approach these cases with more hope of successful treatment.

FACE COMPOSED OF TWO
RIGHT HALVES

ORIGINAL FRONT FACE

FACE COMPOSED OF TWO
LEFT HALVES

PREDOMINANT PERSONALITY UNIT

Face composed of two right halves of
original front face—no difference from the
original face but the same lack of Personality.

AXIA PERSONALITY

Front face photograph of a Mongolian
idiot.

DORMANT PERSONALITY UNIT

Face composed of two left halves of original
photo—no Personality but just flat idiocy.

p. 192

Our aim should be directed towards the discovery of the exciting cause, whether that cause is physical, psychic, or psycho-physical. If we discover this cause and bend our energies towards uprooting it, a successful result can be confidently awaited.

Before closing this chapter on the Mechanism of Personality, it is well to make clear to the reader what is in the mind of the author with regard to the PREDOMINANT PERSONALITY UNIT being tinged with a foreign sex element. In the writer's opinion the PREDOMINANT PERSONALITY UNIT is sex tinged only in the psychological sense, the procreative sex element being located invariably in the DORMANT PERSONALITY UNIT.

That a perverted sex inclination might arise in the foreign sex-tinged PREDOMINANT PERSONALITY UNIT can be readily understood, and sex perverts are invariably found to be suffering from an exaggeration of the PREDOMINANT PERSONALITY UNIT.

ADDENDUM

An apology is tendered to the reader for some of the material appearing in this addendum as it undoubtedly repeats in a measure what has already gone before.

As the subject PERSONALITY is one of vital importance, the writer thought himself justified in putting forward these further views in order to make himself as clear as possible.

Even now he is not at all satisfied that he has succeeded in demonstrating the analysis of Personality in a manner which could be termed effective. At the same time, it is his earnest hope that it will enable the practitioner to make some sort of an attempt to reach the sub-conscious mind and so be better equipped to deal with the difficulties existing in the inner mind of his patient.

We have endeavoured to prove the existence of two distinct Personalities in the individual, and we have offered as evidence in support of this the

N

two entirely different personalities exhibited by the synthetic individuals obtained by bisecting the face photographically and building up two new faces from this operation.

We have put forward the theory that the PREDOMI-NANT PERSONALITY UNIT is the component unit of the Axis Personality blend which exercises the major influence in life, and it is the unit which carries the foreign sex tinge.

From photographic evidence we see clearly that the facial characteristics exhibited by this Unit bear a very close resemblance to the features of the original or Axis Personality, and it is only fair to assume that their sub-conscious reactions would carry a similar intimate relationship.

In other words, this PREDOMINANT PERSONALITY UNIT in the normal individual for weal or woe originates, directs and governs in a major degree the subconscious output of the Axis Personality and stamps it with its distinctive colour.

In the normal person the subordinate or DORMANT PERSONALITY UNIT plays an inconspicuous role and in normal circumstances exercises little or no influence on the subconscious reaction of the Axis Personality. It bears little or no physical resemblance to the physical characteristics of the Axis Personality. Under abnormal circumstances, as we have seen, for example, under the influence of alcohol, there is a marked change in the Axis Personality. There is a loss of balance, an absence of customary control and temporarily a new Personality arises, wild, extravagant, strongly animal in type.

In the male subject who has taken too much alcohol, we notice the salient primitive male inclinations—roughness, combativeness, and eroticism.

In the female we have displayed for our observation the salient primitive female inclinations—emotional overaction, hysteria and eroticism.

Which of the two component Personality Units is affected in the greater degree by alcohol ?

We have endeavoured to prove that the PRE-DOMINANT PERSONALITY UNIT is the major factor in the Axis Personality blend. If the alcohol stimulated this Unit we should, naturally, expect an exaggeration of the characteristics of the Axis Personality, and the individual should display more marked control over his acts and inclinations. In other words, he would present an accentuated picture of his normal Axis Personality.

Instead of this we see pronounced lessened dominion over acts and inclinations which are basically primitive.

It must, consequently, be assumed that the DORMANT PERSONALITY UNIT is the Unit stimulated by alcohol. From the above logically we must conclude that the PREDOMINANT PERSONALITY UNIT is the site of our higher instincts and emotion—our judgment, our intelligence, our power of control, our purely psychic side.

As the human being is a Psycho-physical creation, it naturally follows that the physical side requires appropriate attention and this must devolve upon the DORMANT PERSONALITY UNIT.

The DORMANT PERSONALITY UNIT, therefore, is the mechanism entrusted with the care of our physical condition. It supplies us with the strength and energy we require and is the Unit which harbours our physical sex centre.

Where we have these two PERSONALITY UNITS working in harmony, the result is a sound, solid, functioning Axis Personality and the individual is normal and free from Psychic abnormalities.

The Axis Personality of the individual depends for its existence and effective function on an adequate supply of PSYCHIC FORCE.

Whilst the output of PSYCHIC FORCE is adequate, both these Personalities are supplied with the quantity they require for their normal functioning.

Thus, in the full vigour of adult life, when the elaboration of PSYCHIC FORCE is at its peak, we see the mental and physical powers at their zenith also, and the individual revels in the Golden Hours of Life.

This means to say that the PREDOMINANT PERSONALITY UNIT has a full supply of PSYCHIC FORCE at its disposal and, as a consequence, the individual has reached the high-water level of his intellectual output.

In the same way the DORMANT PERSONALITY UNIT drawing upon abundant supply of PSYCHIC FORCE endows the person with physical and sexual power to the full.

If disease strikes the subject even in the high noon of life, the supply of PSYCHIC FORCE is lessened and there is an immediate fall in the intellectual output and an immediate lessening in the physical vigour.

The PREDOMINANT PERSONALITY UNIT, in other words, bereft of its rich supply of PSYCHIC FORCE is unable to function at full capacity and intellectual brilliancy is dimmed.

In the same way the DORMANT PERSONALITY UNIT with a lessened PSYCHIC FORCE supply at its disposal can no longer maintain physical vigour, and, as a consequence, energy and sexual power are during the illness markedly diminished.

When the illness passes and the endocrine glands are enabled to turn their endocrine secretions once again to the elaboration of PSYCHIC FORCE, normality returns and the subject once again resumes his psychic and physical powers.

As age advances and the endocrine glands undergo the universal degeneration of all things physical, their output grows gradually less, and PSYCHIC FORCE falls away pari passu.

The PREDOMINANT PERSONALITY UNIT, gradually deprived of its PSYCHIC FORCE, fades correspondingly in its vigour until the subject arrives at psychic senility. In the same way the failing PSYCHIC FORCE gradually starves the DORMANT PERSONALITY UNIT of its power until terminal physical dissolution results.

We have seen how the fusion of the two Personality units in a harmonious blend gives us a normal Axis Personality and a consequent normal subject.

We have watched the action of these two component units of the Axis Personality in health and disease and how they are vitalized by PSYCHIC FORCE.

It is of interest to examine here, in the light of what we know, how this PSYCHIC FORCE is distributed to the two component units and to note their consequent individual reaction. It may be taken for granted that our reactions, mental and physical, are dependent upon the amount of PSYCHIC FORCE within us at the moment.

This amount is regulated by the (for the moment) efficiency of our endocrine glands. As we have seen, it is abundant and plentiful in the golden hours of life, and falls on the advent of disease or age. At any period or in any circumstance in life there is a quantity " X " at our disposal.

Now let us examine how the two Personality units divide this PSYCHIC FORCE amongst themselves.

In the highly intellectual we see all the energies and all the resources of the individual used in the pursuit of an idea. Take a painter absorbed in his work, his psychic side is pre-eminently in the ascendant, it may even be to the neglect of his actual physical needs. On the lines of our theory his PREDOMINANT PERSONALITY UNIT is grabbing an unwarrantable, an illicit amount of the total PSYCHIC FORCE output. It intoxicates itself with this plethora of PSYCHIC FORCE, aggrandises and accentuates itself. Simultaneously, there is a fading of the DORMANT PERSONALITY UNIT (whose charge is the physical side of our subject).

There is not an adequate amount of PSYCHIC FORCE left over after the depredations of the PREDOMINANT PERSONALITY UNIT to vitalize normally the DORMANT PERSONALITY UNIT, and the physical of the individual consequently suffers.

This stimulation of the PREDOMINANT PERSONALITY UNIT by the spur of the desire to achieve an object gives us the other side of the picture obtained by alcoholic stimulation.

Stimulation of the PREDOMINANT PERSONALITY UNIT by the desire of accomplishment results in the aggrandisement of *this* unit and the result is psychic. Stimulation of the DORMANT PERSONALITY UNIT by the administration of alcohol brings about the aggrandisement of *this* unit and the result is physical.

When the PREDOMINANT PERSONALITY UNIT of the painter is stimulated by the desire of accomplishment it becomes, as we have seen, accentuated, aggrandised, and the starved DORMANT PERSONALITY fades in vigour.

If this stimulation is carried to excess, there is an eventual breakdown, just as over-stimulation of the DORMANT PERSONALITY UNIT may lead to a breakdown. The PREDOMINANT PERSONALITY UNIT, whose characteristics are sweetness, consideration and control, has now bloated itself with a surfeit of that PSYCHIC FORCE to which these traits owe their being. The result is an accentuation of these same characteristics and our subject becomes morbidly sensitive, morbidly considerate, morbidly controlled and restrained to the point of being frightened to do even ordinary things. In a word, his psychic state becomes one of general anxiety.

On the physical side, the DORMANT PERSONALITY, bereft of the PSYCHIC FORCE required to maintain its position, has sunk into the background, and lacking the power to maintain physical normality allows the physical side to degenerate.

Thus we get the physical weakness, lethargy, lack of energy and loss of sexual power which characterise this state. These manifestations on the physical side and the anxiety on the psychic give us our complete picture of the psycho-neurotic condition.

Accentuation of the DORMANT PERSONALITY UNIT by the administration of alcohol gives rise to primitive animal physical inclinations and hyper-sexual bent. There is an accompanying fading of the balancing or

controlling influence of the PREDOMINANT PERSON-
ALITY UNIT. This is due to an unwarranted amount
of the PSYCHIC FORCE evolved being commandeered
by the now rampant DORMANT PERSONALITY UNIT.

If the stimulation be excessive or prolonged, we see
the DORMANT PERSONALITY UNIT rise to complete
control, and there is an accompanying temporary
total eclipse of the PREDOMINANT PERSONALITY UNIT.

In this condition we have the temporary dominion
of the animal and the temporary dethronement of
reason. This state we term insanity—Alcoholic
Dementia.

In which of these two Personality Units does the
repressed sex complex lie ?

Under the stimulus of alcohol we see the rise to
temporary power of the DORMANT PERSONALITY
UNIT, and simultaneous with that rise we have to
admit a marked exaggeration of the sex instinct.
If, therefore, we can assign a definite locale for these
repressions it must surely be in that Personality Unit
which, apparently, is most intimately related to sex,
viz., the DORMANT PERSONALITY UNIT.

Let us for argument's sake admit this for the moment
and let us analyse the situation thus created along
the lines which we have followed in our consideration
of the influences which acted on the component
Personality Units.

The DORMANT PERSONALITY UNIT is the home of
the sex instinct ; therefore, the propagation or the
repression of this instinct must be determined in this
territory.

If the DORMANT PERSONALITY UNIT is plentifully
supplied with PSYCHIC FORCE, the physical condition
of the subject, according to our theory, is at the zenith
of power and it must be taken for granted that the
sex instinct is equally exalted.

The maintenance of both these states demands the
supply to the DORMANT PERSONALITY UNIT of an
adequate quantity of the total PSYCHIC FORCE
evolved.

This PSYCHIC FORCE once supplied must be utilised, and if not utilized the DORMANT PERSONALITY UNIT must in time become engorged with that FORCE.

Sublimation is an admitted Escape Mechanism and we can use up a great part of the FORCE by this means. We can engage in increased physical output in the way of harm work or games, and so divert part of the FORCE which would normally go to the furtherance of the sex instinct.

We can call in the assistance of the PREDOMINANT PERSONALITY UNIT and urge it to appropriate to itself a quantity of that PSYCHIC FORCE which normally would go to the DORMANT PERSONALITY UNIT. This is done by increased mental occupation. As a desperate measure we can reduce the food supply, thus lowering the vitality and reducing the total amount of PSYCHIC FORCE elaborated and ensuring a greatly reduced supply to the DORMANT PERSONALITY UNIT.

By these three admitted methods we can keep in control the PSYCHIC FORCE in the DORMANT PERSONALITY UNIT or, at least, that part of it ear-marked for the propagation of the sex instinct and no harm will result to the psychic system.

On the other hand, if the sex instinct Force is repressed ; i.e., if the PSYCHIC FORCE allocated to this instinct is neither curtailed in production, sublimed in external action, or utilized in the sex function, we must of necessity get accumulation of that FORCE in the DORMANT PERSONALITY UNIT.

We have seen how a plethora of PSYCHIC FORCE in either Personality Unit and consequent exaggeration of that unit tends to imbalance of the Axis Personality of the individual. In sex repression we have an accumulation of unused PSYCHIC FORCE of a particularly strong type—the sex type—the result is aggrandisement of the DORMANT PERSONALITY UNIT.

This aggrandisement demands increased effort on the part of the PREDOMINANT PERSONALITY UNIT in an effort to maintain control. Such effort entails the deflection of a part of the PSYCHIC FORCE normally allocated to the PREDOMINANT PERSONALITY UNIT to perform its necessary functions. These functions, intellectual effort and the maintenance of psychic order, become increasingly difficult as more and more PSYCHIC FORCE is drawn off to combat the growing dominance of the DORMANT PERSONALITY UNIT. At last a point is reached when the PREDOMINANT PERSONALITY UNIT is no longer able to maintain the conflict and a nervous crash results.

Of what practical use to us is this analysis of the Personality ?

Can it help us in the prevention of the Psycho-neurotic and early Psychic states ?

Can it help us in effectively treating these states once established ?

The author's answer is an emphatic affirmative.

In Psycho-neurosis we have advanced the theory that the PREDOMINANT PERSONALITY UNIT is the component unit chiefly affected. In this condition the basic feature is exaggeration of the normal or Axis Personality.

We all have subconsciously a very definite opinion of our worth. This self-appreciation is located in the PREDOMINANT PERSONALITY UNIT which, as we have claimed, looks after our psychic output. Exaggeration of this unit, naturally, postulates exaggeration of its functions; therefore, we have an increase in our estimation of our personal worth.

We all have a degree of sensitiveness which feeling is likewise located in the PREDOMINANT PERSONALITY UNIT. This likewise becomes exaggerated in the general exaggeration of the PREDOMINANT PERSONALITY UNIT, and the same is true of all psychic attributes.

This generalized exaggeration of our psychic side we group under the name of exaggerated Ego, and could be more truthfully classified as EXAGGERATED PREDOMINANT PERSONALITY UNIT.

When this exaggeration of our inherent psychic characteristics is carried beyond a certain toleration

point, these characteristics become abnormal, even
obnoxious to our neighbours and the unhappy possessor
is dubbed as a neurotic.

The syndrome of this condition is :—

Restlessness, peevishness, irritability, depression,
loss of confidence, headaches and insomnia.

To sustain and nourish these unwelcome visitors the
PREDOMINANT PERSONALITY UNIT takes quite an
illegitimate amount of the PSYCHIC FORCE elaborated.
The result is that the DORMANT PERSONALITY UNIT is
on short ration. As a consequence its care of the
physical side falls away and we get evidence of physical
upset such as :—

Loss of energy, weakness and general fatigue.

This completes the picture of psycho-neurosis and
displays its relationships to the Axis Personality and
its component units.

What brings about this condition ? We have seen
that an adequate amount of PSYCHIC FORCE nourishes
and maintains the Axis Personality in a normal condition and the result is psychic and physical harmony
and well-being.

If any condition arises within the body or mind of the
individual to interfere with the elaboration of this
FORCE in adequate quantity, the result is psychic and
physical upset, i.e., definite Axis Personality change.

In the physical, disease, trauma or toxins definitely
interferes with the normal functioning of the endocrine
glands and there is a consequent immediate falling off
in the quantity of PSYCHIC FORCE. The PREDOMINANT
PERSONALITY UNIT deprived of its normal working
share of this Force is unable to maintain the normal
psychic status of the subject and the result is psychic
debility.

The DORMANT PERSONALITY UNIT, unable to obtain
the quantity it requires to maintain normal physical
vigour, allows the physical side to slip and the result
is physical debility. Combination of these two units,
under these circumstances, gives us an altered Axis
Personality with the evidences of psychic and physical

debility we have quoted above. This is psychic-neurosis of physical origin.

On the psychic side any destructive subconscious happening involving worry and anxiety throws a strain on the psychic fabric of the PREDOMINANT PERSONALITY UNIT. To meet this strain it appropriates an illegitimate share of the PSYCHIC FORCE and gives us the psychic hyper-activity of psycho-neurosis.

Again, any toxic substance which causes over-activity of the DORMANT PERSONALITY UNIT, as in alcohol, resulting in profligate expenditure of PSYCHIC FORCE, induces the psycho-neurotic state.

We have advanced the theory that the PREDOMINANT PERSONALITY UNIT is the Unit which deals practically exclusively with the psychic side of the individual, the DORMANT PERSONALITY guarding and guiding the physical.

The PREDOMINANT PERSONALITY UNIT, therefore, is the guardian of our emotional states. Consequently, in a psycho-neurosis of emotional psychic origin, this Unit would be the scene of conflict.

When the Psycho-neurotic condition takes its origin in the physical, as in drug or alcohol addiction, disease and trauma, the DORMANT PERSONALITY UNIT is the battle-ground.

It must not be inferred from the above that the psycho-neurotic state is regarded by the author as a purely psychic or a purely physical condition. The condition is essentially a psycho-physical one, and here the writer disagrees with the Psycho-analytic school, who seem to concentrate their energies on treating the psychic state of the patient, whilst the old Weir-Mitchell school treated the purely physical and let the psychic work out its own salvation the best way it could.

When a psycho-neurosis develops, owing to purely adverse psychic circumstances, the physical condition is immediately affected in sympathy, and we are soon left in no doubt as to the reality of this.

When the disease has its origin in some purely physical condition we, of course, get an immediate

sympathetic upset in the psychic or PREDOMINANT
PERSONALITY UNIT. If we can succeed in locating the
origin of the condition in one or other of the Personality
Units, it gives us a much closer contact with the trouble
and enables us to treat it with more precision and confidence, as will be seen from the following.

A Psycho-neurosis of purely psychic origin we regard
as located in the PREDOMINANT PERSONALITY UNIT.
Such a psycho-neurotic state arises from two main
causes :—

(a) *A Psychic irritant,* such as FEAR, WORRY,
ANXIETY or some other destructive emotion implanted
in the subconscious.

This gives us our rampant form of Psycho-neurosis,
and is characterised by manifest high nerve tension,
irritability, garrulousness, restlessness, headaches and
insomnia.

The characteristic of this type of Psycho-neurosis is
extravagant expenditure of nervous energy.

(b) *Inadequacy of Psychic Force.* This inadequacy
is due to hypo-production of PSYCHIC FORCE, brought
about by disfunction of the endocrine gland group.
The DORMANT PERSONALITY UNIT is also enfeebled,
due to the PSYCHIC FORCE inanition, and it is unable to
function with normal vigour.

The syndrome in this form is generalized weakness
and depression.

These patients are listless, apathetic, unable to
do any mental or physical work, and are sunk in continuous depression.

The condition demanding treatment here is PSYCHIC
FORCE insufficiency, which must be brought up to
normal.

Before proceeding further, let us finish with these
two forms of Pscyho-neurosis as found in the PRE-
DOMINANT PERSONALITY UNIT.

The first condition we attribute to a psychic irritant
and obviously the ideal treatment is the uprooting of
this. It is rarely if ever advisable to attempt this at the
beginning, and here is the reason. The PREDOMINANT

PERSONALITY UNIT for the maintenance of this morbid visitor has commandeered an illegitimate amount of the total PSYCHIC FORCE elaborated. Inflamed by this engorgement, the PREDOMINATING PERSONALITY UNIT is pouring forth this FORCE in extravagant profusion, and any attempt at probing tends to further waste of the all-vital PSYCHIC FORCE. Our aim must therefore be to allow the irritant to remain at rest for the moment, to curtail its malignant activities and put an end to the profligate expenditure of PSYCHIC FORCE.

This is done by damping down the activity of the PREDOMINANT PERSONALITY UNIT. Just as we can stimulate the activities of this unit by the administration of cocaine or hashish, so by sedatives we can slow down these activities.

This is the treatment termed by the author " Putting the Mind in Splints."

What is the effect of this treatment ?

The higher faculties are no longer so receptive, no longer so sensitive, and pay less and less heed to the stings and pricks of the psychic irritant. As a consequence, there is under-action in place of over-action, and the wastage of PSYCHIC FORCE is abruptly terminated. After a period of this treatment two things have happened, viz. : —

(a) The inflamed psychic engine (the PREDOMINATING PERSONALITY UNIT) has cooled off.

(b) The PREDOMINATING PERSONALITY UNIT is rich with the accumulated PSYCHIC FORCE.

It naturally follows that there is a corresponding increase in psychic strength. The patient has recovered confidence, hope and the power to fight. His mind, refreshed and vigorous, is now ready for tactful handling.

The psychic irritant is then brought to the surface and logically examined from every angle. Its potentialities for evil are closely surveyed and measures planned to meet the evil. The situation is examined and re-examined until the PREDOMINATING PERSONALITY UNIT is almost bored by this continuous review.

Eventually the venom is extracted by this mental catharsis and psychic harmony once again prevails.

The second form of Psycho-neurosis associated with the PREDOMINANT PERSONALITY UNIT is due, as we have shown, to PSYCHIC FORCE insufficiency having its origin in under-production.

The first aim, naturally, must be directed towards a curtailment of PSYCHIC FORCE expenditure down to the absolute limit. All production, both psychic and physical, must cease and the patient be compelled to rest from all activities.

The reason for the under-production of PSYCHIC FORCE must be uncovered, as it is simply stupid to expect a restoration of Psychic Normality until this is done.

In the case of females the cause, in the vast majority of cases, will be found in ovarian dysfunction originating in hæmic abnormality. In the case of males, unhealthy living or some underlying physical ailment will be found to be the cause.

Whatever the reason, it is worse than useless to attempt psychic restoration until the physical condition is definitely clarified. If it is not possible to do this effectively the hope of successfully treating the psycho-neurotic state is meagre.

———————

Psycho-neurosis associated with the DORMANT PERSONALITY UNIT is, as we have seen, of physical origin.

Trauma, disease and vicious habits. Each of these conditions must undeniably interfere with efficient endocrine production and as a consequence there is a falling off in the quantity of the PSYCHIC FORCE produced.

The result is debility, due to psychic inanition, and we have manifestations both physical and psychic of the Psycho-neurotic state.

In trauma our first aim, obviously, is to repair the damage, restore physical well-being, and when this is accomplished we must turn our attention to bringing the PSYCHIC FORCE supply to its normal level.

This is done by limiting expenditure of that Force to a minimum and giving the endocrines plenty of time to recover their strength and their full working capacity. A too early return to full activity with a corresponding strain on the enfeebled endocrines which they are as yet unable to bear, is followed invariably by a nervous crash and possibly the permanent establishment of a condition of nervous semi-invalidism.

Disease.—Infectious fevers, for example, as we have demonstrated, leads to a suspension or, at all events, a markedly weakened effort of endocrine function. There must, of necessity, be a corresponding falling off for a time at least in the production of PSYCHIC FORCE, and here again we get the established syndrome of the Psycho-neurotic condition.

As in trauma, after the toxins have been eliminated, the underlying Psycho-neurosis can only be effectively treated when due time is given to the endocrines for their re-establishment in vigour.

The venereal infections deserve special mention under this heading as, in the author's opinion, these infections bring invariably in their train the Psycho-neurotic states as surely as day follows night. Whether the infecting organism be the gonococcus or the Spirochæte Pallida, the patient remains a de facto neurotic.

This assertion is not difficult of acceptance when we reflect on the ravages on the psychic made by the unchecked development of the syphilitic organism.

Vicious habits.—Alcohol and drug addiction have been fully dealt with elsewhere and are only mentioned here inasmuch as the DORMANT PERSONALITY UNIT is the unit affected by their activities. We have seen how alcohol produces its effect, spurring the DORMANT PERSONALITY to an extravagant expenditure of PSYCHIC FORCE, and leaving the patient bankrupt in that Force after his exhibition. Drug addiction proceeds along similar lines, and full consideration of the treatment has been given in the Chapter devoted to this subject.

Our last of the conspicuous vicious habits is masturbation, and we shall attempt to analyse how it acts in
the production of Psycho-neurosis.

We have allocated the sex centre a site in the
DORMANT PERSONALITY OF THE INDIVIDUAL.   We
know, generally speaking, that the individual of physical
type, that is the strong, vigorous, healthy animal, is
more sex inclined than his refined intellectual physically
inferior brother.

In other words, a strong DORMANT PERSONALITY
UNIT has conspicuous physical superiority and conspicuous sex instincts also.

These two conditions are, as we have seen, dependent
upon the abundant amount of PSYCHIC FORCE allocated
to the DORMANT PERSONALITY UNIT.   If the sex centre
for the expression of its instinct urges action, it requires
PSYCHIC FORCE for such action.   As the opportunity is
never absent in masturbation, this action can be
practised without restraint and the consequence is the
expenditure of a harmful quantity of the PSYCHIC
FORCE allotted to the DORMANT PERSONALITY UNIT.

Unable to maintain its normal part in the Axis
Personality blend, owing to the extravagant expenditure of its PSYCHIC FORCE by the sex element, it loses
its grip in the psychic scheme of things.

This has two harmful effects :—

(1)   The loss of physical vigour generally.

What proof is there of this being so ?

Ask any trainer of race-horses and listen to his
statement regarding young bloodstock.

Owing to this habit of masturbation amongst
young colts it is necessary to castrate over 50%
as otherwise they would be useless for racing purposes.
This is due to loss of vigour, and what is true of the
equine must equally be true of the human animal.

(2)   Psychic upset.

That there is a psychic upset or disturbance of the
Personality is undeniable.

There is a never absent shame and guilt complex.
Something is being done which contravenes the

laws of Nature, something which is indefensible and wrong.

This comes about, in all probability, from the fact that the DORMANT PERSONALITY UNIT, robbed of its needed PSYCHIC FORCE, loses its vigour, that vigour which is necessary to maintain the harmony of the blend of the Axis Personality. The shame, the guilt complex, the anxiety, located in the PREDOMINANT PERSONALITY UNIT, in turn drain this Unit of its normally necessary PSYCHIC FORCE and weaken its vigour.

The result is a loss of vigour in both PERSONALITY UNITS, evidenced soon by a weakened Axis Personality. In other words, Psycho-neurosis is established.

This attempt to link up the component PERSONALITY UNITS with different forms of the Psycho-neurotic condition may enable us to understand more clearly the development of the graver forms of Psychic upset.

The author's conviction is that, when insanity develops in a hitherto mentally sound subject born of mentally sound parents, that such insanity is a progressive Personality degeneration which originated in Psycho-neurosis.

We all know by the toxin of alcohol we can produce Dementia in a comparatively short period. We all must admit that the chronic alcoholic undergoes a progressive Personality degeneration from the mild through the severe Psycho-neurotic condition until he arrives at a point where he is no longer a fit and proper person to be in his own control. In other words, he is psychotic.

Let us observe this case closely from the beginning to its final exit and follow the action of the alcoholic toxin in its onslaughts on the psychic of the individual.

The first immoderate stimulation acted, as we have seen, on the DORMANT PERSONALITY UNIT and brought out all the sex characteristics of the subject.

He became quarrelsome, combative, inclined to boast and anxious to exhibit his physical strength. There was an accompanying increase in sex inclination.

O

This exhibition demanded an extravagant expenditure of PSYCHIC FORCE, and the following morning saw our subject suffering from a general temporary bankruptcy of that FORCE.

The courage of the previous night was replaced by apprehension, the great physical strength by lethargy and the abnormal bien-être by malaise.

Here we have both PERSONALITY UNITS in a state of temporary inanition brought about by profligate waste.

In other words, until rest, warmth, food and a cleanser of the body restores normality the subject is in a condition of temporary Psycho-neurosis, and exhibits every symptom, psychic and physical, of that condition.

If this conduct is persisted in with regularity the patient must enter into a condition of chronic Psycho-neurosis.

Both PERSONALITY UNITS deprived of their required Psychic Force are now in a condition of chronic inanition and the Axis Personality must of necessity degenerate. The psychic output grows gradually less, owing to the weakened effort of the PREDOMINANT PERSONALITY UNIT, and the physical condition simultaneously degenerates owing to the enfeebled DORMANT PERSONALITY UNIT losing its influence.

In these circumstances it naturally follows that the endocrine gland group suffers in the general physical rot, and their output dwindles.

Now, we have the two PERSONALITY UNITS attacked from two sides—

(a) by extravagant expenditure of PSYCHIC FORCE under the alcoholic stimulation ;

(b) by curtailed supply of PSYCHIC FORCE owing to interference with endocrine function.

The logical outcome is that in the course of time the PREDOMINANT PERSONALITY UNIT, systematically starved of its vitalising force, has no longer the strength to maintain contact with reality and responsibility departs.

The DORMANT PERSONALITY UNIT similarly treated has no longer the vigour to exercise vigilance over the physical and bodily degeneration becomes manifest.

Here we have a gradual psychic and physical degeneration from the normal through the Psychoneurotic states until psychosis and physical dissolution is reached.

The Schizophrænic state supplies us with a picture equally vivid.

The growing maiden, generally about the period of puberty, falls away in physical health. This generally starts as digestive inefficiency—constipation. The food, too long retained in the digestive tract, evolves gases Indol and Skatol. These by osmosis are absorbed into the blood-stream. This poison-laden blood, naturally, has an adverse effect on the efficiency of sympathetic action, thus further lessening intestinal activity and tending towards more marked constipation.

Again, this poison-laden blood nourishing the gland system must interfere with their function. We are left in no doubt of this by the action of the ovary, whose secretory function is immediately interfered with, as is evidenced by menstrual abnormality. If the secretory function of the ovary is interfered with it is only logical to assume that its incretory function is also affected.

And if the ovary is affected in this adverse manner, we have no reason to assume that the Pituitary, Suprarenals and Thyroid have escaped.

If these glands are affected by the poison-laden blood, and we must assume that they are, a serious condition must consequently arise, as these are the glands whose internal secretions elaborate PSYCHIC FORCE.

Both the PERSONALITY UNITS are instantly affected by this interference with their PSYCHIC FORCE supply and a gradual degeneration due to inanition sets in. The development now parallels the condition in alcohol though perhaps it is not so rapid.

In the case of the girl the toxin is autogenous and unless stopped the progress will be even more marked and destructive than in alcohol.

After a period of manifest physical ill-health the girl becomes nervy. Very soon she gives evidence of definite Psycho-neurotic symptoms.

These fluctuate in gravity for a time until there comes a decided psychic change.

The girl becomes odd in her manner and this condition gradually increases until it becomes alarming. Eventually a point is reached where her teacher or her parents detect abnormal lines of conduct and a doctor is summoned.

He confirms the suspicions of the parents—certification follows.

Let us examine the picture here from the onset to certification.

The normal girl at puberty time has a physical upset. This may be due to the strain of her oncoming new state or may be caused by something much simpler as, for example, by an attack of influenza or even unsuitable diet.

Whatever the cause, the alimentary system is thrown out of order and constipation results. The blood, laden with the poisoned gases of too long retained putrefactive matter, affects the entire nervous system of the girl and her whole glandular system. As a consequence of this glandular upset there is a diminution of their internal secretions and, as a result, a diminution of PSYCHIC FORCE.

The two PERSONALITY UNITS, deprived of their required quantity of PSYCHIC FORCE, naturally degenerate. Their harmonious working is disrupted and they begin to work independently of each other, each in its own debilitated manner.

We can readily visualize, if some effort is not made to reinvigorate the glands and so increase their FORCE output, this cleavage must gradually grow until the gravest form of mental disorder ensues.

Our energies in treatment, therefore, must be primarily directed towards the elimination of toxins to permit of efficient endocrine function.

In addition to this every effort should be made to encourage increased endocrine secretion in order to maintain the production of PSYCHIC FORCE at the highest possible level.

By these two methods we have the best means of preventing PERSONALITY degeneration into the psychotic state or rescuing the individual from that state and restoring him to normality.

CHAPTER XI

DEPRESSIVE MANIA

Differential diagnosis between the Manic Depressive and Pyscho-neurotic states.

THIS condition does not enter the category of functional nervous disorders, and, like Schizophrænia, properly speaking has no legitimate place in this work.

As, however, there is more difficulty experienced in differentiating between the PSYCHO-NEUROTIC and the MANIC DEPRESSIVE states than there is between PSYCHO-NEUROSIS and any other Psychotic condition, it may be as well to point out the salient characteristics which separate them.

Many times the question has been put to the author : "How do you distinguish between a severe case of Psycho-neurosis with all its morbid imaginings and a case of Psychosis or a so-called 'border-line' case ? "

The writer does not recognise what is termed a "border-line" case. A patient is either of pathologic mentality or he is not, and to classify him as standing astride some psychological Mason and Dixon line is as absurd as the statement of a patient who came to the writer and told him, during the taking of his personal history, that he had had a slight touch of Syphylis in his youth. This "border-line" diagnosis does infinite harm oftentimes. If the patient, as most frequently happens, is a simple case of Psycho-neurosis and gets better under efficient treatment, as he normally should do, some kind relation or friend is bound to remark : "You have done wonderfully well. You know you were a border-line case, and, thanks to Dr. ——, you have pulled through. You are a marvellous result." Anyone in contact with the Psychoneurotic can visualise the harm such a thunderbolt can work.

Here is a rough but workable definition of the difference between the Psycho-neurotic and the Psychotic states. Simple examples are appended in order to make this difference more easily appreciated. If a diagnosis is based on the essential elements in these definitions, an error is unlikely to arise.

PSYCHO-NEUROSIS

The Psycho-neurotic reaction is an abnormal response to a normal mental stimulus.

Example—The Psycho-neurotic gets a fleeting attack of indigestion, which may persist over a period of days.

We are all subject to an occurrence of this nature. It is annoying. It is painful. It is inconvenient. In the normal man this annoying, painful and inconvenient stimulus is countered by an alteration of diet, or perhaps a little bicarbonate of soda, and is completely forgotten.

In the Psycho-neurotic, on the other hand, the response is grotesque in its intensity.

This perfectly natural, simple, pain stimulus is vested wtih mortal importance, and maybe registers on the victim's consciousness the onset of gastric cancer.

Thus, we see the response is out of all possible proportion to the importance of the stimulus. In other words, it is an absurdly abnormal response to a normal mental stimulus of pain.

PSYCHOSIS

The Psychotic reaction is the reverse of this. It is a normal response to an abnormal mental stimulus.

The Psychotic is a fantastic sovereign in a fantastic kingdom, where his ideas, and his alone, obtain.

To illustrate this. In Delusional Insanity one of the commonest delusions is that the food offered to the victim has been poisoned. No amount of reasoning will persuade him to the contrary. He refuses the food. His reaction itself is quite normal—no sane person would accept food which he had sound reason to believe was poisoned.

The stimulus arising in the mind of the Psychotic that the food was poisoned is abnormal.

Thus, in Psychosis we have a fantastic mental stimulus arising in the subconscious evoking a normal and rational reaction from that same subconscious.

It is of profound interest to note that these two mental conditions—PSYCHO-NEUROSIS and PSYCHOSIS, which superficially appear to resemble each other so closely at times, are yet on intimate examination fundamentally different in their structure.

As has been stated at the beginning of the chapter, the MANIC DEPRESSIVE is the subject who provides the greatest difficulty.

It requires patience and skill, especially in the primary taking of the history, to prevent the possibility of error, and this is a type of case where error is very heavily punished.

It is well to emphasise this point here by relating what befell the author lately.

A professional man (not a doctor) persuaded the author to take over the care of a nephew of his alleged to be suffering from a nervous breakdown, which necessitated his giving up his work.

The family history was elicited in the usual manner from the uncle, and in it there was nothing pointing to mental instability in the family. The patient entered the nursing home a few days later.

He was a man in the early forties, physically a fine specimen, intelligent and well educated.

He had served in the war, but his military history had little or no bearing on his neurosis as far as could be seen.

He had been less fortunate, however, at the Court of Venus than on the Field of Mars, having contracted Gonorrhœa, which, whether through a particular virulence or inefficient treatment, had given the poor fellow a very trying time. In addition to numerous scars on the thighs and perenæum, he had an abdominal scar indicating that a supra-pubic operation had been performed.

With this plethora of ætiological material for a Psycho-neurosis of multiple origin, Gonœrrhœal, operative and war, the author admittedly was lax in going more carefully into the family history with the patient himself. Frankly, the evidence displayed in favour of a Psycho-neurotic condition was so overwhelming that everything else was entirely overshadowed. A good result from treatment was expected, and eagerly awaited.

Before leaving the patient, however, a casual question elicited a rather peculiar answer, and the author, somewhat perturbed, spent a further hour with the patient.

The doubt aroused would not be stilled, and orders were given that the patient be placed under the care of a special nurse day and night for the time being. The nurses were instructed to give a detailed account of his conversation, general mental attitude and general conduct.

Four days of this supervision elicited nothing noteworthy. The special nurses were withdrawn and the patient was treated under the customary conditions.

His progress seemed uninterrupted, and though manifestly a man of naturally reserved and rather taciturn type, he became quite talkative and interesting.

When the rest part of his treatment had come to an end, and the second or active part was due to commence, the patient was allowed out for a drive the evening before commencing his morning walks.

On these walks the average patient is aroused at 7 o'clock or 8 o'clock, and goes forth alone to do half an hour's walking exercise, which is systematically increased.

The author saw the patient on his return from the drive on the evening before commencing his morning exercises. He had conducted himself excellently, seemed in good spirits, but an unaccountable doubt kept prodding and spurring the writer's mind, and refused to be repressed. Calling the matron, it was requested that a nurse should accompany the patient on his first walk in the morning and furnish a detailed report of what happened.

In the morning at 7.30 he sallied forth, accompanied by his nurse, and he seemed in excellent spirits, keeping up a general conversation quite gaily.

It was necessary to cross a street of rather heavy traffic, and as they stood on the pavement to wait to cross the patient suddenly made a plunge with the intention of throwing himself under a bus. Fortunately, the nurse was on the alert, and she held on to him sufficiently long to thwart his intention. He broke from her grasp, dashed into the centre of the road and jumped on a bus going in the opposite direction. He was overpowered, given into the care of the police, and returned to the nursing home.

No attempt was made to question him at length regarding the motive for his conduct—unfortunately, it was all too apparent.

A closer inquiry into the family history revealed the fact that an uncle was under restraint suffering from the same mental illness—Depressive Mania.

The fault was the author's. The doctor is always to blame. When he takes the responsibility of a nervous case no pains should be spared in eliciting every particle of evidence, personal and family, which has a bearing on the case.

In this instance reliance was placed on a slipshod family history taken from a layman, who probably or possibly saw no connection between the man in the asylum and the nervous condition of his nephew.

The writer, fascinated by the fact that the case had characteristics which dovetailed into pet theories of his own, neglected to take the essential history in a proper manner.

The moral is, " Leave your pet theories in the study and take the essential facts of every nerve case in intimate detail."

At first glance Manic-depressive Psychosis does resemble closely in the depressed form the Psychoneurotic condition. Inasmuch as Manic-depressive Psychosis is by far the heaviest contributor to the suicide list, it is incumbent on the physician in attendance to take every precaution that no case of this type escapes his detection.

The appended salient features of Manic-depressive Psychosis should make an error almost impossible.

1. *Family History*
   Many of the foremost authorities on the subject boldly assert that a heavy percentage (60-80) of Manic-depressives have a family history of Psychosis.

2. *The Onset*
   When a man, hitherto regarded as normal, level headed and restrained suddenly becomes flamboyant, boastful, talkative, and when this phase is succeeded by a period of irritability, moroseness and taciturnity, we have a cardinal symptom of this condition.

3. When the patient suddenly emerges from this condition and returns to his old normal self for a period, he furnishes us with a further basic symptom.

4. The Manic-depressive invariably attributes his mental misery to his own unworthiness and sees no possibility of his rescue by outside aid.

5. The Manic-depressive rarely displays a physical train of symptoms of conspicuous import. He may be emaciated, due to voluntary abstention from food, and have the drawn appearance we associate with the insomnia invariably found amongst the sufferers from this condition.

THE PSYCHO-NEUROTIC

1. *Family History*
   The family history in the Psycho-neurotic may reveal well-defined evidence of Neurosis on both sides, but rarely of Psychosis on either.

2. He is generally of a high intellectual type, and if he has inherited his malady is invariably of a high type.

3. *Onset*
The onset is gradual and the patient unhesitatingly attempts to give a specific extraneous cause for its commencement. The course is slowly progressive until checked by treatment, when recovery is gradual and slow.

4. Almost invariably there is a physical syndrome, and these cases suffer from vaso-motor and gastrointestinal disturbance during their illness.

In conclusion, we might say justifiably of the Manic-depressive that :—

" In his hypo-manic or manic phases he is a " vaunter without a single sense of shame.

" In his Depressive state he is a psycho-hypo- " chondriac without a single trace of humour."

No attempt is made here to dilate further on the Manic-depressive Psychosis. It is hoped that the points brought forward to illustrate the condition when placed alongside the salient features exhibited in the Psycho-neurotic state, may enable the busy practitioner to make an accurate differential diagnosis between them.

CHAPTER XII

SUICIDE

Suicide in Psycho-neurosis.
Suicide in Psychosis.
As an aftermath of war.
As a result of financial upheaval.
Suicide and the Coroners' Courts.
The prevention of suicide.

OF recent years the daily Press makes distressing reading owing to the apparent increase in the number of suicide cases.

Various causes are put forward to account for this. That it is the natural heritage of the World War in the minds of some is accepted as a blanket reason. Others equally insist that the world economic upheaval is the chief factor.

These two causes must be accepted as accounting for a percentage of the cases of self-destruction to-day. We must not, however, overlook the fact that by far the greatest number rush to end everything for reasons in no way connected with either war or finance.

From a fairly extensive acquaintance with nerve-shattered war victims, the writer can state that they seem to bear their, at times, grievous burdens with a philosophic resignation almost superhuman. They appear to have steeled themselves to their mental and nervous ills, displaying the same courage which animated them in the trenches.

Here and there one sees a wearied sufferer tried beyond human endurance drop despairingly from the ranks and take his life. Even in these cases close scrutiny will, as a rule, reveal that a super-added blow, such as ill-health or unemployment horror, has dealt the final fatal thrust. Yes, suicide amongst war

survivors, even the quasi-mentally wrecked, is comparatively small—a tribute to the gallantry of the
fighting soldier.

The second apparent heavy reason, the present world
economic situation, claims a much higher percentage
amongst those who voluntarily put an end to their
existence.

The well-balanced and not too emotional peoples
who inhabit the British Isles do not fly readily to
self-destruction as compared with our Continental
neighbours.

The writer, in conversation with a rather cynical
American friend, made the remark :—

" I see there was a heavy frost last night.   The
" middle of September is surely very early for
" frost in the United States ? "

" Well, I suppose it is, and I guess we may look
" forward, as a consequence, to seeing half the
" ponds in New Jersey choked up with
" despondent German market gardeners to-
" morrow,"

was the reply.   This rather callous remark prompted
the idea of looking up the suicide ratio in different
countries, and it is consoling to know that the British
peoples are low in that list.

That the economic blizzard of the past six years
blasted a pitiable number out of existence in unthinking panic is undeniable ; yet though this number has
been heartrendingly great, yet a searching analysis
would reveal that in no way does it approach the
number who take their own lives through the most
prolific cause—PSYCHO-NEUROSIS.

PSYCHO-NEUROSIS untreated, lightly treated, or
badly treated would cover 80 per cent. of the cases of
suicide which occur to-day, and the 20 per cent. remaining is a too liberal allowance left to include those
cases directly attributable to war, economic stress and
indisputable insanity.

War cases we have lightly touched upon, and have
endeavoured to demonstrate that the number of

suicide cases of pure war origin, untrammelled by some over-riding condition such as sudden ill-health or unexpected economic or domestic embarrassment, are miraculously few. Reflection and careful examination will substantiate this statement. On the economic side, when we consider the universality of the crash tumbling everywhere financial emperors from their thrones and bringing them literally to the " bread line " in life to consort with the destitute victims of that same cataclysm, we must concede that in the tragic circumstances the suicide rate has been, on the whole, remarkably small.

Here and there a world name, for years tinselled up in apparent financial omnipotence, gets caught up in the tornado. His magnificence, ripped and tattered and torn to shreds, a scarecrow of its former resplendency, rushes the wizard brain into panic resolution and avidly he plunges into the gloom.

Their numbers are few, and their passing is only marked by the cynical or envious amongst us.

On the economic side a much larger number of suicide victims, unfortunately, belong to a class whose whole efforts have been directed towards the provision of a happy life's evening, unclouded by monetary worries. These poor victims of the storm, too old or too weak to work, and unaccustomed to depend on anything but their own efforts for existence, see no refuge but the tomb, and in panic confusion rush to pull down the curtain on their own lives.

Again, we state that a careful study will demonstrate that this six-year financial tempest, on the whole, has not exacted the enormous total of human life by suicide that we are at first apt to assume.

The next consideration is the number of suicides due to unsound mind. To judge from the verdicts almost unvaryingly issued by coroners' courts, practically 99 per cent. of persons who commit suicide are of unsound mind. In the writer's opinion, this verdict in the vast majority of cases is not only false and absurd, but very definitely harmful. The statement has already been made in this chapter that 80 per cent. of suicides are victims of PSYCHO-NEUROSIS, with no previous provable evidence of insanity.

What proof or proofs can be advanced in support of this statement ? Three proofs are submitted for the reader's consideration :—

(*a*) In an ordinary public asylum for the insane the percentage of suicide cases and specially watched as suicide cases is surprisingly *small*. The number of suicide cases actually occurring in asylums is negligible, though opportunities must present themselves often during the years of their detention despite the utmost vigilance on the part of the executive. This statement must be taken in conjunction with the fact that a considerable portion of an asylum population is made up of Depressive Mania cases—the most determined suicide section in the Psychoses. This proves that the insane are far from being universally suicides.

(*b*) When an intending suicide is rescued or happens to survive the attempt, a very small percentage repeat the performance. These survivors live out their lives giving no evidence of mental unsoundness, thus proving that the act was impulsively born of sudden panic and absolutely repented of. In other words, it was a highly exaggerated Psycho-neurotic manifestation of the Escape Mechanism, in which true mental unsoundness played no part. Those survivors who make a second or third or final attempt successful are definitely in the Manic Depressive category, and should be recognized as such on careful examination when first seen.

A case has occurred quite recently where a brilliant man in the Civil Service swallowed a lethal amount of one of the barbituric group. Immediately repenting of his act, when he found he was about to die, he telephoned for a friend to take him to a doctor that his life might be saved. Unfortunately, he died *en route.*

This is a clear manifestation of a panic impulse instantly regretted when logical consideration demonstrated the consequence.

(c) *Suicide Compacts*—These are, unfortunately, everyday occurrences, as demonstrated in the daily Press.

The customary verdict when both have succeeded in their object is " Suicide whilst of unsound mind." Does it not strike one as peculiar that two normal individuals—at least, two individuals hitherto regarded as normal up to their tragic act—should suddenly go insane simultaneously and take their lives ? It is conceded that this could possibly occur, but is it likely ?

When one happens to survive the law steps in and tries the survivor for culpable homicide and metes out punishment accordingly. The law evidently must regard the survivor as sane, and, consequently, responsible for his actions. That the law is right is fully borne out by the subsequent life of the survivor, because the writer, at all events, is unable to recall a single case where the survivor made an attempt to repeat his act.

In 1918 the editor of that famous journal, *The New York World*, shot his wife. He was arrested shortly afterwards and pleaded successfully that it was a suicide compact, stating that after he had slain his wife his nerve failed him and he was unable to carry out his part.

He was sent to Sing Sing Prison for life. Whether it was a genuine suicide compact or not the judiciary of New York had manifestly no qualms about his mental responsibility.

When the writer interviewed this man in Sing Sing Prison in 1928 he certainly had no doubts about the WISDOM of the verdict of the New York Bench.

This effort to prove that the vast majority of suicides are Psycho-neurotics and not insane is done with two specific objects, viz. :—

(1) To spare not only mental anguish to the surviving relatives, but, what is far more important, to prevent the commission of definite mental damage in the surviving members of a family.

P

The coroners' court is vested, and very rightly vested, with an atmosphere of ponderous majesty, if not, indeed, of infallibility in the eyes of the people. When a solemn conclusion is arrived at by a jury of substantial citizens, and this conclusion is further garnished by the coroner (usually a medical man) stating that the deceased died through his own act whilst of unsound mind the effect on the relations must be appalling.

If the victim is simply a Psycho-neurotic and took his own life at a time when panic had overwhelmed his subconscious mind for a moment (which is the writer's contention) what must be the result ? If he is a Psycho-neurotic (as in the majority of cases he is) the brothers or sisters will, in all probability, have a similar neurotic taint, and a horror-fear of insanity is forced upon them.

If the victim happens to be the father of a young family the children soon learn the truth. In all probability they will have inherited the Psycho-neurotic taint of the parent, and it requires no effort of the imagination to visualize the painful and definitely harmful effect a pronouncement of insanity on their dead father makes on their subconscious minds. Over and over again the writer has been consulted by descendants of a suicide to know whether they should get married. They suffer agonies of apprehension lest they might transmit insanity to their children.

When coroners' courts have not specific evidence of unmistakable psychosis before the commission of the act of self-destruction, it is wrong and definitely harmful to bring in a verdict of insanity.

(2) The second object in attempting to prove that the vast majority of suicides are suffering from Psycho-neurosis and not Psychosis is to prevent suicide, or at least to attempt to prevent suicide by appropriate treatment.

If a Psycho-neurotic committed suicide within two years after being treated the writer would hold himself responsible for gross inefficiency in his handling of the case, or for a wrong diagnosis, i.e., accepting and treating a case of Depressive Mania as a Psycho-neurotic.

If a case is a true case of Psycho-neurosis, no matter how severe the form in which the malady presents itself, it should, if efficiently treated, be steered safely past all danger of suicide.

A careful examination must be made into the family and personal history. A searching scrutiny of the life, habits, exercises, virtues, vices and weaknesses of the subject is essential. This conscientiously done there is little or no danger of the case being confused with Depressive Mania.

As regards treatment, put the patient if possible in a nursing home specialed by nurses day and night. These nurses are instructed never to relax vigilance over the patient for a moment during the ten days of his intensive treatment. They must keep a case sheet filled in with remarks about his diet, his diges-tion, his sleep, his ideas, everything important or (seemingly) unimportant.

The " Mind in Splints " treatment, *vide* chapter on Treatment, is started immediately, and the quantity of the draught regulated to keep the patient in a defi-nitely drowsy condition during the day and deeply asleep at night. The heart's action, respiratory and digestive systems are closely watched and the patient is only allowed blanket baths during the period.

At the end of ten days the patient is taken off the mixture during the day, but is given a draught at night to ensure sleep.

On the second day, after the cessation of the " Mind in Splints " treatment, the chief causative factor of his nervous condition is freely discussed. His mental reaction is closely noted. If he still betrays ANXIETY, RESTLESSNESS and MARKED MENTAL UPSET the treat-ment is resumed for another five days. The author has rarely found it necessary to do this.

When the patient, clearly orientated, gives definite proof that he can face the situation which was fast precipitating his total nervous crash, discuss that situation with him from every angle. Make him display it in its worst aspects. Insist on him dragging forth its most harrowing details into the light of day. Insist on these details being recounted again and again. At night ensure sleep by the draught and repeat it if required.

Review the whole harrowing situation next day. Encourage his fighting it out—appeal to him from all angles of appeal. Compel him to purge his mind of all the irritating mass of material again and again during the day. Always ensure a peaceful night's rest by the draught and clear out the bowels thoroughly with saline in the morning.

From the third day allow the patient to have the type of bath recommended in the chapter on Treatment.

Again drag from him in every detail the causative elements and maintain this attitude until he can face the situation with comparative ease.

Now come walks and exercises, always accompanied by a nurse for the time being.

At the end of two weeks the patient enters on routine treatment, and the operator should know exactly where the patient's mental attitude to life stands. If the treatment has been rigorously carried out and the patient has responded well, the result should be good, and the patient stand in no danger of taking his own life.

CHAPTER XIII

PERVERSION

Homo-sexuality.

Sex and its relationship to psychic and physical development of the individual.

Anatomical construction of male and female.

The Psychic development and sex.

Example of "reversion."

The sex-hybrid.

The only child.

Perversion of the normal sex instinct.

Cure for perversion—co-education, etc.

IT may seem strange to the reader to find a chapter devoted to this subject in a book dealing with the Psycho-neurotic states, but it is a very definite Psycho-pathologic condition, and must be classified under some specific psychic heading.

By " Perversion " here we mean Homosexuality and Homosexuality alone.

This is definitely not a Psychotic state. Some of the greatest intellects down through the ages have been Homosexualistic, but exhibited no evidence of psychic degeneration in any other form.

With regard to other forms of Perversion, such as Sadism, Flagellation, etc., they seem definitely psychotic in type, as is evidenced by the frequency with which the practitioners of these vices are associated with crimes of violence, often terminating in death.

The Homosexual, as we have stated, is not psychotic according to accepted standards. Does he therefore come into the Psycho-neurotic category ?

The author's experience of this type of case is not extensive, but even the few cases treated by him were very definitely Psycho-neurotics, and had that malady in a conspicuous degree. That is the only explanation offered for the inclusion of this chapter.

Whether the reader agrees or disagrees with the classification is immaterial. The main point is that Homosexuality is more rife amongst us than is generally imagined, and what will probably cause greater surprise is the statement that under certain circumstances it is contagious. Not many years back a secondary school known to the author as a school where the strictest supervision was exercised, was invaded by this evil from outside, and a surprising number of boys fell victims. So serious was the affair may be judged by the fact that seven of the outside principals got jail sentences ranging from three years to ten years.

This incontrovertible fact gives us of the medical profession abundant food for thought and compels us to concentrate our attention on the question invariably asked of us by the laity, " How does it arise ? " If we can account for or give even a feasible explanation (no matter how feeble) of its origin, we have taken a step forward in tackling this problem. If we accept it, as to-day it is practically accepted as an insoluble problem, we can never hope to deal with it.

Penal treatment, to those who understand the human mind and the torturing urge in these unfortunates, is only vindictive, stupid and futile. It only applies to a negligible percentage, and is in no way preventative or curative. In face of this statement, which cannot be denied, what steps can we take ?

The writer begs leave to place before his readers what we definitely know about sex in its relationship to both psychic and physical developments. From these facts, indisputable facts, we can formulate a theory of the causation of Homosexuality and map out a line of treatment calculated to guide the sex-life of the individual into its orthodox channel.

Let us take first of all the anatomical construction of the human male and compare it with the anatomical construction of the human female in order to demonstrate the very slight differences which exist between them.

Male—In general the male body is built for strength, stamina and speed. The head is larger, the features coarser and the major portion of the face covered with hair. The chest, broad and deep, is devoid of superfluous fat and a coarse hairy growth is usually manifest, even covering the rudimentary breasts. The thorax tapers gradually to meet the strong, narrow and small pelvis. The legs lean, muscular and sinewy indicate a suitability for their designed function—speed, load and endurance.

Female—In general the body is soft, fatty, flabby and not designed for either speed, stamina or rough usage. The head is small, the features fine, regular and devoid of hair. The chest is small and plentifully covered with fat. The breasts are prominent and rounded. The skin is soft, velvety and devoid of hair. The thorax slopes markedly, but gracefully, to the tapering waist, the grace of which is still more accentuated when it meets the broad flattened illiac crests of the pelvic girdle. The thighs are soft, flabby and rounded, their inner faces almost in juxtaposition when the heels are together, plainly indicating their inutility for heavy, fast or rough work.

These are the salient differences, the basic desiderata in the male and female physical make-up. We, however, see examples, and not infrequently, where the male corpus is definitely female in type, and we meet females who have practically the true male anatomical structure.

In these misfits close observation will reveal the female-bodied male unconsciously performing acts, such as running, throwing a stone, etc., in the manner in which we would expect a normal female to carry out these actions.

The same applies to the male-bodied female, and in modern athletics this type can make a very respectable show against even the front ranks of the athletic male.

What is the point in this comparison?

That though the line of demarkation in the general

anatomical development of males and females is
pronounced and unmistakable, yet that line can be
and is frequently crossed, and we find males with
female type bodies and vice versa.

Now, let us take anatomical characteristics common
to both :—

It will be noted that these characteristics are linked
up entirely with the sex function.

Male—Two breasts and nipples rudimentary in
function, made up of fatty tissue and rudimentary
lactiferous glands.

Female—Two breasts with nipples, capable of
secreting milk, made up of abundant fatty tissue and
functioning lactiferous glands.

Male—Two extra-abdominal procreative organs
of certain embryological origin, whose specialized
epithelium forms spermatozoa.

Female—Two intra-abdominal procreative organs
of similar embryological origin, whose specialised
epithelium forms ova.

It must be admitted, therefore, that the physical
characteristics devoted to sex are common to both
anatomically and embryologically and only differ in
specific function.

THE PSYCHIC DEVELOPMENT AND ITS RELATION TO SEX

The Freudian school maintain that a baby sucking
its thumb or toe is carrying out a symbolic sexual act
—that may or may not be accepted by the reader.
That a baby feeding at its mother's breast is doing
something which is a definite link up in the psychic
chain dictating sexual stimulation can be readily
accepted. That the mother feels this stimulation is
not denied, and to the author's mind it is not at all
far-fetched to think that the subconscious of the child
is similarly activated. Be that as it may, close observation of children reveals the fact that they are highly
sexual, and it seems immaterial to them whether the
playmate is of their own or the opposite sex.

Here the writer advances the theory that the child in its very early years is bisexual, with both hetero and homosexual proclivities. That in the ordinary natural normal progress of development the homosexual radix fades and the heterosexual radix flourishes. That this normal development should and must occur in the male child is easily understood if we accept the sex-stimulating effect of breast feeding with the mother or foster mother as the love object. Here we are getting subconscious sex stimuli poured along the orthodox channel *ab initio* with a magnificent chance of remaining in that channel. This, at first sight, is counteracted by the fact that the female child breast-fed must also have the mother as its love object, and, consequently, tends towards the abnormal in its sex development.

No ! The subconscious sex urge (if we admit an urge at all) under the stimulus of suckling, must be towards the anatomical sex structure of the individual. The proof of that lies in the fact that the percentage of homosexualists is negligible as compared with the normal, and we presume that the vast majority of children are breast-fed. How, then, does homosexuality arise ? It is developmental.

The circumstances attendant on the earliest days of the child (if we accept the breast-feeding theory) are all favourable to the development of the heterosexual radix and the gradual " fading " of the homosexual tendency. The word " fading " is used here advisedly, as the author is forced by his experience to state that he has dealt with two cases in adult life where the homosexual instinct flared up into activity after years of apparent heterosexual function.

When the child is weaned and handed over to the care of the nurse, the first battle for its sex development may begin, more especially if the child is a female. A patient of the author's, a Lesbian, told him that the first sex stimulation she could remember was when her nurse practised certain sexual acts on her. Here we have a case of primary sex stimulation originating

234 NERVES AND THE MASSES

between two members of the same sex and developing
into full-blown Lesbianism.

Another instance of rather a mixed type was afforded
by a youth of twenty years. He was of fairly average
physique and of just average intelligence. He came
from one of the Colonies, had a commission in a famous
regiment, but, owing to nervousness whilst in charge
of men on parade, it was impossible to confirm his
commission, and partly at his own request he was
allowed to resign and join the ranks. After a period
he was found physically unfit, according to his own
story, and discharged the Service.

Possessed of plenty of money he went on a debauch
in London, and wound up by forming an intimate
companionship with an old degenerate. Alcohol, late
nights and general debauchery broke down his nervous
system, and he was a pitiable object when first admitted
for treatment.

In his history he related that after his discharge
from the Army he was in contact with numerous women
in London. After indulging himself with these in
every imaginable way he at last grew sated and
" reverted " to Homosexuality. REVERTED is the
word he used himself.

He told his story then that when a child of nine
years old at school an older boy had practised certain
sexual acts on him. He said that at the beginning
this revolted and horrified him, but subsequently he
became accustomed to it and liked it. After leaving
school, however, he had not continued as a Homosexualist, but had practised Hetrosexuality with
apparent frequency. In London, prior to his reversion,
he had become sated with normal sexual excesses and
easily turned towards Homosexuality for further
sensation.

Here was a case of a young man of twenty-one who
knew nothing of the psychological significance of the
history he gave. He specifically stated that in his early
childhood his abnormal sexual experiences at the
beginning revolted and horrified him, and, subse-

quently, casting aside his abnormality, he pursued a normal sexual life, only to revert to Homosexuality when he was sated with too much Hetrosexuality.

That this case was developmental admits of no doubt in the author's mind. If this youth had not been contaminated at a period in his life when his subconscious mind was in a condition to suffer the greatest possible damage from such contamination, there is every reason to believe that there would have been no Homosexual taint in his make-up. This is evidenced by the ardent desire he expressed to rid himself of this abnormality, and that this desire was genuine was backed up by the proof that for years he had avoided the perverted life.

What this patient's final history was is unknown to the writer, as he returned to the Colonies to the care of his people.

Before passing on to the consideration of the possible development of the perverted type, let us glance for a moment at the development of the half-way or sex-hybrid.

A male child born alone into a family is born under circumstances of the gravest import. It is not for a moment suggested by the author that this circumstance gives rise or may give rise to any condition of perversion, but it is suggested that in a lamentable percentage of cases there is distinct danger of the male characteristics of the child being over-smeared with the female characteristics of its mother to its detriment. In other words, the child runs the danger of having his manhood " kissed to death."

This opinion is sure to give rise to a resentment amongst those readers who are only sons, but where they do not possess characteristics of this type they have to thank a strong-minded mother or a strong-minded father (or both) for their escape.

Take a child, an only male child, left all day to the care of an over-affectionate mother. In the ardour of her motherly instinct she kisses, caresses and fondles the child. There is no opposition to his desires, no

matter how extravagant. He is rarely, if ever, chided.
He is pampered, petted and fondled and softened until
his natural combative male instinct is smothered over.
In other words, his natural rough, tough masculine
subconscious fibre has become sodden and enfeebled.

What is the result of this in adult life ? The victim
emerges from the Fontleroy chrysalis to become the
over-mannered " young gentleman." The curious thing
to be noted is that these over-excellent manners pervade
all ranks of society, and one can find the effeminate
mannered man of this type in the roughest strata of
life.   The word " effeminate " here must not be interpreted as of Homosexual significance, as Homosexuality in this type is no more common than it is
amongst the rougher brethren. This type is character-
ized by a timidity towards life in general. Life is too
rough for them, and subconsciously they wish to return
to the protective influence of their mothers.

It is an incapacitating state. The victims of this
condition are difficult to classify. They are not necessarily neurotics, although they resemble them. They
are not necessarily perverts, although oftentimes
blamed for this. As a rule they are non-productive, as
their characters never permit them to assume any
definite responsibilities. They go through life victims
of persistent, although good-natured persecution, which
they accept with a grand indifference, ascribing it to
abysmal lack of culture in their persecutors.

This is a pathetic class, and, as a rule, are entirely to
be pitied. To treat them in the adult state is pure
waste of time. They are untreatable. They have fixed
their subconscious on a plane midway between the
sexes—a situation in absolute isolation from both.
These are the exponents of Freud's Oedipus complex.

Again, it must be emphasized that when an only son
is fortunate enough to be born of a mother with good
sense and virility of mind, who recognizes that the
shaping of the male subconscious requires special care,
then we may have an even more excellent result than
when the child is born one of a large family.

The softened type to which we have been referring can be seen at times in a big family. The position is generally held by the eldest or the youngest son. Here mother love seems to be poured out in an abnormal degree, and unless there is a corrective influence from some other member of the family, the type we have just described is almost sure to result.

What applies to the mother in a minor way applies to the nurse of the family. Here, again, we have got long and intimate contact with the subject, but as the role of nurse will be further examined later in this section it is not proposed to dilate upon it now.

It is recorded that a famous Jesuit once said : " Give me the boy until he is seven years old ; I have no fear for his future." What the learned Father, who must have been a profound psychologist, wished to convey was that the subconscious mind, which is the basis of character, is impressionable, malleable, ductile and avidly receptive up to the age of seven. The character stamped on it at this period is ineffaceable and fit to overcome any enemies who may assault it in its passage through life.

As has been said, this softened type of male is pathetic and very unfitted for life's battle. He rarely leaves home, and seldom or never marries, all his affection being concentrated on his mother. Treatment after the tenth year is definitely hopeless. The harm has been done. The victim is suspended in character neutrality. His outlook is colourless ; his life motive is colourless ; his soul is colourless, and in adult life he sows not neither does he sin. Yet this is a state which definitely yields to treatment if treatment is entered upon at the proper time. The only danger is the mother, and the type of mother who brings about this condition is very often almost impossible to deal with. An effort must be made to get her to understand, and the task is a very difficult one, that her over-affection is definitely detrimental to the future of the child. It must be impressed upon her that this affection is pathologic, abnormal and has to be curbed.

It is advised that the mother pass as little time as possible with the child in its waking hours, and in no circumstances should she take it to bed with her and fondle it after the third year. All efforts at pampering the child and clothing it in a luxurious and effeminate manner must be strongly checked. The father, where possible, must make an effort to see the child daily and keep before him everything which has a bearing on future male life. The games the child is permitted to play, the toys which are bought for him, the picture books chosen to develop the subconscious acuity must be exclusively of a type which awakens interest in the normal male mind. Encouragement should be given to the child to play with boys of his own age and praise unlavishly bestowed on him for the performance of feats that are manly.

For any delinquency the mother should be persuaded to inflict the punishment necessary, and she should be taught to steel her heart against giving her natural sympathy.

Praise and commendation should come exclusively from the father.

The boy should be sent to a school for boys at the earliest possible age, and at ten years it is advisable that he be entered as a boarder.

By this means one can strangle in early life those softened characteristics which would be so incapacitating and so fatal to the man in adult life.

The above has been written exclusively about the male as it has never been the fortune of the writer to encounter a female of this type. One can safely hazard a guess that the number can by no means compare with the number of males so tainted. The mother, after all, is the member of the family in constant contact with the developing subconscious of the child. Her maternal instinct poured forth in a plus quantity over the developing male subconscious can believably do a definite amount of harm, whereas it is impossible to conceive how it could possibly harm the developing subconscious of the female child.

Nevertheless, one sees from time to time solitary girls in a family with definite external masculine traits. The mother here will be often found to harbour a grievance that the girl child is not a boy, and partially neglects it. The child, subconsciously feeling this, leans towards the father, and a subconscious effort to please tends to stimulate what she knows to be her male parent's desire.

What is the lesson to be drawn from this type of case ?

That this type exists is undeniable, and that it is purely developmental must be admitted. Here we have a practical obliteration of sex under the influence of circumstantial maldevelopment.

To the writer's mind the obliteration of sex is a much more difficult accomplishment than the bringing about of sex abnormality.

When we consider the physical, and especially the physico-sexual similarity, both structurally and developmentally, which exists in the human body, we must be prepared for a sporadic crossing of the border line. But that developmental environment is capable of destroying man's strongest instinct brings forcibly before us that vicious circumstances are easily able to convert the normal into the abnormal.

We have seen how the child in its earliest years is bi-sexual instinctively. We have seen how, in certain circumstances, this bi-sexual child can grow up to become what might with full justice be described as a neutral thing.

We know that there exist human beings where a perversion of the normal sexual instinct does occur. Is this perversion innate ? In other words, is it impossible for the perverted person to be normal ? The answer of the writer, from his own experience, is most emphatically No. It is developmental. In support of this he begs leave to quote a case which he treated just after the termination of the European War.

This case was sent by a genito-urinary surgeon whom the patient had consulted. As the patient's outstanding complaint was that he thought his abdomen was ripped open and his intestines were hanging out, the surgeon was in no mood to waste his time over him and sent him along to the writer.

The patient's age was 28.   He was physically a magnificent   specimen   of   manhood,   standing   over 6 feet, and had fought excellently through four years of war and was wounded.

At first general inspection he gave the impression of a softness almost effeminate, and not at all consistent with a man who had passed four years in the great struggle. His voice, a high-pitched treble, tended to accentuate this feeling, and his general mannerisms, which were over-polite and lacking in male brusqueness, filled the effeminate picture in detail.

On being asked plainly what was his complaint he replied that he was perfectly happy in every way except that he was obsessed by an idea, which he was unable to throw off, that his abdomen was ripped open and his intestines were hanging out.   There was no great amount of mental pain manifested by the patient in the appalling circumstances. He accepted it with a complacency entirely incomprehensible, but this complacency was not based on any doubt of the basic reality of his abdominal condition. His family history yielded nothing of pertinent interest. It was good on both sides and his personal history contained nothing startling.

It may be interpolated here that the author at this time was an ardent devotee of Freud, and was doing his feeble best to get results by the Psycho-analytic method.

On being questioned as to his hobbies, games, etc., the patient stated that he was very interested in the Boy Scout movement, and gave all his spare time to it. At the 'Varsity he had never gone in for athletics, although he looked ideally built for a Rugby Forward. He slept well except for occasional war dreams.

On being further questioned about his dreams, especially those of sexual significance, he stated that only twice in his life had he had nocturnal emission. Pressed on this point he confessed that, as far as he remembered, no female had figured in the dream. One of the dreams he remembered with clarity was that he was clambering up a pole in pursuit of a boy who was climbing the pole, and whilst he was climbing after the boy emission occurred. He attributed this to pressure against the pole.

On being questioned as to his ordinary life, he said that women made no appeal to him. He had never had and had no desire to have connection with a woman, nor would he admit any similar attraction towards his own sex. One could see that his statements were in every way reliable, as he was really a very fine type in most respects.

Considering the nature of the symptoms complained of, the author in his enthusiasm approached the case with the greatest confidence, feeling certain that the war was the fundamental factor in the patient's condition.

For many weary months he dragged the unfortunate patient up and down the war front, from the Belgian border to the Swiss frontier, trying to elicit from him what he (the author) thought would be the causation factor in his complex. When he was wounded at Ypres and sent down the line one memory stuck prominently out in his mind. He saw a wounded soldier lying on a stretcher with blood oozing from his body, and forming the idea that the wound must be in the soldier's abdominal wall, which had probably been torn open by a shell fragment, promptly fainted himself.

When questioned as to whether he had actually seen the abdominal condition, he admitted that he had not, but that the idea arose in his mind. This was the start of his own abdominal condition, and from that day he had been unable to shake off the hallucination.

The author was very cock-a-hoop, and for the moment saw the complete recovery of his case. This hope was short-lived, however, and weary weeks passed with the patient remaining in *statu quo*.

At last the war theatre was abandoned and the patient was taken back to his earliest childhood memories. He recalled eventually what proved to be a factor of vital importance in his case. He stated that when he was six or seven years old one day he was walking with his nurse. His mother returning from shopping met them outside the house. She stopped to speak to the child before entering the house, and when she had gone the nurse said to the child, " Do you see your mummy ? She is very fat, with a large tummy. There is a living baby inside your mummie, and in a short time that baby will come out and you will have another little sister or brother." The baby, of course, eventually arrived, and the child, puzzling over in his subconscious, could only come to the conclusion that the baby had arrived through a splitting of his mother's abdominal wall.

The idea persisted for a time that this was the method by which all children made their entry into the world, until the patient, in later life, learnt about the maternal passages, when the idea faded from consciousness.

The hallucination cleared up promptly, much to the author's satisfaction and no small amazement. A difficulty remained, however, and a great one, inasmuch as the patient was by now fully aware of the fact that he was a Homosexualist, although a nonpractitioner. This worried him a lot, and an effort was made to win him from this tendency. It must be understood that he had never committed a Homosexual act in his life, but admitted that his tendency would be towards this rather than normal sexuality.

He was advised to seek the acquaintance of a woman friend and to pass as much time as possible in her society. It was pointed out to him that he was to make no effort to push forward any sexual idea with regard to her, but to try to cultivate simply a pleasure at being in her company. Manifestly, it was lucky, because he eventually married the girl, who had stuck by him during his difficult period, and he is now the father of a family.

The writer was unable to assist the patient in any way towards this ideal termination beyond suggesting the initial step of picking out an understanding and companionable female. The patient's efforts, plus her assistance, brought about the fortunate termination.

Let us examine this case in the light of the material which we have at our disposal. How did the first sexual impression implanted by the nurse influence the sexual trend of the child towards perversion ? The writer has to admit that he has not even a theory to advance for such development, and he has submitted the case to several prominent disciples of the Freudian School who can give no satisfactory answer. He has had to rest content with the conviction that the nurse laid the seeds of this perversion in some way, but he has not one single satisfactory proof in support of that conviction.

Is there a cure for perversion ? In the writer's opinion coeducation must be a powerful influence in directing the sex interest into its normal channel. Coeducation has many opponents, inasmuch as it is considered by them to call forth precocious sexual inclinations. That there is an undoubted danger of this cannot be denied, but as this method of teaching could terminate at ten years of age, it is highly improbable that much damage could have been done at this age.

The advantage of coeducation is that the subconscious sex instinct has had time to grow and develop by Hetrosexual or normal stimulation, with a consequent atrophying of the Homosexual or abnormal instinct. After all, Homosexuality is almost a luxury evil, being far more commonly met with amongst the leisured classes than amongst the teaming millions, whose early school life is coeducational.

Few will deny that boarding schools are prominent breeding grounds for this evil, and as the poor have not got these at their command there are fewer opportunities for the development of this vice in their class.

In view of the evidence advanced by the second case set forth in this chapter, treatment of Perversion may not be the hopeless thing it appears to be at first sight.

In the case of the twenty-year-old Colonial youth, his earliest sexual experiences were definitely Homosexual. Later in life he shelved this tendency and became normal. Still later, after a sexual debauch in the normal manner, he reverted to Homosexuality. Here there were three changes in the sexual life of the young man voluntarily accomplished without any assistance.

In the other case quoted we have a subject non-practising, but very definitely Homosexual in type. Merely on the suggestion of the writer he submitted himself to an attempt to educate himself to be sexually normal and succeeded.

In view of the evidence afforded by these two cases, and in view of the fact that we know the normal can and do become perverted, it is not beyond the bounds of reason to expect that encouragement, care and teaching should be able to guide the pervert into the path of sexual normality.

For a further consideration of the possible origin of Perversion (Homosexual) see Chapter X.

CHAPTER XIV

ALCOHOL AND DRUG ADDICTION

ALCOHOL

THE treatment of the alcoholic, at some time or other, falls to the lot of every man who practises the Art of Medicine. Few members of the Medical Profession, to whichever branch they belong, can escape coming in contact with him.

The surgeon dislikes operating on the alcoholic, inasmuch as he knows that his chances of a good result are considerably lowered in a patient of this type.

The anæsthetist thoroughly dislikes him and he makes his art at times a difficult one.

Even the gynæcologist and obstetrician do not entirely escape from contact with this type.

The unfortunate physician, however, has the unenviable lot of carrying these individuals through life, and, as a general rule, the recompense obtained is poor in comparison with the trouble they give.

The immoderate user of alcohol is, obviously, not a popular subject for treatment. The work is arduous, the results at times disheartening, and the recompense in no way commensurate with the worry involved.

The alcoholic is, as a rule, seldom of high moral worth, and when reinstated in a condition of health which is, at least, comfortable, he is apt to regard his recovery as being brought about mainly by his own consent to deprivation rather than to the efforts of the physician who gave him the strength to deprive himself. Again, his peculiar mental disposition buoys him up with the absurd idea of his potentiality to resist the captivating draught and his powers to right himself again even if he does take a little too much.

Into what category should the alcoholic be placed ? Is he a definite psychotic type ? If not psychotic, does he belong to one of the Psycho-neuroses groups ?

The chronic alcoholic who daily drinks himself into a condition of alcoholic stupor is definitely psychotic. He deliberately—i.e. with what deliberation he possesses—places himself daily in a position in which he is not a fit and proper person to be in his own control. On this basis obviously he is certifiable, and the author would have no hesitation in certifying such an individual. Institutional treatment—i.e. an Institution which treats certified lunacy cases — is the proper habitat for this type.

It is useless and a waste of time and money to attempt reformation. There is no hardship attached to the Institutional procedure, as the individual soon loses his rampant craving for alcohol and settles down to Institutional life in that complacent mental attitude so commonly met with amongst the senile dements.

Under such circumstances the patient is kept clean, comfortable and out of harm's way. He is not in a position to fall into the fire whilst in a drunken stupor or to set the house alight and endanger others, or do the thousand and one irresponsible things which he is capable of doing if living his own life. Release for probationary periods soon serves to indicate beyond dispute that no matter how long the interval has lasted over which the alcohol has been withdrawn, the first opportunity of access only leads to the customary debauch. In these circumstances, especially as the mental powers will be found to have degenerated beyond the point of feeling the loss of contact with externals, it is much wiser to recognize the impossibility of release and to regard Institutional detention as the safest solution of the problem.

THE PSYCHO-NEUROTIC TYPE OF ALCOHOLISM

The immoderate use of alcohol, which falls short of the class just spoken of, is, in the opinion of the writer, a definite Psycho-neurotic type.

The author is prepared for the vials of wrath to be poured upon his head by those who regard the immoderate or even moderate use of alcohol as a vice. Again the author repeats, in the face of this hostility, that alcoholism is a symptom of general nervous exhaustion of the INHERITED or ACQUIRED Psycho-neurotic type.

The INHERITED type of Psycho-neurotic provides by far the overwhelming proportion of immoderate users of alcohol. This type, as we know, are spendthrifts and dissipators of nervous energy. They are always out at elbow and down at heel from a nervous force point of view. Under the spur of their badly controlled emotions they are continually short of PSYCHIC FORCE. Their extravagance keeps them in a perpetual condition of PSYCHIC FORCE hunger, and they look for anything in the nature of drinks, drugs or further excitement to damp down the perpetual gnaw of their minds.

The SUBCONSCIOUS PSYCHIC FORCE which Nature has locked away from their profligate expenditure can be raided by the stimulus of alcohol, and raid it they do on the faintest pretext. Their minds aglow with the new found FORCE, they are once again ecstatically happy and tread the Elysian Fields freed from the pain and worry of the moment. Everyday life teems with

examples of this type of alcoholic. Their æsthetic sense
prevents them from sinking into the bestial condition
of the sot, and a few rare ones even display their
brightest mental efforts under the stimulus of alcohol.
They are incapable, however, of sustained effort ; their
work is spasmodic.

Reference is made again to that chapter where
the treatment of the victim of INHERITED PSYCHO-
NEUROSIS is mentioned (Chapter III). This type, with
the superadded alcohol adornment, unfortunately
calls forth the same comment as regards treatment.
It is possible to treat him for his alcoholism, to restore
his physical and nervous energy for a time, but when
an exciting moment arrives he plunges into another
debauch of PSYCHIC FORCE expenditure. He soon
exhausts his normal supply, and, living only for the
moment, again returns to alcohol, blasting into his
PSYCHIC FORCE reserves to carry him through his
revels.

In a short time there is the usual collapse, and he
reverts to his customary state bankrupt in PSYCHIC
FORCE.

In treating the alcoholic who is a victim of ACQUIRED
PSYCHO-NEUROSIS, there is every hope of a permanent
cure. The alcoholism in cases of this type is but a
symptom of the pathologic nervous state, and if the
nervous condition is effectively treated, the alcoholic
tendency clears up of its own accord.

Treatment for the alcoholic condition must of
necessity come first because it is impossible to get at
the underlying nervous state effectively if the body
is being continuously upset by alcoholic stimulation.
In other words, it follows the rule definitely laid down
in the chapter on Treatment that the first step in
treatment must, of necessity, be a thorough physical
cleansing.

Alcoholism may be divided into :—

(1) Acute Alcoholism ;
(2) Chronic Alcoholism.

Acute Alcoholism—This form is very rarely met with. It is a condition where alcohol is taken suddenly and in an enormous quantity. The patient becomes unconscious and sometimes even dies. Alcohol taken under these circumstances is a poison pure and simple, and the treatment required must be sought for in a Toxicological Treatise.

Chronic Alcoholism is the condition with which we are immediately concerned, and which we regard basically as arising from a Psycho-neurotic state, INHERITED or ACQUIRED, in the victim.

Let us examine the mechanism in the development of what we regard as the chronic alcoholic. We start with him as a normal citizen. He begins his day with a normal amount of PSYCHIC FORCE quite adequate to enable him to discharge his daily duties without undue fatigue. He returns home in the evening having used up his CONSCIOUS PSYCHIC FORCE in the day's work. After a time he retires to rest, gets a normal night's sleep, replenishes himself with CONSCIOUS PSYCHIC FORCE and is ready in the morning to accomplish another day's work.

This is the twenty-four-hour cycle of the average healthy normal man using up the normal PSYCHIC FORCE with which Nature supplies him and replenishing it with rest and sleep. The desire for alcohol never enters into this picture.

The same individual gets pneumonia and returns to work too early. He recognizes he is " run down," as he himself expresses it. As a matter of fact, the true state of affairs is that his ENDOCRINE GLANDS, exhausted by the struggle against his pneumonia, exhausted in their efforts to build up his physical strength, are unable to make the additional effort needed to supply him with the energy he requires for the discharge of his normal duties. In other words, he is suffering from ACQUIRED PSYCHO-NEUROSIS, exhaustion type.

In the middle of the day all, or practically all, of the CONSCIOUS PSYCHIC FORCE which Nature has been able to place at his disposal has been used up. He feels unable to go on, and, in reality, he is unable to go on. Some kind friend, noticing his pale, drawn and exhausted appearance, suggests a stimulant. He takes it and, after a short period, he is flooded with a new supply of PSYCHIC FORCE. The alcohol gets the credit for such energizing. This, on the surface, seems to be so, and if it were so alcohol would be a marvellous aid in life. Unfortunately, however, this is far from true. The alcohol acts as a blasting force on the reservoir of SUBCONSCIOUS PSYCHIC FORCE, Nature's most jealously guarded asset. This energy is thrown into the depleted reservoir of CONSCIOUS PSYCHIC FORCE, and remains at the disposal of the individual.

When he returns home in the evening the fatigue is more marked, following the alcoholic stimulation. He retires early to bed.

Leaving out of consideration for the moment the digestive upset caused by the alcohol, and the consequent interference with the normal production of PSYCHIC FORCE under ordinary circumstances, we have the following condition of affairs after the night's rest :—

Nature was engaged in her usual work of restoring PSYCHIC FORCE during the hours of rest. In the first place, she takes care to refill the reservoir of SUBCONSCIOUS PSYCHIC FORCE. Her second consideration is to devote what remains over to replenish the reservoir of CONSCIOUS PSYCHIC FORCE.

Owing to the health circumstances the ENDOCRINE GLANDS which produce the FORCE are not working to full capacity. The result is that the reservoir of CONSCIOUS PSYCHIC FORCE is not completely filled. As the reservoir of SUBCONSCIOUS PSYCHIC FORCE is being constantly called upon to build up the body, and the consequence is the reservoir of CONSCIOUS PSYCHIC FORCE receives scant attention and is never capacity full, naturally it follows that CONSCIOUS PSYCHIC FORCE being below normal the work output suffers.

This is abundantly proved by the mental attitude of the individual. He sails forth disinclined to work. He feels that he is unable to work, and, in reality, this is so. After a short time his energy (CONSCIOUS PSYCHIC FORCE) runs down. He can carry on no longer. Suddenly he remembers the stimulant and its beneficent action of the previous day. He takes a stimulant, again he floods himself illegitimately with SUBCONSCIOUS PSYCHIC FORCE and carries on for a further period. When this FORCE is absorbed and he finds himself exhausted he has another stimulant, and so it goes on until the close of his day's work. On his return he gives evidence of utter exhaustion as well as signs of alcoholism.

During the day he expended all the CONSCIOUS PSYCHIC FORCE at his command, and once, twice, three or four times has ravaged his store of SUBCONSCIOUS PSYCHIC FORCE by alcoholic stimulation. Overnight Nature does her utmost to repair the damage. She fills the reservoir of SUBCONSCIOUS PSYCHIC FORCE first, as is her custom, and this has been depleted to such an extent by the previous day's depredations that but little is left to go into the reservoir of CONSCIOUS PSYCHIC FORCE. Consequently, the individual is disinclined to go to work. He now definitely is unable to go to work without stimulation. Alcohol is again called upon to lend its ghastly assistance, and the man starts to run his entire life on his SUBCONSCIOUS PSYCHIC FORCE reservoir.

If we can imagine this conduct carried on over a lengthy period of time, it is easy to grasp how an individual slips into the continuous use of alcoholic stimulation in order to be able to maintain his position in the scheme of things.

To make this theory of the establishment of Chronic Alcoholism clear the author begs permission to represent it graphically :—

THE NORMAL MAN
In the Morning

C. P. F.
Conscious Psychic Force.

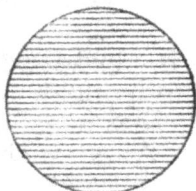

S. P. F.
Subconscious Psychic Force.

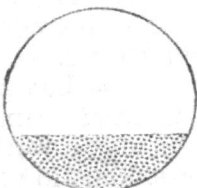

C. P. F.
In the evening after a normal day's
work, seven-eighths depleted.

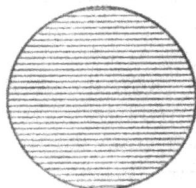

S. P. F.
In the evening after a normal day's
work—still intact.

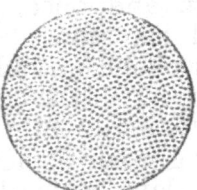

C. P. F.
Refilled after a night's rest, ready
for the next day's work.

S. P. F.
After a night's rest still unused—
intact.

AFTER ILLNESS
(Acquired Psycho-neurosis Through Illness)

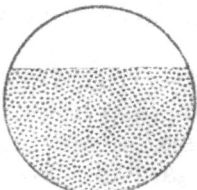

C. P. F.
Reservoir of Conscious Psychic Force.
In the morning reservoir only two-
thirds full.   Nature devoting one-
third to rebuilding body.

S. P. F.
Reservoir of Subconscious Psychic
Force—still intact.

C. P. F.
Reservoir at midday. Conscious
Psychic Force at lowest ebb. Subject
fatigued, unable to work.

S. P. F.
Still intact.

C. P. F.
After alcoholic stimulation. Force
blasted over from reservoir of Subconscious Force and transformed into
Conscious Psychic Force at the
voluntary disposal of the individual.

S. P. F.
Subconscious Psychic Force reduced
in reservoir under stimulus of alcohol
and transferred into reservoir of
Subconscious Psychic Force for
voluntary use.

The Same Case—Evening

C. P. F.
Ravished Psychic Force used up and
reservoir practically empty.

S. P. F.
Reservoir still half empty as when
robbed by alcoholic stimulation.

Circle with dot markings represents
Reservoir of Conscious Psychic
Force, and is stamped C P. F.

Circle with transverse bar markings
represents Reservoir of Subconscious
Psychic Force, and is stamped S. P. F.

The Same Case—the Next Morning after Nature's Effort to Restore Psychic Force by Rest

C. P. F.
After Nature has refilled Subconscious Psychic Force reservoir, only a small quantity remains in reservoir of Conscious Psychic Force. This is evidenced by disinclination to work and speedy exhaustion.

S. P. F.
Nature refills Subconscious Psychic Force Reservoir.

The Same Case—after Two Hours' Work

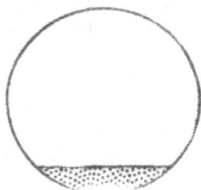

C. P. F.
Absorption of practically all available Conscious Psychic Force—exhaustion.

S. P. F.
Reservoir still intact.

The Same Case—after Alcoholic Stimulation

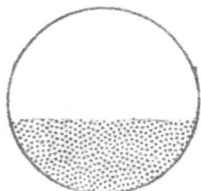

C. P F.
Partially filled after first alcoholic stimulation.

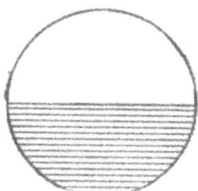

S. P. F.
Partially depleted after first alcoholic stimulation.

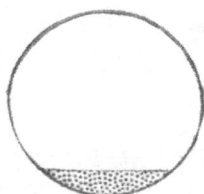

C. P. F.
Again exhausted and just prior to second alcoholic stimulation.

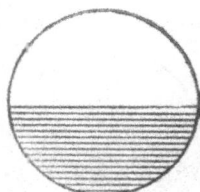

S. P. F.
State prior to second alcoholic stimulation.

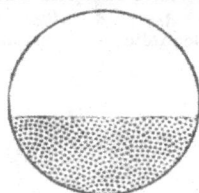

C. P. F.
After second alcoholic stimulation, partly refilled.

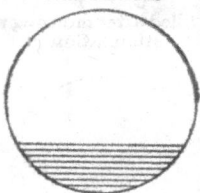

S. P. F.
After second alcoholic stimulation, further depleted.

Return Home

C. P. F.
Reservoir practically empty—exhaustion.

S. P. F.
Reservoir well depleted.

The Next Morning

C. P. F.
Minimum quantity. Disinclination to go to work without alcoholic stimulation.

S. P. F.
Reservoir refilled overnight and intact before alcoholic stimulation.

After Alcoholic Stimulation

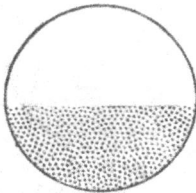

C. P. F.
Partially filled after morning alcoholic stimulation.

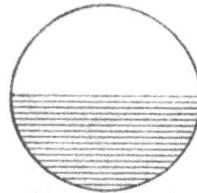

S. P. F.
Partially depleted after morning alcoholic stimulation.

C. P. F.
Conscious Psychic Force exhausted after a few hours and before the second stimulation.

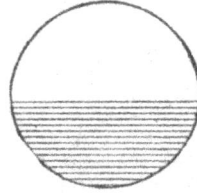

S. P. F.
Subconscious Psychic Force remaining before second alcoholic stimulation.

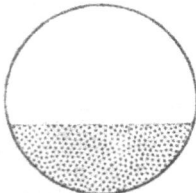

C. P. F.
After second stimulation by alcohol.

S. P. F.
After second stimulation by alcohol

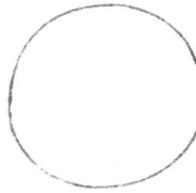

C. P F.
After repeated stimulation no more Psychic Force eventually is transferred to the Conscious Psychic Force reservoir and no attempt is made at exertion.

S. P. F.
The Subconscious Force reservoir is practically depleted. The remaining Force is for internal use and stuporous sleep supervenes.

From the diagrammatic representation detailed above it will be seen that from the beginning alcohol raids the reservoir of SUBCONSCIOUS PSYCHIC FORCE, and even from the very beginning the subject exhibits some of the objective signs of PSYCHO-NEUROSIS.

Of course, we started off with the theory that the alcoholic was an established Psycho-neurotic, and, therefore, it is to be presumed that he would have both the objective and subjective symptoms of his complaint. When alcoholic stimulation is commenced, however, right from the start these objective signs of PSYCHO-NEUROSIS manifest themselves, if they are not already present. For example :—

(a) the hands become tremulous ;
(b) the patient is easily exhausted and mental concentration is interfered with.

As the alcoholic progresses in his downward career, and as he invades the reservoir of his SUBCONSCIOUS PSYCHIC FORCE more deeply, the subjective symptoms of PSYCHO-NEUROSIS accentuate themselves until they cross over the borderline and appear as a definite Psychosis—ALCOHOLIC MANIA or DELERIUM TREMENS.

It is very interesting to note this extravagant expenditure of SUBCONSCIOUS PSYCHIC FORCE and the consequent psychopathologic manifestations which ensue.

It will be remembered that in the chapter where we considered the mechanism of a nervous breakdown, that we attributed it to a profligate expenditure of SUBCONSCIOUS PSYCHIC FORCE under the stimulus of *Fear*. There we stated that FEAR had the same power as alcohol appears to have, viz., the power of being able to encroach the reservoir of SUBCONSCIOUS PSYCHIC FORCE and permit its escape. In both cases we get a similar result—a temporary collapse of the nervous balance of the individual.

CHRONIC ALCOHOLISM

We have seen a diagrammatic representation of the development of the chronic alcoholic. Now let us look at him in the flesh.

R

When a middle-aged man, accustomed to take alcohol, finds his mental powers slipping and his physical powers falling below what they normally should be at that age he consults his physician. As a general rule, he is sufficiently frank to acknowledge that he is conscious of the fact that he is consuming too much alcohol. He acknowledges that neither the psychic nor the physical engine turns over smoothly in the morning until flooded with a peg or two.

This is the *first* assault on his SUBCONSCIOUS PSYCHIC FORCE.

Again, before lunch he frankly admits that it requires two or three or more aperitifs to put him in a mood for his midday meal, this despite the fact that he has had only an apology for a breakfast.

This is the *second* assault on his SUBCONSCIOUS PSYCHIC FORCE.

The midday meal is washed down with more alcohol in the shape of beer, spirits, liqueurs or port.

In the afternoon he confesses to a mental heaviness which seriously impedes his work, and as the normal working hours draw to a close he confesses that he feels exhausted physically and mentally, and takes the first opportunity of having a bracer.

Another assault on his SUBCONSCIOUS PSYCHIC FORCE.

He feels better after the first bracer, and much better when the sixth is reached. By this time he proceeds home, and just one more before preparing for dinner is the natural order of things. Dinner is accompanied by beer or wine or spirits, liqueurs or port, and this closes his alcoholic allowance for the day, with the exception of one, two, three, four or more customary whisky pegs before going to rest.

This type is by no means uncommon. It would appear at first sight that no one could consume daily such quantities of alcohol without ruining his health and his general capabilities. The fact of the matter is that many men do carry on and carry on with apparent efficiency and passable health until the saturation point is reached. This saturation point is eventually reached by all, though it differs in different individuals, but when it is reached the individual is left in no doubt of his position. It is at this stage he seeks medical advice.

Before examining our subject let us hear what is the burden of his complaint :—

" Doctor, I have gone to pieces lately. I have " lost all the zest of life ; my work has become a " burden to me ; the confidence in my ability to " carry on has disappeared utterly because I " know that I am unable to do my work efficiently.

" When I awake in the morning I look forward " to the day with dread. I feel quite unfit to get " up.

" Food is abhorrent to me. In fact, I very often " vomit.

" To struggle to the office is an effort, and " when I arrive there my mind is utterly bewildered " and I do not know where to begin. What is " almost worse, I have lost all connection with the " work I did yesterday or last week, and I am " afraid to start lest I blunder into some wrong " track and make a mess of things.

" It is a godsend to me when I can go outside " and have a drink or two to brace myself up. " After this, for an hour or two, I can get through " a certain amount of work, but it is an effort " and a great strain, and the approach of lunch " hour is welcome.

" Two or three aperitifs give me some sort of " an appetite, and very often I eat more than is " really good for me.

" After lunch, when I return to the office, I " must confess I am no longer nervous and rest- " less. Quite the opposite. I am contented and " happy, and would like to go to sleep if that were " possible. I do not feel like work ; in fact, my " brain is not clear enough for work, and I " just pedal along taking care to commit no " errors.

" This is bad for business, doctor, and I feel
" there must be a change or there will be a crash.

" When I go home at night I have no real
" appetite for dinner. It is a pleasure when this
" is over and I can settle down to a book or a
" game of bridge to take my mind off myself and
" my affairs.

"And, doctor, the worst feature is that unless
" I have three or four or more pegs before going
" to bed I do not sleep, and the night is passed
" in horror.

" I cannot imagine what has happened.   I
" never felt like this until the last three months,
" and now, frankly, I have come to you because
" I am really frightened."

How accurately this clinical picture follows the
diagrammatic representation of the alcoholic's progress.

The above is a thumb-nail sketch, an absolute
facsimile, of the story which all bring to the consulting
room when they have reached the landing stage—the
saturation point. Outraged Nature has kicked ; she
will tolerate no more abuse. Life will now be lived
under her sternest command because her confidence
has been abused.   Liberties may be taken, but the
penalty exacted frightens the life out of the most
venturesome. The body has reached a state where it
plainly gives evidence that it cannot and will not
render service unless alcohol is rigidly excluded
from it.

Let us look at the physical picture of the victim.
As a rule his age is in the early or middle fifties, and,
as he sits in the chair, he holds his body all tensed up.
He is incapable of relaxing and is made " jumpy " by
even mild physical examination.

The face has lost its normal contour and gives evidence of holding superfluous fluid in the tissues. His
eyes lack lustre. His lids are heavy, puffed and pouched
underneath.

When he is stripped it is seen that his torso is
covered with a cuirass of soft blubbery fat. The fat

infiltrated muscles of the abdominal wall have sagged outwards under the pressing weight of the overloaded atonic stomach and intestines, and lumps of hideous adipose tissue heap themselves upon and destroy the outline of his pelvis and thighs.

His body is hypersensitive and shrinks from even the cool touch of the examining stethoscope and the skin turns gooseflesh when the clothes are removed.

When the mouth is open the breath is foul and heavy and the tongue is coated with a yellow liverish coat from the tip to the pillars of the fauces.

Examination of the heart reveals a fast, soft, ineffective sound, betraying the feeble fat infiltrated organ that lies beneath.

The pupils are dilated and react sluggishly.

The knee jerks—plus, plus.

The hands exhibit a coarse tremor.

This presents a picture of the psychic and physical side of the alcoholic who has arrived at Nature's extreme point of tolerance. He is perfectly aware of his own position ; perfectly aware that he is at last face to face with two alternatives—treatment or death to his efficiency. Yes, perhaps even physical death.

It is pointed out to him that his digestive system is in a state of revolt, and he is well aware that his nervous system is running riot and is practically out of his control. His liver, the chemical factory of his body, is in chaotic disorder and is no longer making an attempt to deal with the abnormal work to which it has been subjected for years.

All these truths are as apparent to the victim instinctively as they are to the physician, and he is asked to make up his mind.

The author has never brought any influence, apart from the obvious state of affairs, to bear on the patient as to what line of conduct he should pursue. The treatment is not pleasant and entails considerable sacrifice on the part of the patient. This should be pointed out to him, and he should be given time to consider fully the situation.

If, after having given the matter due consideration, the patient expresses a definite desire to undergo treatment, it should be made clear to him the nature of the treatment which he has to undergo for the recleansing and refitment of his body. He must be assured that he will be restored to a physical state of well-being which will enable him to resist the craving for alcohol. At the same time, it must be firmly pointed out that the treatment does not include the provision of a private guardian angel to take alcohol out of his hand if he wishes to resume his vice. Yet, apart from that, he would be fortified against the lure to an extent where any man of character should be capable of successful resistance.

The specific treatment for alcoholism used by the writer is the work of Doctor Lambert, of New York, and he (the writer) has found it incomparably the best form of treatment which he has met. It comprises the full drug administration for the four-day period ; the full food and liquid to be taken during the time of the active treatment ; the temperature, pulse rate and remarks about the patient's general and mental condition during this treatment.

After undergoing the Lambert Treatment and a period of rest the writer, regarding the alcoholic of this type as being a Psycho-neurotic with marked exhaustion symptoms, undertakes to treat the patient for this condition in order to build up his physical system to a point where there is still less likelihood of a relapse. This treatment will be gone into in detail in due course.

To treat a patient successfully by the Lambert System it is almost essential that he should enter a private nursing home. When treatment is undergone in a patient's own home surroundings he looks forward to visits from different members of the family and friends. This is not at all desirable during the four or five days when he is undergoing the intensive form of treatment. The nursing home limits itself to strict regime, and the patient conforms more easily and settles down more fully to what he knows is rigidly established routine.

The patient therefore enters the nursing home and retires quietly to bed. The day nurse on the case is in attendance and the operator makes a careful physical examination, paying particular attention to the vascular and urinary systems. Very often these cases exhibit a marked degree of gastric irritability, and this must be cleared up before treatment proper commences.

In all cases a certain amount of nervous movements are present owing to the withdrawal of the immoderate quantity of alcohol, and it is well that a quietening draught should be given to settle down the general nervous condition of the patient. Dilute alcohol in small quantities may be given every two hours during the first twenty-four hours and every four hours during the second day, and practically withdrawn the third day.

Although it must be understood that there is no objection to giving a small quantity of alcohol at times before the treatment commences, or even during the first forty-eight hours of the specific treatment, it can be taken as a standard that it is an advisable thing to give the patient three or four days complete physical rest before entering on Doctor Lambert's Specific Treatment. This will enable him to stand the rather exhausting 96 hours which this treatment entails.

On the day the patient commences treatment, the usual hour fixed by the writer is 3 o'clock in the afternoon, the nurses who are to take charge of the case must both be present. The specific medicine is carefully measured into the capsules in which it is taken. The Blue Mass is got ready, also Compound Cathartic Pill. The treatment sheets are carefully explained. The hours for the increase in the specific medicine doses are specially pointed out, and it is impressed on the nurses the necessity that careful notes should be made of the physical and mental state of the patient every four hours.

If the patient vomits the nurse is instructed to get the operator on the telephone at any hour of the day or night, informing the doctor of the particular hour during the treatment at which this occurred, as, for example, the thirty-fifth hour from the beginning of the treatment. The operator has a duplicate treatment sheet and knows exactly the amount of specific medicine being taken at the time, and will give orders as to what is to be done in the circumstances. If by any chance the nurse is unable to get the operator, the administration of the specific medicine is stopped forthwith. The patient is given a large cup of coffee, and if this is vomited another cup is given. The specific treatment is not resumed until the operator has been in touch with the nurse.

It is impossible for the nurse to make any mistake, inasmuch as every step of the treatment is definitely outlined, and nothing can arise if ordinary care is exercised by the nurse in attendance.

For three days after the cessation of the treatment the patient is left more or less to his own resources. He can get up and sit about his room in a dressing-gown, but it is not advisable to attempt to go out. He is not allowed to sit up long enough to over-fatigue himself, as is liable to occur owing to the drastic nature of the four days' treatment.

Sleep is ensured at night by a draught if necessary, and the patient is encouraged to rest himself as much as possible.

The author is accustomed to regard the patient now as a case of ordinary Psycho-neurosis.

The treatment has unloaded the liver, cleansed out the entire digestive system and soothed the frayed nerves of the subject.

On the fourth day after treatment has finished, the patient is aroused at 7 o'clock. A saline draught is administered, followed by a cup of tea. When the bowels have acted he puts on heavy clothes and goes for a brisk walk. He comes back to his bath and massage, has his breakfast and rests for an hour, exercises before and after lunch. The general routine treatment outlined in the building-up of an ordinary case of Psycho-neurosis is carried out.

At the end of the second week Organotherapy treatment is entered upon.

The exercises and treatment are maintained for six weeks before the patient is allowed to return to his normal surroundings.

The patient will now state that he feels well ; he is well, and intends to remain well. The craving for alcohol is nil, and it is pointed out to him that the reason for this is that his body is in good general condition ; his digestive system is efficient ; his nervous system is functioning properly, and this is evidenced by his general activity, his mental clearness and his ability to sleep at night without adventitious aid.

It is impressed upon him that as long as he maintains his body in this state of well-being that the desire for alcohol will not present itself. At the same time he is reminded that a return to his old routine habits may subject him to an insidious temptation under which he may fall almost accidentally ; that even a slip is dangerous to him and may result in a condition of affairs actually more serious than what obtained before.

It is pointed out to him that he is in a condition to resist with a minimum of will effort any relapse into alcoholism, and that a relapse will, in all probability, mean irrevocable injury to both his health and his efficiency. He should be encouraged to seek out for himself a new method of daily life as far as possible, and make a definite act of determination to keep his physical condition at the highest point of efficiency consistent with his age.

Supervision over a period of twelve months is advised, and if the character of the patient is sufficiently strong there should be no doubt about the result produced.

DELIRIUM TREMENS

Delirium Tremens is a condition which is not infrequently met with in general practice. There is a considerable amount of danger in the condition, inasmuch as the body is generally weakened down through lack of food owing to the disordered state of the digestive system. In addition to this, the excitement and struggling impose a very severe strain on the heart and blood vessels, probably already damaged by alcoholic excess.

Naturally, in the psychic state of the patient, proper precautions are taken that he is not left at any time without adequate supervision.

The patient is put to bed between blankets and kept warm by the application of hot-water bottles, the idea being to conserve all the energy output possible as the condition is basically extravagant expenditure of PSYCHIC FORCE under abnormal excitement.

1/100th grain Hyoscene is administered hypodermically, and a draught consisting of :—

Chloral Hydrate	grs.	20
Potassium Bromide ...	grs.	20
Sodium Bromide	grs.	20
Tinct. Hyoscyamus ...	mins.	20

is given.

If this is well retained and the patient still remains excitable, it may be repeated in two hours. If at the end of the third hour the patient has not quietened down the Hyoscene injection may be repeated. This is usually effective in inducing sleep.

As a general rule, the mental condition quietens down completely in 24 to 48 hours. The draught outlined above is administered three times daily over a period of time, usually about a week, until the exhausted nervous system has refitted itself.

For a further three days after the draught has been withdrawn the patient is allowed to get up and walk about his room ; sleep, of course, being assured at night by the draught if necessary.

He is now in a fit state to undergo Lambert's

Treatment, and should experience no difficulty in withstanding the rigorous 96 hours during which it lasts.

DRUG ADDICTION

Can drug addiction be cured ?

This is a question which is put to the physician with unfailing regularity as each case is brought to his notice. There is no question which is harder to answer specifically.

When the habit has been established over a long period the hope of success of the treatment will, naturally, be commensurate with the length of that period.

In the second place, the personal character of the addict is of outstanding importance. Where the victim has fallen into the fell clutches of drug-taking, but has sufficient strength of character to resist the craving for self-saturation, then there is proportionate hope for a successful exit.

Thirdly, the physical condition of the patient, manifestly, must have a profound bearing on the ultimate result. If one is face to face with a weakling of poor physique then there are two immediate apparent obstacles to the cure :—

(a) The weak physique is scarcely able to stand up to the drastic physical treatment entailed, and either the patient has to interrupt treatment as his physical strength will not stand the strain, or the physician has to modify it to such a degree that a thorough physical cleansing in the circumstances is impossible.

(b) When the craving has been definitely overcome, it has to be remembered that only half the task has been completed, and there still remains the physical building up to be done. If the physical make-up is of poor quality, it is almost impossible to bring the body to such a state of well-being that it will be able to exist on its own natural nervous output, and not again seek extraneous and fatal assistance from the favourite drug.

The drugs most commonly used are :—
Morphia, Cocaine and Heroin.

Opium smoking is met with, but rarely in the British Isles.

Hashish is practically confined to the East.

Marahuana smoking, according to reports, has become popular in the United States of America, the habit having crossed the border from Mexico.

Morphine addiction is, probably, the most popular form of drug vice. It has to be admitted, unfortunately, that a heavy percentage of these cases have their source of origin in medical treatment. Medical men in particular are highly represented in this unhappy list.

It generally begins in an effort to alleviate pain, and it can be quite readily understood that a medical man, knowing its potentialities in this direction, and faced with the necessity of carrying on his work when racked with pain, falls readily into the trap.

It is surprising with what suddenness the habit grips the victim and how soon a complete mastery is established.

Morphia produces marked physical as well as psychic changes in the user.

On the physical side pallor is an outstanding characteristic. The face is deadly white or sallow. The jaws are drawn and sunken. The eyes, staring and set back in their hollow sockets, look out upon the world with a gaze of profound depression when a stimulating dose is needed, or sparkle with supernormal brilliancy after a recently administered injection.

The body generally is emaciated and the skin in that condition we designate " goose-flesh."

Itching all over the body is a pronounced feature, and the inability to keep warm is also very noticeable.

The tongue is foul and heavily coated, constipation invariably being present.

On the arms and legs puncture points dot the entire surface, and septic sores, healed or active, can be seen all over the skin.

On the physical side, when the patient is under the drug, there is a feeling of general *bien etre* which reflects itself upon the mind and maintains the victim in a pleasant state of excitement.

The jerky muscular movements disappear and a false euphoria radiates the face with a glow of self-confidence and self-assertion.

As the effects of the latest injection die down anxiety dawns in the eyes again. The patient becomes restless, is unable to sit still, and the feeling of self-complacency is replaced by one of irritability and moroseness. Body jerks, spasms and twitchings soon reappear, and general bodily irritation makes scratching almost irresistible.

The effect of Morphia, on the psychic side, we see in the uninterrupted deterioration of the personality of the individual. A slow progressive rot begins in the morale, and its progress advances unchecked until it is totally destroyed.

Every ethical idea, every good impulse, every thought of responsibility or duty is remorselessly crushed under the pressure of the craving. Nothing is permitted to stand in the way of the desire to obtain the drug.

These patients become liars, deceivers, utterly unscrupulous, and not even human life itself is safe if it stands in the way of their obtaining the drug.

The author treated a case, some years ago. A patient who had been taking 28 grains of Morphine Sulphate daily by injection, according to his own story. When he came under notice the greatest amount he was taking was 10 grs. daily. He said that he had reduced himself voluntarily this amount over a period of 12 months, and was genuinely anxious to break the habit.

He was put on a regular four-hourly dose, being steadily reduced before radical treatment was contemplated, and had, apparently, done extremely well. After six weeks his dosage (from memory) was about two grains in the 24 hours, one-third of a grain being given with clocklike precision every four hours. This kept him in a condition of comparative comfort, and he made no complaint.

One morning, at 3 o'clock, he woke up and called for the night sister on duty and demanded his dose. The sister reminded him that this was not due until 4 o'clock, and under no circumstances could she give him an injection before that hour. He became insistent, and she, in the face of his threatening attitude, told him that this dose was kept in the night superintendent's bureau, and, consequently, it would be impossible for her (the sister) to obtain it. With a cunning which is characteristic of the drug addict, the patient told her that he knew she carried an emergency ration in her poison cupboard and demanded the keys. She refused, and he attacked her. Fortunately, a patient in an adjoining room heard the struggle and released the sister from what was practically a murderous attack.

This gives us some idea of the deterioration which the character of the addict undergoes. This patient normally was quiet, inoffensive, well educated and of good family, but, under the stimulation of this terrible craving, all these fine feelings were jettisoned, and he reverted to the primitive.

TREATMENT OF THE DRUG ADDICT

Where there is a sincere desire expressed by the patient to rid himself of the craving, and where there is a good sound physical make-up, and, in addition to this, the age is under fifty, it can be said that there is a strong hope of successful treatment.

The following is the method adopted by the author when examining the patient. It may seem drastic to the general reader, but after fifteen years' contact with these cases all the care taken has been demonstrated to be absolutely essential.

First of all the patient is questioned as to :—

    (a) How the habit started. Whether to alleviate pain or whether through contact with vicious companions.

(*b*) The duration of the habit.

(*c*) The greatest quantity of the drug taken in twenty-four hours, and the method employed in its assimilation.

(*d*) His domestic status, how it has been affected by the drug-taking.

(*e*) His definite reason for desiring a cure.

A *thorough* physical examination is essential. If there is any physical condition causing continuous pain, which condition cannot be treated successfully, reject the case for treatment. It is hopeless to expect a beneficent result. If there is a physical condition, for example, some obscure disease of the pelvic organs in the female causing continuous depression, or some gastro-intestinal condition in the male producing the same effect, it is hopeless to cure Morphine addiction. These patients will relapse, no matter what is done for them.

If there is a psychopathic or near psychopathic element in the case the prognosis is not favourable.

If the patient is over fifty years of age and the habit is of long standing, prospect of a successful cure recedes.

These groupings are put forward bluntly and frankly because it is depressing to spend time and worry in attempting to cure this dreadful evil and find oneself in the middle or at the end of treatment up against an insurmountable barrier which precludes the possibility of a successful termination.

There is a large class of Morphia users, outside these groupings, which are definitely amenable to treatment. First of all there is the foolish young man or young woman, the thrill seekers of this hectic age, who has been induced to take a shot of Morphia by some vicious-minded person. It must be remembered that your true morphinist, by some malignant mental twist, is ever avid to make conversions. The bravado of the neophyte, plus the feeling of sudden well-being, acting generally on a reckless unthinking mind, lays the foundation all too readily.

This class, in the majority of cases, does give definitely good results.

A second and much larger class, from which the physician is entitled to expect a happy exit, are those to whom Morphia is administered in illness for relief of pain. If seen early, and if of good sound physique, there is no reason why they should not be rescued from this appalling vice.

No matter what the state of the patient is, treatment can only be successfully undertaken in a nursing home, and even here every precaution has to be taken that the vigilance of the physician and nurses is not being successfully eluded.

The preliminary examination made by the author may seem harsh, but experience has demonstrated that it is entirely necessary. The patient is stripped and thoroughly examined physically. This should be carried out without wounding the susceptibility of the patient in any unnecessary manner. The pyjamas or nightdress is handed to the patient and the articles necessary for toilet purposes are laid out in the bedroom after they have been thoroughly examined. All other clothing, except bedroom slippers, is taken away. Dressing-case, trunks, handbags, etc., the whole impedimenta of every description is removed out of reach of the patient. In other words, the patient has, at his or her hand, the bare necessities for toilet use and the bare clothing requisite for lying in bed.

It must be remembered that the moral character of these patients, in the majority of cases, has deteriorated to such a point that they will stoop to any level which their cunning suggests to them to indulge in their vice.

It is better to exact a promise that no visitors should be received during the treatment period if possible, or only visitors who have the highest sense of the responsibility of the treatment being undertaken. The author practically excludes visitors.

The nursing staff must be personally known to the

physician, and must be of unimpeachable trustworthiness.

The patient is now in bed and settled. The first part of the treatment is a lecture where he (or she) is given to understand exactly the position relative to the physician. It is plainly demonstrated that a cure can only be effected by absolute obedience to the letter of the rules outlined, and any breach of these rules will involve the patient being withdrawn from the nursing home.

The patient is assured that a certain quantity of the drug will be administered by a competent attendant every four hours. This quantity will be sufficient to maintain him in a degree of comfort which will entail no hardship, and, at the same time, permit of no indulgence in a luxurious debauch. The drug will be administered punctiliously at the times laid down. It can be administered solely by the attendant at these times, and no condition could arise to justify an injection except at the specified hours.

The amount of the drug administered must be known only to the physician and the attendant, the patient being simply guaranteed that it is given in sufficient quantity to prevent suffering.

In this way there is a steady diminution of the drug, and the sufferings associated with abrupt withdrawal are entirely eliminated.

The patient is put to bed in a room the temperature of which is kept round about 70°. He is kept in bed with hot-water bottles continuously beside him. The object of this is to conserve every atom of PSYCHIC FORCE the body produces. Heat also acts as a nerve depressant and allays restlessness and excitability, which are distressing features of these cases.

Free elimination of the bowels by drastic catharsis is necessary. The patient is encouraged to drink liquid in abundant quantities. Under these conditions bodily secretions long strangled by the toxic drugs are once again enabled to manifest their beneficent influence on the body to restart their repair efforts as the gradual

S

imperceptible withdrawal of the drug pours less and less poison daily into the system. As the beneficent secretions gradually assert their power, strength returns and the nervous system clarifies itself gradually and the patient feels less and less the need for the drug.

The regularity of the administration given exactly at the specific hours, the relief promised by the administration at the appointed times, quieten the suspicions of the patient, and the lessening quantities are never noticed.

When the drug has been finally withdrawn, rest at night should be ensured by giving the following draught :—

> Rx
>
> | | | |
> |---|---|---|
> | Potassium bromide ... ... | grs. | 20 |
> | Sodium bromide ... ... | grs. | 20 |
> | Chloral hydrate ... ... | grs. | 20 |
> | Tincture of Hyoscyamus ... | grs. | 20 |

followed by free purgation in the morning.

After this treatment has been maintained for one week, and the drug entirely withdrawn over that time, the patient is now put on Doctor Lambert's Treatment to cleanse out the entire system and give the purified body a chance to rebuild itself with completely fresh materials.

After the Lambert Treatment there is the usual building up according to the scheme outlined by the author in the chapter on Treatment.

The patient is discharged fit and well, equipped for the battle of life, with no desire to return to the drug if he exercises in any normal degree the will power which has been restored to him.

This treatment may seem long to the physician who is not accustomed to deal with drug addicts. It may seem harsh to those who are not acquainted with this appalling malady. It cannot be curtailed, however. It cannot be modified from what is outlined here.

Morphia is a ruthless enemy productive of moral death practically from its onset, and eventually premature physical death.

If cases are selected with care, as outlined at the beginning of this chapter, and treated with the rigorous attention displayed here, good results can be counted on.

COCAINE and HEROIN differ in their effects on the psychic of the individual, but treatment is along exactly the same lines as outlined in the treatment of MORPHIA addiction.

CHAPTER XV

TREATMENT OF PSYCHO-NEUROSIS

The Operator—his relation to the patient.
The Patient—his health, habits, amusements, etc., in relation to his illness.
Treatment proper—" Mind in splints."
> Analysis of immediate difficulties.
> Building up of Physical well-being.
> Psychotherapeutic treatment.
> Administration of Hormones.

Concluding remarks.

THE author does not presume to advance for a moment that his outline of treatment is ideal The treatment, however, put forward has been constantly applied over a period of fifteen years dealing exclusively with this type of case. Reasons will be given for the different steps taken in the method employed.

The setting in Psychotherapy treatment embraces two individuals, as well as the method employed. The subject is, naturally, the individual of outstanding importance in the treatment, but a close second follows the operator. The method employed must be dictated by the type of individual under treatment.

For example, to push along in a harsh manner a neurotic case with definite hyperthyroidic symptoms tends only to increase the anxiety and fear elements, and, consequently, imperil the outcome.

On the other hand, to permit the phlegmatic, listless, hypothyroidic type to go its own way would be fatal from the point of view of ultimate beneficial results.

A few words here with regard to the operator will not be out of place, and whilst the author makes no claim whatsoever that his technique is faultless, or even good, he is forced to state that there are certain things which must be avoided if the patient is going to make satisfactory progress.

The operator should approach a case with his mental attitude ready to be moulded entirely on the patiently elicited story of the subject. This means to say that the operator with an entirely unbiassed mind listens intently to the story of the patient's immediate and present worries.

He must assimilate sympathetically everything which is put before him, no matter how grotesque, betraying no personally felt emotion of surprise or incredulity.

When the immediate state of affairs has been grasped in as full detail as possible, this should terminate the interview from an active point of view for that day. A few words of consolation should be given to the patient and an appointment at the earliest possible day for the next interview is arranged.

On the patient's return for the second interview, if there is a desire manifested to amplify the worries and woes of the primary meeting, do nothing to check the flow of information. Everything stated by the patient voluntarily or by judicious questioning is of the utmost value in giving the operator a close-up of the character, nervous condition, mode of life and general ideas of the subject.

If satisfied with the present personal history the patient is questioned as to his family history and a close scrutiny should be made of the history of his immediate personal relatives.

This procedure, if carefully done, will exhaust the time at the operator's disposal at the second interview, and will give the operator time to reflect upon whether he feels that he can do the case justice.

The physician, before proceeding further with the case, must be in a position, with the facts at his disposal, to know whether he is really capable of handling it. If he feels that he is capable of doing so, let him meet the patient at the third interview radiating confidence. If he is diffident about his ability to cope with the condition it would be much better for him to pass on the case.

The operator must remember that he is using his conscious mind, a feeble instrument at best, to put right the subconscious mind, an instrument of superhuman worth. It must be palpable to everyone, therefore, that the subconscious mind of the subject in its acuity will immediately detect any evidence of diffidence in the mind of the operator and summarily reject him. That there could be no hope of beneficial treatment under these circumstances is apparent to all.

When the operator meets the subject, therefore, for the third interview he must have made up his mind definitely that he can and will administer benefit. Every action of his must convey this to the patient and convey it in a convincing and subtle manner.

The personal history is now taken in as much detail as possible, assistance being given at proper places to encourage the patient to talk. It must be demonstrated to the patient that his entire confidence is required, that he has got to overcome his feelings in every way in order to expose anything in his mental or physical relationships which may have a bearing on his present condition. In a word, the patient must be encouraged to analyse himself and to dig from his subconscious mind past events which cause unpleasant memories.

The writer invariably informs the patient at the beginning of treatment that he (the writer) cannot cure the patient's nervous condition, that he has never cured a nervous condition in his life, that that lies solely in the power of the patient *under the guidance of his adviser*. To be able to give the advice necessary for the patient to bring about his own salvation it is essential that the operator should know everything possible that goes through the mind of the patient. The author exemplifies this by asking the patient to suppose himself in the position of witnessing a gruesome traffic accident resulting in the mutilation and death of a friend on his (the patient's) way to the consulting room.

The patient is asked to consider what his state would be supposing the catastrophe had occurred half an hour before. He is forced to admit that he would be shaking, excited generally, agitated and distressed. If, when he has been made to relate in detail the circumstances of the tragedy, he is again compelled to tell his story, and for the third time made to repeat it, he will have to admit that his excitement and agitation, on the third recital, would have been reduced by 50 per cent. It is pointed out to him that if the recital of the story is continued again and again he would finally reach a point where he would tell the story practically devoid of agitation and almost with ennui.

This illustration is apparent to most neurotics. The essential thing for the operator to remember is that these people are intelligent and, in reality, it is that very intelligence which has brought about their uncomfortable mental state. They thoroughly understand that the recital of even a grave horror too often repeated soon becomes boring. As a matter of fact, this type of mind tires very easily, mental exhaustion being one of its most prominent features, and it tires just as easily of its horrors when they are brought prominently to the fore again and again.

The author has found that these patients often exhibit a morbid curiosity regarding mental states in general and endeavour at times to draw from the operator examples of different mental states which he may have met during the course of his professional career. It is inadvisable for the operator to indulge these inclinations, as the following story will illustrate :—

When treating a patient very early in his (the author's) career the patient asked a question about capital punishment. As the treatment had really finished for the day the author began to discuss this matter. The patient asked whether death was instantaneous in hanging, and the author replied that he was convinced that it was not, going into the details that as the brain was the centre of life and feeling, it must remain sensitive and active for some considerable period—in fact, until death supervened from ordinary strangulation. As the patient was a man of the world it never occurred to the author that the detailed proof brought forward to sustain his theory would have any harmful effect. As a matter of fact, quite the opposite occurred. The unfortunate patient went home and ruminated all night on the awful possibility of a human being dangling at the end of a rope alive and sensitive for a period of time. The result was, to put it briefly, a considerable retrogression on the patient's part and a recurrence of the objective symptoms connected up with his own condition which had long before disappeared.

On another occasion, the author, dealing with a case of severe claustrophobia, specially marked towards tube travelling, was convinced that the patient had made such progress that it would be an advisable thing for her to go down to the tube and test herself thoroughly out. The result was disastrous. The patient was not at all fitted to undergo the ordeal. She relapsed badly and quite rightly refused to continue under treatment by the author.

Here are two examples of things the operator should not do. The first is not to discuss affairs which are abnormal if these affairs are not directly connected with the patient. These people wallow in the abnormal, have a morbid pleasure in listening to its recital at times, then go home and scourge themselves into a condition of psychic depression about matters in no way connected with their particular state.

With regard to trials of strength or searching for proofs of progress, the operators will be advised to allow these essays to emanate from the patients themselves.

The operator who is content to bring his patient to that state of existence where he is able to cope with the ordinary affairs of life and fulfil his duties with comfort has done all that is required of him. These mental fabrics are never made of the stoutest material, and, where the practitioner has proofed them against the ordinary wear and tear of everyday existence, his job is well and efficiently done.

The object of the operator manifestly from the beginning is to inspire the patient with confidence in his powers to help him (the patient) to create self-confidence in him, to help him to re-establish in himself ability to regard the ordinary trials of life as something with which he is quite fit to contend.

If the operator succeeds in awakening that confidence his task becomes easy in direct ratio to the degree with which this has been brought about.

If the operator is unable to awaken in his patient the confidence that he can rehabilitate himself, the operator is doomed to failure.

Not only must the patient be assured that he can get back all his mental strength and happiness, but he must recognize that this rebuilding comes largely from within himself and that the operator acts only in the role of a wise guardian in its accomplishment. When the subject thoroughly grasps this, and when he is beginning to notice some slight degree of improvement in his general nervous condition, if he is convinced that this is due very largely if not entirely to his own effort, he strains at the leash in his desire to accelerate his progress and has no fear of relapse as the foundation work is his own.

FINANCE

The question of finance is one which must be thrashed out before treatment is undertaken. Freud definitely stated that no patient can receive effective psychotherapeutic treatment unless he is free from the financial worries attendant on that treatment, and, therefore, in these days of universal financial worry, effective psychotherapeutic treatment would seem to be limited.

As, however, the treatment outlined in this book does not attempt to put before its readers the methods of the great Master, his rigid financial rule does not apply. Nevertheless, it is abundantly clear to anyone

that the patient should understand from the beginning
what his financial obligations are. If a patient, in the
middle of treatment, when definite progress is beginning to manifest itself, starts to worry about where he
stands financially, it is abundantly manifest that
progress will be interrupted.

These patients, whose main characteristic is their
self-centralization, after a time begin to lose this self-
centralization under treatment. Their worries project
themselves or tend to project themselves more and
more towards externals. An ever-present external with
the vast majority of us is monetary standing.

If the patient therefore at the beginning knows what
his commitments are in this respect it roots out the
possibility of the financial element being a pain focus
during treatment.

It is practically impossible for the ordinary operator,
or, indeed, for anyone, to do psychotherapeutic work
gratuitously. In the first place the time absorbed is
very great, and, in the second place, it is well to impress
on these patients that something very definite and
substantial is being done and remuneration, consequently, is required.

The operator has no extraneous aids, as, for example,
tonics and other visible appliances. As a consequence,
patients are liable to conceive the idea that the progress made is entirely due to their own efforts, and
when a certain advance is made they think they will
be able to carry on by themselves without expert aid.
This is a disastrous mental attitude because a half-
treated patient will most certainly relapse and his last
state is immeasurably worse than his first.

The attitude of the operator should be as firm in this
the financial regard as it is in all his relationships with
the patient. Every act of his should be positive and
open to no question. The patient, consequently,
understands from the beginning exactly what his
commitment is, and lays his plans accordingly. By
this means the anxiety, disappointment and irritation
are completely removed from his mind, and as his

condition improves he has no pain focus from the financial point of view to impede his progress.

DOMESTIC STATUS

As will be apparent to everyone, the domestic status of the patient is of overwhelming importance. If the atmosphere of the home is bad, effective treatment becomes almost impossible. The practitioner owes a duty to himself as well as to the patient, and that is that he demand every favourable circumstance in order to bring his work to the desired conclusion.

If strained relations exist between members of the family, if there is a focus of irritation from the household due to any specific cause outside the patient's own psychic abnormality, that focus must be got rid of if a satisfactory result is to be obtained.

It is quite apparent that no matter how earnest and hard working the operator may be, he is only in contact with the subject for an hour, and whatever benefit he may strive to obtain in that time can, and will be wiped out if the patient has got to return to a hostile or even uncongenial atmosphere.

Here, again, the operator has got to be adamant. At times it may be very difficult to carry out this strong attitude, but as no beneficent result can be obtained where there is a hostile atmosphere in the household, it is easier to face the situation at the beginning rather than have the mortification of witnessing a bad result at the end of treatment.

This practically means for the operator that in certain cases he is left with no alternative but to insist on a complete change of surroundings and a complete break with the existing circumstances of the patient. This insistence will at times give rise to strong opposition, usually on financial grounds, but it should be clearly explained that if improvement or cure is to be effective a definite change is essential.

The author invariably sends patients to a nursing home—minimum two weeks to six or eight weeks or longer in many cases. This is necessitated by his particular method of treatment in the first place, and, secondly, because he recognizes the great advantage of a complete break with existing ties.

When the patient returns, as at some time he must return, to the family circle, his orientation to everything is completely changed for the better if a good result has been obtained by the operator. Matters which irritated him and formerly drove him to a near frenzy have now faded in their intensity, and he takes pride in his ability to overcome them. Thus, he gains strength from his weakness, and taking pride in that manifest strength his nervous stability grows from day to day.

COMMERCIAL STATUS

A man who is facing a severe business crisis obviously is not an ideal subject for psychotherapeutic treatment. It is the duty of the operator to get as intimate a grasp as possible of such a situation and arrange what can be done to meet it.

The patient, face to face with threatening bankruptcy, for example, which can only be avoided by his remaining at the wheel personally, would derive no benefit from a treatment which would even temporarily detach him from his work. Such a patient is intolerant of anything in the nature of treatment. His mind is not in a fit condition to accept mental consolation when that mind is the cockpit of a thousand turbulent emotions.

This does not mean to say, however, that the operator has no function at this period. He has an overwhelming task and responsibility, as this is the type from whom a heavy percentage of our suicides are recruited, and it is within the province of the skilful psychologist to steer the patient safely through the threatening crisis.

The ideal thing would be to keep in daily contact with the patient, encouraging him and demonstrating to him that his affairs are not of cataclysmic importance. The moral support thus given and the physical support lent by ensuring good rest at night and keeping the body as well as possible by exercise and amusements, will tide over the vast majority of cases in these crises.

SUMMARY

To summarize briefly the attitude of the operator when he sees his patient for the first time :—

(1) It is essential to listen closely to the immediate complaints of the patient. To trace the origin of these complaints as accurately as possible, and to find out all the circumstances which tend to aggravate the condition.

(2) Careful details of the family history must be patiently elicited.

(3) A careful and intensive examination is made of the personal history and habits of the patient.

(4) When the foregoing points have been fully investigated the operator should question himself as to his ability to treat the patient. If he feels capable and confident he must demonstrate to the patient his capability and confidence. There must be no hesitation or doubt in his mind, because the patient's subconscious mind will detect any hesitancy on the operator's part, with fatal results as regards the beneficial outcome.

(5) The patient's confidence must be carefully won, not only by a display of sympathetic understanding of the situation, but a definite assurance of the patient's ability to extricate himself from his difficulties by understanding assistance.

(6) It is advisable for the operator to confine himself strictly to the patient's particular state and refuse, even under pressure, to cull examples from other morbid mental states.

(7) Never try the patient's advance too highly by submitting him to ordeals which he may not be able to sustain.

(8) Encourage, on the other hand, all efforts on the patient's part which prove to him the progress he is making.

(9) Before outlining a specific method of treatment discuss with the patient whether it is entirely possible and feasible, and if it is not do not insist upon its being carried out.

(10) Once a line of treatment is definitely suggested, let no whim or fancy on the patient's part turn the operator aside from its being carried out.

THE PATIENT

After listening to a preliminary recital of the patient's troubles and gathering as far as possible all their ramifications and relationships, it is not advisable to press on along this line just for the moment.

The personal history is the next item of importance, and this must be exhaustively taken from all angles—health, habits, amusements, hobbies, occupation, social and financial standing.

Health—The age of the patient, any illnesses contracted, operations performed, etc., have to be carefully noted. His position in the family, whether he comes as the eldest, in the middle, or the youngest, the number in family, and his parents' age at the time of his birth.

Habits—Tobacco, alcohol, drugs.

Amusements and Hobbies—The games played at school, the exercise he takes now, his different hobbies.

Occupation—The profession he follows, its nature and surroundings, the number of hours worked.

Social Attitude—Whether fond of mixing with people generally or of the reticent solitary type.

Financial Standing—Whether he suffers from financial worries or is contented in this respect. Extravagant or penurious in habit.

When this list has been exhaustively searched it will be found that a pretty complete external picture would be had of the patient's life, past and present.

Let us examine these different headings in detail :—

Age—As regards age, the author, for his own purposes, classifies the dangerous periods of life in both male and female as :—

    (*a*) The onset of puberty;

    (*b*) The middle distance ; and

    (*c*) The change of life.

(*a*) *The onset of puberty* is satisfactory when sex development is normal and Nature changes over into the top gear of life. This change, momentous though it be, usually gives little trouble, if any. If, however, anything occurs to interfere with the smooth working of that change, there is an immediate jarring of the nervous system. Debilitating fevers or any other debilitating agency, accident, disease, malnutrition, all interfere with this normal change, and the result is nervous upheaval.

Very often, at this particular spot on the road of life, a nervous habit may make itself evident. This may remain throughout life as a simple general nervousness, or be met with in all the varying shades of nervous exhaustion up to psychosis itself.

(*b*) *In the middle period of life,* which the author regards as being between the 28th and 35th year, the nervous system is, or should be, at its prime just as the physical attributes are. If no nervous weakness has manifested itself through hereditary or at puberty, it is not likely to develop at this particular period. When it does it is generally due to debilitating fever, specific infections, accident, operation, or, in the case of the female, child-birth.

(*c*) *The climacteric period* is a time of trial for the human race in general. Nature is changing down the gears in life, and if antecedent circumstances have favoured an easy change there is little disturbance of the nervous system. If. on the other hand, life has been hard through worry, ill-health or some other cause, the gear change down is harsh and the nervous system suffers accordingly.

It will be seen from the foregoing how necessary it is to take a close scrutiny of the age of the patient in determining the line of specific treatment.   If, for example, a girl of 19 comes to the consulting room with schizophrænic symptoms, she is obviously anæmic, and has not seen the menses for six months, it is perfectly apparent that the blood condition screams for treatment before any effort to approach the mental state of the case.   So it is with the other periods in human existence.

Illnesses contracted—Debilitating diseases, fevers, etc., necessarily take their toll from the nervous system of the patient.   Believing, as the author does, that the nervous system is dependent for its vigour on the ductless glands and their secretions, and believing, as he does, that these same secretions are employed in the resistance and fight against disease, it is to be assumed, on this theory, that the general nervous system of the subject must suffer in those persons who have been the victims of debilitating or wasting diseases.

Exactly the same thing applies to heavy operations. Where the brain has been deprived of general sensation by force applied we are content to accept that the person suffering from this force must remain a case of traumatic nervous exhaustion for a period of time. It is therefore not illogical to assume that where the brain has been deprived of consciousness by anæsthesia for four or five hours, that a certain temporary damage at least is done.   In addition to this damage there is the shock to the central nervous system undoubtedly sustained, even if it is not registered in consciousness. These two factors will explain the occurrence of neurosis in post-operative cases.

Position in the Family—The family position of the subject is of interest.   It cannot be specifically stated that the member who comes at the tail end of a long family is invariably an inferior type mentally and physically to the member who made his appearance earlier.   The eugenic hypothesis leads one to believe that the first child of a young couple, other things being equal, should excel mentally and physically the fifteenth child of an aged couple. This is not borne out invariably in practice, but it may safely be assumed that where the parents are young and the child is born early to the union, that the child must have a better chance in life than a late child born to an aged couple. As stated, however, this cannot be universally sustained.

One case, to the author's mind, brooks no contradiction with regard to the child's position in the family. Reference is made to where there is an only child in the family, and that a male child. In these circumstances observation over a period of fifteen years by the writer has convinced him that it is extremely difficult, if not impossible, for that child to be 100 per cent., normal exceptions nothwithstanding. The reason for this statement is given in detail in Chapter XIII.

Habits—Youthful habits have a marked influence on the adult psychic.

Masturbation is the outstanding habit of young adult life, and it is possible that the actual physical damage done here is of slight importance as compared with the psychic damage. See under heading " Masturbation."

Alcohol and Drugs—With regard to these addictions, there is no necessity to dilate on them, as it is perfectly apparent that no nervous system can be treated effectively if it has been constantly saturated with toxic substances.

Alcohol and drug addiction, in the writer's mind, are simply symptomatic of the underlying neurosis and the success of the treatment as regards permanency for these conditions depends entirely to what degree the neurotic element of the victim can be overcome.

As alcohol and drug addiction have a chapter entirely devoted to themselves, it is unnecessary to pursue further this particular section.

Amusements and Hobbies—The amusements and hobbies of the patient give a very clear line to the operator, and an amount of helpful material for him to work upon to the patient's benefit.

The man who has still a desire to play games and has the nervous energy to put that desire into operation, calls forth excellent promise of an ultimate good result. Even a man who physically is incapacitated for active participation in amusements yet still displays his ability and inclination to extrovert in a hobby, is a favourable subject for treatment. On the other hand, the patient who drops everything in the way of amusements and exercises, and who has lost interest in everything except himself presents a very difficult problem.

Occupation—The patient's occupation has obviously an important bearing on his course of treatment and chances of recovery.

To take as an example an occupation which will make itself clear to everyone, let us visualize the test pilot at an aviation works. The duty of the test pilot, as his name implies, is to prove the airworthiness of new machines or machines which have been renovated. It must of necessity be nerve-racking work. Each and every machine is different in its behaviour, and the tryout must vary in every case. The pilot has no means of knowing beforehand what his machine is liable to do in certain circumstances, and as all the tests are designed to test every emergency worthiness, unknown risks must be taken all the time. The strain of this occupation must be terrific, and if a pilot crashes, the crash, superadded to his life of extreme tension, is liable to bring about a nervous collapse. Granted this is an occupation rare and of extreme danger, yet its outstanding characteristics serve to illustrate what a bearing occupation of whatever kind may have on the nervous condition of the patient.

As in the majority of cases it would be inadvisable for the operator to suggest the test pilot's return to his occupation, so in many cases of other callings in life a change of occupation, or, at all events, a modification in the conditions of his occupation is imperative if a good result is to be obtained.

This is one of the difficult barriers which has to be surmounted in the treatment of PSYCHO-NEUROTIC cases, but as the psychologist's profession bristles with difficulties, this obstacle has to be faced, amongst others, which may arise in the treatment of cases.

Finance—Financial fluctuations are much more frequently met with than dangers attendant upon the occupation of testing flying machines, and, in their own way, give rise to strain and exhaustion of the nervous system quite as evident as the strain associated with the physical danger of flying.

A solution must be found for these financial crises by some means. The solution does not necessarily always lie in straightening out the matter from a strictly financial point of view. The patient's mind must be orientated regarding his finance in a totally different manner if a result is to be obtained. This is not impossible, inasmuch as numbers of people change their standing to meet the changed financial conditions. They make this change very often of their own accord without extraneous help either psychological or material and find comfort, mental happiness, and at times even restrengthened nervous force from the change made.

Surroundings—As a basic rule a patient about to undergo treatment for any psycho-neurotic condition should make up his mind if at all possible to make at least a temporary clean cut with his existing surroundings.

The mind of the neurotic is grooved ; grooved in the deep-cut groove of its own painful mental associations. The object of the operator is to shift the mind on to an entirely different groove. Everything which is new and fresh helps this effort. Everything that is routine and established tends to push the mind back into the old painful track.

When a patient is removed from his home or business surroundings a cleavage of a different type is achieved. Things which automatically happen at certain hours of the day cannot happen under the changed circumstances. The mind is compelled to look about and re-establish itself under new conditions. There is an entire recasting of method. There is a different orientation beginning with infinitesimal unimportant things up to a matter of supreme importance—the patient's nervous state.

The patient must, of necessity, accept these changes. He does so willingly, inasmuch as they vary from the old humdrum existence, and, consequently, interest his jaded mind. All these changes aid the operator in forcibly shifting, or endeavouring to shift, the mind from its morbid groove.

Sociability—Where the patient's nervous state inclined him to prefer his own company to that of others, nursing-home treatment is beneficial. He is compelled to accept the necessary amount of attention in the ordinary way. This tolerance may at first be irksome, but as it is imperative the patient soon accustoms himself to its necessity and invariably benefits from it.

On the other hand, if the patient is too sociable and is victimized by a plethora of friends or acquaintances, the isolation of a nursing home is an effective barrier until such times as the patient's exhausted nervous resources are able to withstand the well-meant but oftentimes baneful influence of excessive friendship.

*   *   *   *

The prospective operator will see from the foregoing what a great amount there is to be learnt about the average patient before an attempt is made to begin treatment. Every patient has to be studied thoroughly, and although the lines indicated here will seem exhaustive, it is not to be assumed by any means that this is so.

The patient suffering from psycho-neurosis practically demands from the operator an individual treatment suitable to his particular psychic. The broad lines indicated are essentials, but the final movements of the treatment are indicated by the patient's attitude and response. The operator must recognize that he is dealing with a state of perpetual emergency and must be sufficiently nimble-minded to counter that emergency, and to do so without manifest difficulty. This will necessitate careful parrying at times, and there is no necessity to attempt to solve the problem for the patient on the spot. It is dangerous to do so, because if the *modus operandi* outlined is faulty there is a specific loss of confidence on the patient's part. Confidence in these cases is oftentimes very hard to win. Confidence lost is practically impossible to regain. As in the case illustrated in Chapter VI, to which the reader is requested to refer again, the first attempt to overcome the long-standing abnormality met with no success. The patient was requested to make a voluntary effort at the exercises designed to counteract the abnormality. These exercises of necessity occasioned pain due to old-standing adhesions, etc. In a very short time he refused absolutely to tolerate the necessary pain and stated that if it were a vital part of the treatment he would no longer continue. No effort was made to bring pressure on the patient to continue along these lines, but as the physical difficulty of necessity had to be overcome an equally effective measure had to be devised. An appeal was made to his sporting and athletic instinct when boxing was suggested, and as we must all suffer a degree of martyrdom in the interests of sport he gladly submitted to what must have been greatly enhanced pain.

We thus see how impossible it is to work along stereotyped lines in treating the Psycho-neurotic. Apart from broad fundamentals, the operator must be prepared to devise emergency aids called forth by the victim's specific condition.

Patience on the operator's part is essential, and when he reflects that the victim is not putting forth quaint ideas which are intensely painful to himself, it is easy to cultivate a sympathetic understanding.

Progress may be slow at the beginning and relapses come all too frequently. Nevertheless, there is abundant gratification in work well done when definite improvement manifests itself.

When the family and personal history have been accurately taken, any element in either history which suggests a physical difficulty must be carefully looked into. It is useless to put a patient suffering from anæmia under psychological treatment. The physical condition must be cleared up, or to a large extent relieved, before any radical treatment for the nervous system is attempted. In the same way no benefit may be expected when commencing psychological treatment on a patient debilitated after an exhausting fever, heavy operation or child-birth.

The first effort made should be to clear up any difficulty on the physical side, because if this difficulty persists it will impede recovery on the psychic side, and, later on, in all probability will be a focus around which further nervous troubles will group themselves. The author remembers on one occasion having a patient brought to him from a private home supposed to be suffering from Dementia Præcox. Several features in the history of the case seemed to be distinctly unorthodox, and he suggested an X-ray of the cranium. This turned out to be a very happy chance, inasmuch as a depressed longitudinal fracture of the vertex was revealed on the X-ray plate. There was nothing in the history to indicate where this had occurred, and the mystery was never solved.

It is easy to imagine how futile psychological treatment would be in a case of this nature and how exasperating to find one's efforts go unrewarded.

The patient in question was recommended to see a brain surgeon, and the subsequent history of the case is unknown to the author.

*   *   *

TREATMENT PROPER

When the physical condition, the financial affairs and the domestic and business arrangements are definitely settled, treatment proper can now be entered upon, and the first step is :

(a) *Put the Mind in Splints*

Let us glance for a moment at the mental condition of the patient. His mind is obsessed by dreads, worries and doubts ; his troubles seethe and foam without cessation through his mind. All day during waking hours the brain grinds over remorselessly, never ceasing, never resting.

Whether the subject is at business or at leisure to amuse himself, the wheels of the mind never cease turning. When the day closes rest is sought in vain. The mind, unhampered by externals, has more leisure still to devote to its own morbid output. Every worrying thought, every harassing emotion, is eagerly sought after and tossed into the machinery of the mind for the maintenance of its morbid product.

It stands to sense that if we could shut off the engine of the mind at the time when the patient is supposed to be resting, we should of necessity do that engine a great and beneficent service. In these days of practically universal mechanization, we all know that an engine run for too long a period, or run under bad conditions, soon ruins itself. If this mental engine has had to run all day in the discharge of its duties and all night to deal with the morbid material thrown into it by a disordered subconscious, it overheats after its own fashion, and there is only one inevitable end —the destruction of its efficiency.

It is palpable to all, therefore, that any effort successfully made to slow the engine down must of necessity be of the utmost benefit. Here and now it may be positively stated that this cannot be effectively accomplished by an effort of the will. It is amusing to read a psychologist's suggestion, put forward in a letter to the daily Press, that insomnia can be conquered by the victim leaving his worries outside and regarding his home as holy. If insomnia, the progeny of nervous exhaustion, can be put aside with such facility, why not regard the business office, the consulting room or any other localæ as holy and leave the worries outside there also ?—

If this were possible man would live in a state of mental *bein être* and so free himself from mental troubles at mere volition. No, the effort is beyond human endeavour. The brain needs adventitious assistance to accomplish this. The engine must be artificially slowed down to cool. This can be done and is the first step in treating Pyscho-neurotic conditions. This is what the author terms " Putting the Mind in Splints."

We all know when a finger is injured at the knuckle and infection ensues, that the inflammation persists unless the joint is immobilized. We immobolize the joint by putting on a splint, and the consequent rest allows the wound to heal rapidly.

By sedatives we restrict mental activity and allow the inflamed mind to settle down and resume normality in a similar manner.

This is the origin of that treatment we term " Putting the Mind in Splints."

The patient is put to bed in a quiet room where the brightness is reduced to a minimum. Care is taken to see that there is sufficient warmth and comfort in the bed, whilst the room itself remains well aired. At 3 o'clock in the afternoon a draught is given consisting of the simple bromides with chloral hydrate and hyoscyamus. The dose usually given by the author is 20 grs. each of Potassium Bromide, Sodium Bromide, Chloral Hydrate and 20 mins. of Tincture of Hyoscyamus. The warmth, silence, the dim light and this draught compel relaxation after a time. Patients strung up to the highest tension develop a pleasant lethargy and a gradual contentment and quasi ease manifests itself at the end of an hour.

The patient may read if so inclined, but the idea is impressed upon him that this rest period is one of the most important steps in the treatment, and that no strong effort or mental concentration should be made on the material being read.

At 10 o'clock at night the dose is repeated, the patient is finally made comfortable, and in a short time the generality of patients have succumbed to the combined effects of the 3 o'clock and 10 o'clock doses. Sleep comes, and where it does not the dose is repeated as to one-half after midnight and it is rarely if ever that this fails to be effective.

At 7 o'clock the patient is aroused, no matter what the night's sleep has been like. If he has succeeded in getting seven or eight hours' sleep so much the better. If not, he is, nevertheless, awakened.

Mist. Alba 3 ounces is given now, followed by a cup of tea after an interval of 20 minutes. When the saline has acted the patient goes to the bath and no attempt is made to chill it down or invigorate him in any way. The patient returns to bed, is given his breakfast, the morning paper, and is allowed to distract himself quietly until 10 o'clock.

At 10 o'clock the draught is repeated. Quietness reigns again, strong light is excluded and every effort is made to keep the patient as relaxed as possible until lunch is served at 1 o'clock.

After lunch, the heaviness of the meal combined with the 10 a.m. draught induces a condition of somnolence or, at least, lethargic indifference. At 3 o'clock a draught is again administered and the patient is left to his own resources—to slumber or read or rest in whatever manner he wishes until it is time for the evening meal.

This routine is continued day after day with unremitting care for from 12 to 16 days. The quantity of the draught is raised or lowered as circumstances dictate.

Regarding this draught, the author has invariably found it quite safe ; it is absolutely effective and non-habit forming.

The food at this period should be sustaining but light. Meat should be cut down to the minimum, vegetables and fruit forming the preponderating side of the dietary. Where possible, milk should be substituted for tea and coffee. Smoking should be reduced to the minimum.

The rationale of this treatment is mental rest. Rest is suggested by the quietness of the room, exclusion of strong light, and the comfortable warmth of the bed. All visitors, business communications are forbidden; anything tending to excite the mind is rigidly excluded.

We all know that a wound on a joint remains open on account of the movements associated with the joint. We know that healing commences when the joint is immobilized in a splint and movement becomes impossible. When the mind is put in splints by this method it is unable to turn over under the stimulus of morbid worry and settles down contentedly in a complacency artificially produced.

It is a most extraordinary thing that although comparatively heavy quantities of these depressing drugs are being administered, they interfere to only a slight extent, nevertheless, with the digestive action and the bodily condition is but slightly if at all upset. The saline administered in the morning sweats the previous day's drugs from the intestinal walls and prevents accumulation in the system.

Let us look at the condition of the patient as he progresses under this treatment. On admission he is worried, restless, tense as a fiddle string. There is no desire for food, but if a smoker an insatiable desire for nicotine, or if an alcoholic an unquenchable thirst for drink. The comfort of the bed, the quietness, dim light, and the heavy draught slow down the over-active imagination and blunt the edge of the painful morbid ideas.

The second draught coming soon on top of the first deepens the feeling of lethargy and gradually sleep overcomes the brain. When the patient is awakened in the morning the body is cleansed of the overnight draught but the brain remains less susceptible to pain stimuli. The warm morning bath cleanses and soothes without stimulating the brain. The return to a comfortable warm bed and quiet surroundings tends to maintain a feeling of indifference. When the morning meal is taken and the morning draught administered two hours later it is an effort for most patients to remain awake. Even in the least susceptible, the mental anguish of the previous day is very markedly lessened.

As treatment progresses day by day, the indifference to worry becomes more evident. The mind settles into a state of complacency and the patient practically slumbers all day and sleeps all night. It is impossible for the mind, under these conditions, to retain its acuity and so it is impossible for the turbulent mental morbid impressions to wound it.

It is thus easy to imagine that a man tossed and tumbled by a multitude of painful emotions emerges after fourteen days rest in quite a different psychic atmosphere. Where he formerly displayed panic, confusion and disorder, there is now a tendency to develop order, discipline and hope. Things are viewed in quite an altered perspective and situations are logically examined which before only gave rise to expressions of utter hopelessness.

At the end of the " mind in splints " treatment the author can almost visualize the rested brain saying " Thank God for that respite."

This treatment differs radically from the Weir-Mitchell treatment of yesterday. In the Weir-Mitchell treatment the patient was confined to bed and kept from making any physical effort. Unfortunately, the prevention of physical effort allows more time to be devoted to psychic effort, just exactly what is not wanted in the psycho-neurotic. One can contemplate with horror a victim of Psycho-neurosis being compelled to lie immobile with nothing to check the mental engine from grinding over at a thousand revolutions per minute.

The forced feeding idea in the Weir-Mitchell treatment may have done something to bring about a mental lethargy through food intoxication, but the author cannot quite grasp how this was accomplished.

At the conclusion of what may be termed the intensive part of the foregoing treatment, the patient is allowed to sit up for about four hours the first day, and eight hours the next day. The morning and afternoon draughts are now finished with, but the evening draught is still given at 10 o'clock to foster a good night's rest. This draught is gradually tapered off each night over a period of seven days, at the end of which time there should be no necessity for its continuance.

During the two days' rest the patient is allowed to occupy himself much as he pleases. There is no effort made to approach him from the point of view of psychic treatment.

On the third day, after breakfast, the patient is once again carefully examined and any difference between his condition now and his condition at the beginning of treatment is carefully noted. This has special reference to his heart rate, his blood pressure, and his nervous reflexes. The patient's weight is also taken and compared with his weight on admission.

On the fourth day the patient is awakened at 7 o'clock in the morning, and the Mist. Alba is given followed by a cup of tea. When this has acted he is warmly clad and sent out to do a walk of roughly one mile. When he returns a bath is ready waiting for him at a temperature of about 100 degrees. After he has soaped himself and washed all over he is told to turn the cold tap on and gradually reduce the temperature to 70 degrees. This change of temperature will cause no discomfort if the patient keeps the water thoroughly agitated around him. The tonic effect is extraordinarily beneficial and there is no strain on the central nervous or vascular systems as obtains in giving a cold bath. The patient returns to bed, has massage for half an hour, when breakfast is served. He may read the morning paper or any light literature if he wishes. He is left alone after breakfast for two hours. The physician's visit at the end of this time will often find the patient comfortably slumbering.

This early morning walk is designed to open the pores and aid sweat secretion. Thus we have the body starting the day under ideal conditions, the three excretory systems having operated to the full.

The patient must be closely questioned as to the effect of the early morning walk ; throwing strain on the heart at this time is to be avoided, so the length of the walk and the rate at which it is undertaken must be carefully graded by the practitioner. As fitness develops the walk is increased both in distance and in rate. The object to be attained is a definite perspiring of the body during this exercise. Wet weather or cold is no obstacle. Provision must be made against the elements, and as the patient returns immediately to a bath and complete change of clothing there is no risk whatever in doing his general health any damage.

This treatment is kept up for ten days, every morning, and is followed by the two hours' rest after breakfast as previously outlined. At the end of this two hours' rest the patient gets up, dresses and goes for a walk at a gentle rate. This walk must have some specific-object, either to visit a place of interest in the neigh bourhood, to make a specific call, or do some message of definite import.

When the patient returns he washes and prepares himself for the mid-day meal. After this meal he is encouraged to rest for another couple of hours, light literature being provided unless the patient prefers to sleep.

In the afternoon he should be encouraged to watch games if not physically fit to take part in them. If physically fit, golf is ideal for two or three hours.

On his return the patient has an ordinary bath, changes his outdoor clothes and has his evening meal round about 7 o'clock. The evening is spent at cards, chess, billiards or indoor games, or by occasional visits to the theatre or picture house.

There is no object in the patient going to bed before 11 o'clock. Very few adults of the present day are inclined to sleep before midnight and it is difficult to expect that a patient with nothing particular to do all day, that is nothing that could really fatigue him, to be able to go to sleep before 12 o'clock.   When one of these "nervy" patients is sent to bed too early and does not feel inclined to sleep, he becomes restless and irritable.   This very often deprives him of sleep until two or three hours later.   If, on the other hand, he remains up until he is more or less desirous of seeking rest, he falls asleep early and naturally.

The writer does not mean to suggest that the patient should be allowed to engage in exciting games of bridge or any other brain stimulating effort.   It is supposed that he has had half an hour or an hour's leisure to settle down before retiring to his room. The bed should always be comfortable and warm, but there must be an abundance of fresh air at all times.

This type of patient is very often worried at night by harrowing dreams and wakes up in a state of panic not knowing his surroundings.   This tends to terrorise him and it is usually advisable, therefore, to place a dim burning night light in the room.   This should be sufficiently conspicuous to illuminate dimly but to cause no glare or annoyance to the patient.

As we have said, this routine is maintained from ten to fourteen days and it will be noted that no effort has as yet been made to enter upon psycho-therapeutic treatment.

Let us examine what purpose has been fulfilled by the treatment the patient has received before entering upon the psycho-therapeutic administration.   He has spent fourteen days in bed.   During that time his mental powers have been damped down sufficiently low to make it impossible for him to worry.   This has been artificially produced, but the brain has benefited to an extraordinary extent.   Sleep, formerly insufficient in a marked degree, has been established in superabundant quantity.   During the waking hours the morbid sensitiveness has been blunted and the inflamed mind rested.   The fears, worries and anxieties have lost their virulence to a great extent.   Definite progress can now be claimed.

The succeeding fourteen days, occupied in toning up the body, cleansing it to its innermost regions as well as possible, and giving the mind outside interests, has strengthened the progress established by the mental rest obtained in the first fourteen days.

It will be noted that every effort is made to prevent the brain occupying itself with the troublesome affairs which formerly clogged it up. In the first treatment there is taken out of its power the ability to deal with any mental problems. In the second treatment every effort is made to occupy every waking moment of the patient with things external to himself and, as far as possible, removed from his old worries. The patient's mind, at this time, forcibly rested for fourteen days, and deliberately distracted for another fourteen days, will be found with a completely different orientation. The worries, no longer so poignant, give rise to the belief that the mind is reasserting its mastery.

The restored sleep undoubtedly strengthens the mind and enables it to stand courageously up to its trials. The cleansed body, fresh with exercise and renewed vigour, gives a mental feeling of general well-being. All these beneficial stimuli crowd themselves into the mind expelling the torturing thoughts which have lain there, replacing them by confidence, hope and courage. The mind is now ready for psycho-therapeutic treatment.

Before passing to a consideration of the psycho-therapeutic treatment in these cases, we must first examine the two treatments now administered in the light of the theory advanced by the author as to the causation of Psycho-neurosis.

It will be remembered that in the chapter devoted to the Aetiology of the Psycho-neurotic states, the theory was put forward that these states were due to profligate expenditure of SUBCONSCIOUS PSYCHIC FORCE under the stimulus of fear or some other morbid emotion. Secondly, that the exhaustion condition invariably found in Psycho-neurosis was a direct consequence of that profligate expenditure.

When the mind is " put in splints," as the author terms it, to limit its activities to the greatest possible extent, what is happening ? The bodily function, activated by the sympathetic, are of necessity carried on in the usual way. This, of course, requires the expenditure of FORCE, but this expenditure, for all practical purposes, is the only expenditure, and it is infinitesimal in amount.

Morbid mental processes, heart palpitations, head-aches, muscular tremors, excitable movements, and all the paraphernalia which we associate with the Psycho-neurotic syndrome, are rigidly cut off.

These are the conduits which so lavishly drain the PSYCHIC FORCE from the subconscious mind, and as this FORCE is being constantly evolved in the body, and as its expenditure is rigorously controlled, the result is that the subconscious mind rises from a state of PSYCHIC FORCE bankruptcy and becomes opulent in that respect.

As to the second part of treatment, the body is cleared by the action of the three excretory systems, and, as a consequence, the blood is at its purest and richest. This blood stream, inundating the ductless glands, with its life-giving elements in their best state, must cause a corresponding increase in the gland activities both quantitively and qualitatively.

If our theory is right that the internal secretion of these glands is the material from which PSYCHIC FORCE eventually is elaborated, then nothing but good can result from this treatment, and nothing but good does result.

The mind, rich, confident and strong in its new resources, no longer evades the issue. The old dreads, fears, imaginings are valued in a new light, and the reinvigorated mind no longer stands appalled at ghostly phantasies.

The physical condition rapidly improves, new energy surges through the body, every organ takes on a new lease of life, and a benign circle of health, strength and contentment replaces the old vicious circle of debility, lethargy and mental terror.

With the mind in this state, it is now possible to approach it from the Psycho-therapeutic angle. It is now safe to drag the rattling skeletons from their cupboards in the subconscious and expose them to the light of reason and common sense.

The dark mists of unknown dreads and buried fears evaporate before the sun of the new found courage and confidence which light up the innermost recesses of that mind.

* * * *

PSYCHO-THERAPEUTIC TREATMENT.

The writer endeavoured to follow the strict Freudian principles over a period of three years. Openly he confesses to have failed. He does not presume to offer a criticism of a method which everyone must admit has been revolutionary in the treatment of the psycho-neurotic states. As stated in the foreword, he blames his own technique or lack of it and had perforce to carve out a pathway of his own making stimulated by the immense benefit which he had experienced from the works of the great German psychologist.

That it is impossible to treat successfully the Psycho-neurotic states without some form of analysis must be admitted by all who treat patients suffering from this malady.

It was borne in upon the writer early, however, that as the subconscious field was limitless it must surely contain other pathologic fauna and flora than sex.

Disease, accident, ill-health, specific infections, heredity, domestic and financial worries, all these presented themselves individually and collectively to the author's mind as fertile seeds capable of producing an all too plentiful pathological harvest in the boundless area of the subconscious mind.

Driven on by the urge of this theory an attempt was made to grapple with the outstanding happening which was the direct cause of the springing up in subconsciousness of the crop of fears, dreads, doubts

U

and despairs which batten on the fertility of the mind
and destroy its usefulness.

As an example, and everyday life teems with these
examples, a friend of the writer committed suicide
some years back. He was a man of outstanding genius
as a financier, in the prime of life at forty-eight years
old, and physically fit, with a zest for living equal to
that of any youth of twenty.

Possessed of the Midas touch, from nothing he had
conjured millions, literally millions, out of the air and
enjoyed to the full everything which such vast wealth
could purchase. It could be truthfully said that he
held the Four Aces of life in his hand—youth, health,
brains and wealth.

The market suddenly crashed and overnight, practically speaking, he crashed with it into the shades.

Let us examine the picture from a psychological
point of view and endeavour to determine the exciting
factor in such a tragic end. The brain of the man
could not be classified short of super in finance. He
had started from scratch in life's race, and by intellectual keenness, coolness, audacity and strength
had pitted himself against the giants of the financial
game and won. The strain at times must have been
colossal, and undoubtedly took its toll, but he
betrayed no evidence of this.

His perfect physical condition (he was a teetotaller)
enabled him to carry on where an older, less fit, and
less temperate man could not have sustained the conflict.

What was the cause from a psycho-therapeutic point
of view for the debacle ? Was it sex ? It can be stated
from an intimate knowledge that he had no inhibitions.
Was it insanity ? The family and personal history in
this regard was spotless. This brain had functioned
from youth in a manner that overthrew the most
skilled adversaries in business, despite the fact that
that brain had not the advantage of even an elementary
education.

What then was the exciting cause ? The cause was
an overwhelming and sudden psycho-neurotic explosion

induced by mental worry releasing an uncontrollable deluge of PSYCHIC FORCE in the subconscious, causing temporary panic and confusion, terminating in self-destruction.

This case is a tragic example of the Escape Mechanism acting in an exaggerated manner.

Supposing this victim had called on a physician for his nervous condition on the eve of his tragic exit. What would his (the physician's) attitude be ? After eliciting possibly a family and personal history, including a recital of the threatening circumstances of the moment, what would the operator proceed to do ?

Analyse him for a buried sex complex ? It is manifest that a mind in such turmoil must be left undisturbed and an immediate attempt made to harness its morbid activity until its thought processes have time to fall into orderly array. When this has been accomplished analysis may be commenced. Analysis along what lines ? Some obscure complex buried in the sub-conscious ? No ! Analysis of the exciting cause, the detonator which fired the subconscious explosion.

At the risk of repetition the writer asks permission to bring once again to the reader's notice that important part of Psycho-therapeutic treatment known as Menthal Catharsis. As on this is based the writer's conception of the value of Psychotherapy on the treatment of Psycho-neurosis, its importance will be realized.

The reader is requested to visualize himself for a moment as the spectator of a horrible accident. To make it more personal and thus more gruesome, let us suppose that a friend has just left him and in attempting to cross the road is knocked down by a bus and life crushed out of him in a revolting manner.

The reader would force himself though in a state of collapse to lend what assistance he was able to until the body were eventually removed in the ambulance. What would be the psychic condition of the reader in these circumstances ? He would feel himself on the verge of collapse—that is, he would feel exhausted, his heart thumping against his ribs, his entire body in a state of universal tremor and a cold perspiration bursting out over his face, neck and chest.

These are the cardinal physical symptoms of a case of ACQUIRED PSYCHO-NEUROSIS.

At night he would find difficulty in getting off to sleep, tossing restlessly from side to side, and eventually when he did drop off a hideous nightmare of the horrible occurrence would be filmed on his subconscious mind.

These are the cardinal psychic symptoms of a case of ACQUIRED PSYCHO-NEUROSIS.

He would be, in fact, a temporary Psycho-neurotic (acquired psychic type) shock.

The next day, although his condition will have improved, he will still feel nervy, jumpy and uneasy, and he determines to see a Nerve Specialist. On being asked to what he attributed his condition, the subject relates the occurrence of yesterday. The physician, grasping the position and knowing that the subconscious mind of his patient is still dammed up with the flood of PSYCHIC FORCE let loose by the horrible spectacle, determines to open up and keep open that excellent avenue of escape, viz., the relation of the occurrence.

He will make the patient go over the full story again, relating all he saw in intimate detail. This repetition will be accompanied by an exaggeration of the physical manifestations—sweating, tremors, etc.

The patient, a third, a fourth, a fifth time will be compelled to bring forward the entire story in all its hideous detail. With each repetition the physical and psychic manifestations will become less and less marked, until, if this line be pursued sufficiently long, the story will be given eventually without a single exhibition of emotional or physical upset.

This action on the part of the Specialist is the employment of " Escape Mechanism." It is the opening up of an avenue of exit through which the disturbing PSYCHIC FORCE may make its escape and disemburden the harassed subconscious of its unwanted presence.

This is MENTAL CATHARSIS, and by its means the mind voids the uneconomic PSYCHIC FORCE let loose in it under emotional stimulus.

The foregoing is only given as a crude example of how an implanted morbid emotion of whatever origin acts whilst in the subconscious mind. We see how under its stimulus the subconscious is continually flooded with economically unusable PSYCHIC FORCE. We see how the subconscious in its effort to get rid of this unwanted FORCE employs avenues of escape which give us our physical and psychic symptoms as in PSYCHO-NEUROSIS. In addition to this, it enables us to understand how a complex buried in subconsciousness if discovered can be dragged from its dark recesses, recognized, and its power to work psychic evil destroyed.

In Psychotherapy as employed by the author, the first attempt is made to grapple with the immediate cause of the psychic upheaval. A patient, for instance, may go along for years in comparative comfort and efficiency with some grievous sex complex buried in the subconscious. Though this may cause continuous annoyance and discomfort, it may not be of sufficient import to wreck the ordinary life of the individual. A domestic upheaval, a financial crash, or some strong emotional upset, superadded to this complex precipitates a crash and the patient collapses into a state of profound PSYCHO-NEUROSIS.

After the preliminary brain rest, tackle the immediate exciting cause. Get the patient to change surroundings if these have any bearing on the condition. Insist on having the story in its most harrowing and intimate details. Have it repeated *ad nauseam,* or at least until the patient can repeat it without visible trace of emotion.

When this has been accomplished build the patient up to the highest point of physical well-being, and then make an effort to uproot the deeply buried complex.

This may seem to the majority of readers an all too simple form of psychic treatment, but if efficiently carried out it will demonstrate in no uncertain manner its usefulness.

If the practitioner has the leisure and enthusiasm to attempt deep exploration of the subconscious, then the works of Freud are recommended.

*   *   *   *

The fourth element in treatment is by the administration of the Hormones. Much criticism has been levelled at Gland Therapy treatment and much of that criticism it is to be feared has been levelled by people who have not exhaustively examined the tremendous part which the author is convinced they play in the building up of the nervous system of the Psychoneurotic.

The theory has already been advanced that the entire nervous system depends largely for its strength and efficiency on the ductless glands. From his own experience the author has no hesitation in asserting that by the medicinal use of these glands, either orally or hypodermically or by both methods combined, the most beneficial results have been obtained.

As in most things in life, there is a particular time to commence this administration. It is useless, for example, to take a patient at the height of a nervous collapse and throw gland substances into his system, thus plying him with further nervous energy to continue his nervous manifestations. These nervous outbursts must first of all be controlled and the nervous leakage stopped by the three methods already outlined, viz. :—

(1) By " putting the mind in splints";
(2) By analysing the immediate difficulties which are upsetting the mind; and
(3) By building the patient up to a state of physical well-being.

If this has been successfully done the leakage of PSYCHIC FORCE has been successfully cut off, and the patient is manufacturing by his own resources sufficient PSYCHIC FORCE (nervous energy) for his daily needs

and possibly with a slight overflow for his nervous refitment. This is the period to start glandular treatment.

The glands, exhausted in their efforts to maintain the wastage of PSYCHIC FORCE expended in resisting the mental blizzard, are tired and avid for any or every extraneous aid. Just as Thyroid administered to the myxodematous person rapidly manifests itself throughout the system, so does the administration of the Hormones make this evident in the immediate signs of the recovery of nervous strength and energy.

In a week's time the lethargy and weakness in the patient tend to disappear. Exercise, formerly a drag and heavy burden, soon becomes a source of enjoyment. Mental vigour, muscular energy, activity and brightness sweep away the listless grudging effort of the preceding weeks. The joy of living puts vigour and snap into every effort, and the patient of his own volition demands outlet for more and more effort.

Care must be taken that this sudden revitalizing does not induce a tendency to over-exertion and consequent depression.

The night comes, there is a feeling of grateful weariness due to effort easily sustained, and sleep comes naturally and unaided.

INDEX

INDEX

A

O

P

For Product Safety Concerns and Information please contact our EU
representative GPSR@taylorandfrancis.com
Taylor & Francis Verlag GmbH, Kaufingerstraße 24, 80331 München, Germany

www.ingramcontent.com/pod-product-compliance
Lightning Source LLC
Chambersburg PA
CBHW072050020426
42334CB00017B/1462

9 781032 944500